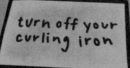

one in a millennial

one in a millennial

ON FRIENDSHIP, FEELINGS, FANGIRLS, AND FITTING IN

kate kennedy

ST. MARTIN'S
PRESS

First published in the United States by St. Martin's Press,
an imprint of St. Martin's Publishing Group

ONE IN A MILLENNIAL. Copyright © 2023 by Be There In Five, LLC. All rights
reserved. Printed in the United States of America. For information, address
St. Martin's Publishing Group, 120 Broadway, New York, NY 10271.

www.stmartins.com

Designed by Omar Chapa

Library of Congress Cataloging-in-Publication Data

Names: Kennedy, Kate (Podcaster), author.
Title: One in a millennial : on friendship, feelings, fangirls, and fitting in /
    Kate Kennedy.
Description: First edition. | New York, NY : St. Martin's Press, 2023.
Identifiers: LCCN 2023027374 | ISBN 9781250285126 (hardcover) |
    ISBN 9781250285133 (ebook)
Subjects: LCSH: Kennedy, Kate (Podcaster) | Generation Y—Social
    conditions. | Young adults—Social life and customs—21st century. |
    Young adults—Social life and customs—Humor. | Popular culture.
Classification: LCC HQ799.5 .K46 2023 | DDC 305.2—dc23/eng/20230807
LC record available at https://lccn.loc.gov/2023027374

Our books may be purchased in bulk for promotional, educational,
or business use. Please contact your local bookseller or the Macmillan
Corporate and Premium Sales Department at 1-800-221-7945, extension 5442,
or by email at MacmillanSpecialMarkets@macmillan.com.

First Edition: 2023

10   9   8   7   6   5   4   3   2   1

For my sister, Kelly.
I may never be on time, but I'll look up to you until the end of it.

contents

Prologue   *1*

Introduction: Passion of the Zeitgeist   *3*

Part I: 1990s

1. Limited To   23

   Pop-up Biblio: American Girls Next Door

2. Back in the Daybed   43

3. You've Got Male   61

4. God Must've Spent a Little Less Time on Me   82

Part II: 2000s

5. Popular-Girl Handwriting   111

   Pop-up Biblio: Saved by the Bell Jar

6. Are We Going Out? Or Out-Out?   151

7. Serotonin, Plain and Tall   178

8. Kate Expectations   200

Part III: Today

9. B There in Five   223

10. The Parent Trap   249

    Pop-up Biblio: To Infinity Scarves and Beyond

11. Pumpkin Spice Girl   281

12. Light at the End of the Trundle   308

Conclusion   *321*

Addendum   *323*

Acknowledgments   *324*

prologue

I often think back to buying beads in a pack, making bead lizards for my BFF's backpack. Eating cereal from a bowl, flipping through American Girl catalogs to the contentment of my "Heart and Soul," the only song I knew on the piano. I think about the importance of being kind, perhaps more importantly, to rewind, and the beauty of never really knowing the time until it got dark. Streams weren't on screens, they were creeks or ravines, and sporting a shark-tooth necklace was what it meant to look sharp. When I think about my millennial existence, I long for when others' approval was none of my business, and being a kid afraid of blacktop knee skids long before I turned to magazines that told me black tops would make me look slim. I wanted to impress my parents and teachers but not yet boys or worship leaders, and I was only envious of the autographs on a classmate's neon cast after a monkey-bar fall. I reminisce about orchestrating digital seductions via AIM, growing up, and trivializing the contents of my own brain, because somewhere along the way, I learned that loving top-forty music or the Mary-Kate and Ashley multiverse wasn't refined. I think about navigating tragedies at a formative age, one where I wished mall-fountain pennies could remedy my pain, before moving on to free smells that Bath & Body Worked just as well. I think about how pop songs and boy bands mismanaged my expectations, and I cared way too much about male validation, because regardless of how much time they said God had spent on me, I hadn't spent enough on myself yet. I think about the sex-and-diet culture and misogyny everything around us would sell; I think about bypassing any and all regard for my own mental health. I was a sorority girl who wanted to rage, trying to reconcile how to feel when you're raised by a church that insisted if you leaned into who you are, you'd go to hell. In my quest for self-love, first, I lived, laughed, chugged my way through early adulthood, not realizing in many ways I was at the pregame for the rest of my life. I think about obsessing over women who were popular or famous and it bringing me joy, but also a needless pursuit of sameness, not realizing the times I was a part of something that felt right but left others out. Amidst the lore of Miss Mary Macks and punch-buggy-no-punch-backs, I have pensive thoughts about becoming a parent but interrupt myself with hot takes about The Parent Trap, wondering if I've been more of a Meredith Blake all along. I think of the girlhood represented by Limited Too, wondering if all girl power was empowering me to do was consume, and how it took twenty-five years after those fitting-room tears to eventually learn to love myself, Too. I've scoured both my journals and my brain, changed some details, locations, and maybe a few names. I'm here to entertain, not instruct, though I do ask for one thing in exchange—by detailing some of my millennial memories, I hope you'll honor yours all the same.

introduction

Passion of the Zeitgeist

When it comes to where I get my spiritual inspiration, I like to think of Britney 6:2 as my John 3:16. Britney Spears, album six, track two, that is. When she said, "There's only two types of people in the world, the ones that entertain and the ones that observe," it was an unexpected and self-actualizing moment for me upon first listening to a song called "Circus." It resonated with me like gospel. I am an observer through and through.

It's hard for me to relate when people say things like "I know nothing about pop culture," "I'm not on social media," or perhaps the only friendship-potential litmus test more effective than someone asking me to run a 5K during the early 2010s themed-race boom: "I don't own a TV." I put these people in the category of entertainer and not observer because it means they have the remarkable ability to entertain themselves without entertainment, absolving them of the desire to watch what other people are doing. I am not this person. Britney follows up in "Circus" with how she's a "put-on-a-show kind of girl," and I am, too, but more like a put-on-a-TV-show kind of girl, who feels more defined by my role as a devoted audience member rather than a performer. I like to quote this scripture when I'm being introduced to people in an entertainment medium, because long before my career started, I was deeply committed to consuming entertainment and being entertained by the world around me, supplementing my lack of lived experience with what I could observe about other people's lives.

It's vulnerable for me to open up these observations to the world, because I think of myself as an Erika Jayne on Opposite Day, meaning if somebody asked me, "How many Fs do I give?" the answer would be all of them. About everything. Ever. All of the time. Friendship, feelings, fandoms, fitting in, feminism. In my bones, I don't know how to not care the most. This book is my big reveal to those involved in eras of my life when I self-identified as "chill," a "no-big-deal" kind of gal after I saw Kate Bosworth in *Blue Crush* or Kate Hudson in *Almost Famous* and devoted my life to appearing "breezy." I'd scrunch my hair, say I loved rock 'n' roll, and sit in basements with boys playing in jam bands, secretly wishing I was listening to fewer instruments and more lyrics, noting the room would be much more inviting with lamp lighting and fewer wall tapestries. "I'm with the band!," I'd swear as I swung my Vera Bradley bag over my shoulder, because nothing gives a groupie an edge quite like mature floral quilting. But I knew that eventually the heart and purse I wore on my sleeve would reveal otherwise, or maybe a statement necklace would state my truth: I was, and always have been, with the bandwagon.

Most of my childhood was unplugged, but I made my first online profile around age ten, and social media introduced me to a whole new layer of information gathering, cultural celebration, and inevitable comparison. Suddenly, I was able to obsess over popular culture and also popular girls, from stars who were "just like us" in *Us Weekly* to the hometown stars I wanted to be just like, fantasizing that my cool new friend would say cute friendisms like "I love us!" weekly. In the early days of AOL and MySpace, having visibility into the personal lives of popular girls after school hours was an ideal way to perform some light discovery on how to infuse my personal brand with more desirable attributes. I cared less about grades and class rank than how I could acquire the subjective glamour that made me eligible for a far more prestigious formal ranking system: the MySpace top eight of upperclasswomen who embodied coolness at a Celica and cellular level. So I'd study group dynamics with the same level of vigor at school, the mall, in youth groups, or online, developing a passion for the millennial girls' zeitgeist that I've carried throughout my life and into my career, with my current full-time job as host of my podcast of six years, *Be There in Five.*

For most of my early life, I felt like an amalgam of the people, pop culture, and zeitgeist around me, forgoing the discomfort of forging my own identity and instead burying it in other people's whose coolness had already been preapproved by society. I would take cues from popular media and popular kids in school to curate a version of me that was not defined by what I liked, but by finding ways to get people to like me. I know that sounds sad, but to me, it was an exercise in resourcefulness. I would grow to like these things, too, and still do; I assume I wanted to ease my self-consciousness in the trenches of adolescent insecurity, hoping to grab on to the J.Crew peacoat-tails of something someone else said was socially acceptable so I could move through the world a little more smoothly. It's hard to explain, but for an observer and somewhat malleable person, acquiring social capital can become a hobbyist venture that you genuinely enjoy.

I think a lot of us now look back and cringe about many of the things we did to fit in, forgetting we grew up during a time when it seemed like avoiding being unique at all costs was the right thing to do. Though to be clear, it cost me a lot; I'm pretty sure I had my net worth tied up in a New York & Company credit card at one point, and I definitely spent a month's hostess earnings on a North Face Denali as an "investment piece." But I blame spending K–12 learning about things like SOHCAHTOA instead of personal finances! If we really want to play financially doomed millennial bingo, I also have had a suburban tanning salon send a collections agency after me and have been tricked into signing up for a credit card not once, but twice, at football games because it seemed reasonable to exchange the potential identity theft for a pilled fleece blanket or a free mousepad. This advertising tactic on college campuses was so predatory it's now illegal, but credit card companies asking for social security numbers at social functions was just one of the many things millennials were up against that we're still paying for.

While my desire to fit in was fueled by my zeitgeisty interests, deep down, it was also a symptom of my sensitivity. I wanted to make other people feel comfortable, and I felt okay only if someone else told me it was okay, if my outfit got okayed, or if I made sure they're okay with me being there. So throughout life, the way I processed my quest to study and follow the herd is through an enthusiasm for words, and my parents encouraged me to rappel into the depths of my feelings with verbal self-expression most of my life. I was an avid journaler, doodler, gel-pen collector, and a member of Shel's Angels, a term I just made up for superfans of Shel Silverstein's poetry. I have archives and archives of poems I've written throughout my life, and to this day, it remains the core cadence of my brain; you'll notice when I get into a rant, it sometimes comes out in a singsongy form, but I tried to keep it at bay. I put a handful of poems in this book, almost as a means to reclaim this hobby I was always embarrassed by. Taylor Swift says she fills the empty lunch tables of her past, and I fill the empty seats at my poetry reading at the local Borders Books & Music when I was thirteen. Throughout, I try to make a case for us all to try and care a little less about being liked, and I thought I'd lead by example and just let my corniness and tendency to get carried away with wordplay finally have a place. It's a trait that has gotten a lot worse with age; I blame listening to too much *Hamilton* from 2016 to 2018.

I feel like when people talk about girlhood, there's a tendency to romanticize and overstate one's complex inner-girl world, and I probably sound like that in describing my sensitive nature or interest in writing, but I think most people probably have a more complex interior than they let on. I don't think I'm deeper than anyone else or want to paint myself as some young, troubled, prodigious artist—far from it. I just was confused by my multitudes; I think many of us were, since we weren't opening up much about our inner worlds, thus assuming other people didn't possess similar complexities and there must be something wrong with us.

True to millennial form, I felt like I existed within endless contradictions. I obsessed over my appearance, but I wrote poetry agonizing over people judging books by their covers. I wanted to be an intellectual and read more books, but I felt happiest reading *Seventeen* and *YM* cover to cover, only to have to cover my ass when I struggled to finish a book for class. I also was an avid reader of yearbooks, where I researched senior quotes I could copy for AIM away messages, along with those hair yearbooks in the waiting area at Hair Cuttery. I'd contemplate an angled cut, a zigzag part, or face-framing layers, always opting for a "just a trim," even though I convinced myself this time would be different and I'd come back to school a new woman. It's interesting to me that for all the time I thought about getting layers, I never felt permission to have them within me; it was such a source of tension for me internally, feeling like a fraud who cared about all the wrong things in life, and worrying their shallow nature meant I wasn't sophisticated or intelligent.

In discussing these experiences on my podcast over the years, I've had so many women around my age echo the same default setting of self-consciousness that's hard to snap out of, and I'm always trying to pinpoint why we cared so much. Why was I worried my hobbies weren't good enough, why did I accept that they'd be weaponized against me? Why would I ever let someone who drafts make-believe football teams make me believe I should be embarrassed by my interests?

For better or worse, this was my experience; pop culture is my sport, these brands were my status symbols, and the times were very different. We didn't know any other way besides trying to stick as close to the status quo, whether you're a younger millennial who did so with Troy Bolton and the other Wildcats, or an older one who got their start at the Peach Pit or The Max. At many points, we experienced a harsh pop-cultural backdrop that was especially unforgiving toward women, and it took me several years to even recognize it as wrong. One of my goals for this book was to be kind and rewind through some highlights of one millennial's life now that I can contextualize it, and see what it looks like from a different point of view.

This book details my life stories, but while writing it, I thought about us: the not-so-few, the not-always-very-proud millennial generation as a whole. I think it's interesting that many of us waited so long to be taken seriously, to grow up and come into our own, hopefully shedding ourselves of adolescent self-consciousness, only to enter the workforce and realize that, to our superiors, we weren't defined by the growth we had achieved; to some people, we represented the enemy. In my first corporate job in 2009, I quickly learned that people, like, *really* didn't like millennials. Or how much I said the word "like." It wasn't always obvious; maybe an eye roll here and there when a process was pointed out as being inefficient by a digital native, or a casual approach to workplace professionalism made someone sneer. I also think I'm uniquely aware of millennial stereotypes because I spent the first several years of my career in market research, aka the business of professional stereotyping, and all my clients in the early 2010s talked about was trying to understand millennials. Our generation's consumer-behavior patterns were a significant departure from generations past, making us harder to target and sell to, and my days were filled with senior executives going on and on about how we all think we're "so special," or we're so entitled, lazy, full of contradictions, and flaky, they couldn't pin us down.

Even though these clichés aren't how I self-identify, I am a walking millennial stereotype for many other reasons. I'm thirty-five, got married later than the median age, am still a proud renter in an increasingly expensive city I should probably leave, and my dog is my child while I wait for some fertility stuff to work out; I suspect part of the difficulty is due to my life's delayed milestones and how that doesn't pause your biological clock. I haven't had a car since college, because I don't like owning things, and in the 2010s, I got reliant on the "millennial subsidy" of the gig economy, and have Ubered everywhere for the past decade. I spent the first half of my career in corporate market research, where I helped advertising clients optimize their campaigns with audience data (buzzwords!), did a stint as a Six Sigma Black Belt (shout-out to business-process improvers!), then left my stable job to pursue the millennial entrepreneurial boss-babe dream after a side hustle went viral and curiosity got the best of me. Why? Find a job you love, and you'll never work another day! It's the millennial way. This was the peak hustle/grind, quit-your-nine-to-five era of glamourizing entrepreneurship, and wow, did this lofty advice poorly prepare me to leave a stable situation postrecession, with no experience, hoping that a can-do attitude and a copy of *Lean In* would be enough to make me the next wunderkind.

There's a quote I often think about when attempting to articulate my experience as a millennial woman. It said, "From the outside looking in, you can't understand it. From the inside looking out, you can't explain it." While I wish I pulled this from a classic novel, it was actually something I read once on a sorority koozie (where I get all my news). Despite Bid Day 2K6 being long gone, I still find it profound in how it represents the way a group's shared experience can feel incredibly disconnected from outsiders' perceptions. When the term "millennial" graces a headline, instead of reading something celebratory, you're more likely to see our generational plight represented in the context of something we've ruined or disrupted, or the ways we've fallen behind, bypassing the sum of our experiences on the inside for the ways we don't appear to add up to other generations on the outside. In the 2010s, the media narrative became so unfavorable toward millennials, I was double-taking headlines about how we single-handedly destroyed economic sectors to make sure they weren't satire.

One of the early influences of this movement was *Time*'s infamous 2013 cover story, whose subtitle read, "Millennials are lazy, entitled narcissists who still live with their parents. Why they'll save us all."[1] The title of that piece was "The Me Me Me Generation," and it fueled the repetition-loving meme generation, inspiring journalists throughout the next several years to position changes in the marketplace as millennials killing off entire industries. We've been blamed in headlines for killing (no joke) movie theaters, department stores, the beer industry, vacations, company loyalty, bar soap, low-fat yogurt, the entirety of the American Dream, and the list goes on. In 2016, I remember experiencing price-point whiplash as we were blamed for the demise of paper napkins and then accused of destroying the diamond industry. The fact that people wanted to support Big Paper more than our desire to minimize waste tells you everything you need to know about how motivated people are to empathize with millennials. Society would rather blame our job-hopping and brunch-going for why diamonds are suffering more than, I don't know, a history of violence and exploitation? To make matters worse, it's hard to defend ourselves, because the act of not taking criticism well can be easily reduced to whiny millennial behavior.

To be fair, every generation has its unfair stereotypes and weaponizing of differences; it's human nature to feel like you know better than younger people with less life experience. Similarly, it's understandable

---

1. https://time.com/247/millennials-the-me-me-me-generation/

to feel like the opinions of people older than you are irrelevant. But over time, I've watched perfectly normal decisions be cherry-picked for scrutiny, as long as it serves a narrative that reinforces our behavior as self-absorbed, easily distracted, noncommittal, and basement-dwelling. Honestly, joke's on them; as a true-to-form nonhomeowning millennial, I don't even find that trope insulting. All I'm thinking is, *Damn, your parents have a basement?! That's awesome.* It's safe to assume this is the same logic being applied lately by content creators that make it seem romantic and adventurous to live in a van by the river. The insults of yesteryear are our new best-case scenarios.

That's why, in my experience, the stereotypes that come along with the label "millennial" are hard to frame as a badge of honor when the term feels more like a criminally adhesive HomeGoods sticker on that frame that I've spent years trying to scratch off. But the term originally was meant to simply represent a group of people coming of age around the start of the new millennium. According to the Pew Research Center, millennials are people born between 1981 and 1996, though generational definitions vary and aren't an exact science.[2] Born in 1987, I'm on the slightly older side of the midpoint, and initially, I couldn't decide if I think these generalizations are a self-fulfilling means to Myers-Briggs our birthdays or if it's a genuinely helpful way to examine the complexities of how a life stage intersects with a particular social, political, and cultural climate. In millennials' case, over time, I've started to understand how it can be a little bit of both.

While I don't identify with all of the common stereotypes, I understand how certain economic and technological shifts during our formative years impacted these perceptions, and how these outside forces

2. https://www.pewresearch.org/social-trends/2019/02/14/millennial-life-how -young-adulthood-today-compares-with-prior-generations-2/

will shape the uncertainty of our generation for years to come. For example, data from the Pew Research Center shows millennials have higher levels of student-loan debt, unemployment, and poverty, along with lower levels of personal wealth and income than preceding generations (Gen X and Baby Boomers) at this life stage.[3] But it's not for all those reasons I just listed, e.g., lazy or entitled; rather, it's because we're a product of our time, having faced the worst financial crisis since the Great Depression when many of us entered the workforce, and two recessions plus a global pandemic prior to age forty, leaving many of us considerably behind on milestones relative to other generations based on economic drivers alone. Another layer of financial implications became prevalent when millennials reached the life phase of having children. Understandably, things like experiencing a delayed building of personal wealth, the inaccessibility of home ownership, and the cost of childcare can impact the timing and affordability of expanding a family. It's certainly impacted the timing of my choices, and later I'll discuss the role of timing in frustratingly impeding your chances as well.

So my clients weren't wrong; we were told we were special by our parents, and maybe some of us had the audacity to believe it. But it turned out we're special in a different way: in the context of having especially disproportionate expectations relative to our realities. When our parents told us we could be anything we wanted, it was within the confines of what reality looked like in the 1980s, 1990s, and early 2000s, but the rules changed. For example, when you're told you need to get a college degree to get a job and become financially stable, only for the job market to change and the college degree to become the thing making you financially unstable, it's a hard adjustment that can affect the rest of your life. I've also noticed among friends and listeners that our coming of age during the information age made for a particularly confusing

---

3. ibid.

early adulthood. We planned our lives without a lot of information, making key life decisions more grounded in traditions, but are now in a world that's inundated with information and, therefore, surrounded by opportunities that didn't exist when we were planning our dreams.

Millennials also uniquely straddle two eras of connectivity, growing up during the most seismic technological advancement of the past century: the internet. We've witnessed the metamorphosis (my favorite Hilary Duff album) of technology and communication not once or twice, but year after year. While everyone experiences how technology influences a given life stage, the timing of your adolescence makes a huge difference. To reduce us to being the selfie-taking selfish generation is to suggest we've been given the world and to fully ignore the timing and implications of when and how the World Wide Web was given to us. While other age groups adapted as adults, we were the first to navigate and thus define the terms of curating an online persona before we could drive, vote, or, in my case, even see a PG-13 movie. We also experimented with our online identities before understanding the immortality of our behavior on the internet (and I'm sure the next several decades of millennials running for office will pay for it and do wonders for our reputation).

The implications of millennials being behind and being the first online have created a reality where our options differ vastly from our parents' (and our former) expectations. This would seem pretty intuitive relative to the passage of time for any generation, but there's something about millennials that feels hard to pinpoint, where I notice many of us feel very tormented by our departure from traditional values. In recent years, after many "pick your brain" conversations following my entrepreneurial venture, I've discovered that members of my generation want to seize the opportunity to pursue passion over a predictable profession, but are torn between the traditional values they held growing up versus the modern opportunities that greeted them once they did. To me, this is the nucleus of the millennial paradox.

Like I mentioned, in many ways, I represent this paradox, having spent the first half of my career in a predictable corporate pipeline, and the second half (up until this point) self-employed following a series of less stable but more fulfilling sources of income. Whenever I tell people about my current career (hosting a podcast about the female millennial zeitgeist), they are noticeably confused, often asking me how it's a full-time job, if I *actually* make money doing it, then asking me what my husband does, assuming he bankrolls it (he doesn't), among a barrage of other semicondescending comments questioning its validity. I get it; becoming a DIY self-appointed niche internet talk-radio host isn't exactly every parent's dream. My urge is to get ahead of the joke, to go full-on Chandler Bing and say, "Could there *be* anything more millennial than a career podcaster?" Yes, actually. One who got there because they started a doormat business they left a stable job for after seeing one singular episode of *Friends*. More on that later.

Even though I'm proud of my career, I constantly feel torn between the two value systems I mentioned earlier. I'm still holding myself to the formula of success that I knew to be true in my youth and feel guilty for my inability to follow it, despite knowing the formula no longer applies. Depending on the day, I'm either living out my dreams or have made a huge mistake in leaving corporate stability. I'm either the poster child or the imposter. I find the uncertainty of my life straying from the formula to be either energizing or consuming. Some days I find myself working toward things like a stable career, having kids, and owning a home, only to wonder if those are things I genuinely want, or if they are things I always thought I'd have, never knowing if their absence makes me conflate grief with desire. Somewhere in between the pursuit of passion and the desire for respect and stability, you'll likely find a lost millennial, recently hit square in the head with thoughts about how they were raised to feel like one in a million, who never thought in a million years they'd find themselves here, in many ways, back at square one.

And if I'm being a whiny millennial, I'll remind you it doesn't stop there; it used to just be frustrating that we're looked down upon by older generations, but recently, we've become the widely memeified laughing-stock of younger people, too. This was to be expected eventually, but I feel like it happened quickly, and it's been a tough transition for the first crew on the internet to feel like it's no longer our territory. Part of me wants to be, like, *Give us a break! We walked so you could hoverboard, Aidan!* But then I realize I'm doing something older generations tend to do that I don't like: holding age and life phases against you, as if we aren't all simply a product of our time, doing our best. I'm honestly okay with the ridicule, for the most part, because Gen Z is way funnier than I ever was on the internet; I was too scared of getting bullied offline to develop my own sense of humor, but they're all about individuality and inclusivity, from what my algorithm tells me. No generational wars will ever cloud something about younger people that I categorically applaud: their prioritization of self-acceptance.

Throughout this book, I'll often bring up how my pursuit of same-ness was troubling in some cases, while in others, pop culture and popular trends served as recognizable identifiers, and prior to being ridiculed for being basic in the late aughts and early 2010s, it was a way to ground your interests in pursuit of what was perhaps the most pervasive adjective of my millennial existence: popularity. Now uniqueness is valued, diversity is thankfully prioritized, and kids get on the internet and tell the world things I wouldn't even admit to my inner circle in my youth, like struggles with self-esteem, mental health, or body image. It's a different time, and we're having to learn who we are all over again against a completely different yardstick.

The point is, I often feel too young to be taken seriously by older generations and, more recently, too old and irrelevant to be considered cool by younger generations, though lately, I've been wondering why we ever left the definition up to people on the outside in the first place. On the inside, we know the truth. Millennials aren't rife with contradictions and allegedly falling behind because we're these entitled, spoiled creatures. We were raised in preparation for a world that no longer exists and are forever trying to navigate the terms. But when you think about the strength of being enthusiastic digital natives, paired with the beauty of many of our simpler, more unplugged upbringings, the contradictions start to look more like balance. I genuinely believe that navigating these disparate worlds makes us dynamic and well-rounded, and our ownership of what makes us unique on the inside is the only way to worry less about how it looks on the outside. I hope that now, given that the oldest millennials have entered their forties, as we step into more leadership roles and gain economic power, we'll finally get the chance to show the world what we're made of besides a suede Ugg.

I wanted to attempt a thoughtful excavation of my experience moving through the zeitgeist because I've always felt like we're a generation defined by stereotypes more than actual experiences, measured by major milestones instead of the moments when life happens in between. When I think about our (rose) golden days, I don't identify with a postrecession haze or blazing feelings of entitlement in the workplace. I haven't lived with my parents since I was seventeen and to own a house is still a huge dream, but those things aren't high on my list in terms of what it means to be a woman of my generation. I don't want to tell stories about how I found myself through pursuits of fine art or academia like I was told I would, I want to tell you about the existential questions I asked myself in a suburban mall at a Limited Too, how an NSYNC song almost made me lose my religion, how I credit my ability to wordsmith far more to AOL Instant Messenger than school, and it wasn't until I thought more about how Jessie Spano made me scared to call myself a feminist that I linked *Saved by the Bell* to my participating in the kind of feminism where you buy mugs with sassy phrases in the name of equality.

While some essays are more intense, introspective, and unresolved, others are celebratory, fun, and light; most are somewhere in between, as one of my missions in life is to be an example of a person who can contain multitudes as vast as the paper napkins and diamonds we destroyed. Even if the theme isn't quintessential to being a millennial, the state of the zeitgeist remains a background character in how I defined myself, entertained myself, or healed myself along the way. As a result, most essays have way too many specific pop-culture references that I won't always explain. While this strategy may not meet the gaze of critical acclaim, it does fit the criteria for a *Gilmore Girls* episode, which is the highest form of art I could strive for. In the same vein, this book may not always pass the Bechdel Test, but it does pass the Bledel Test, where I follow a similar career arc to Alexis Bledel's characters, spending my early years steeped in Stars Hollow fanfare, then moving onto time-sharing denim with friends, hoping to find a boyfriend studying abroad like Kostas in *The Sisterhood of the Traveling Pants*. Eventually, we get to a *Handmaid's Tale*–esque nightmarish dystopia in the late 2010s, but we enjoy ourselves first.

I wanted to open by acknowledging how millennials have been portrayed by outsiders for context, but the rest of the book is actually about one person's experience from the inside. Much of that experience has to do with celebrating the media and culture I grew up surrounded by as a millennial that makes me a product of my time, but it also has a lot to do with what it was like moving through the world as a young, impressionable woman who was easily influenced by the toxicity of her time. That experience isn't unique to our generation; this is something we share as women within and across generations. Even though it may look different depending on our respective environments, we share the experience of navigating formative years of girlhood alongside a social and cultural landscape that shapes us and stares at us, forever existing between looking out at the world and being painfully aware that we're being looked at.

I also want to note there's not one single standard "female" experience; my use of gendered terminology is meant to represent my individual identity as a cisgender woman, and not to exclude or erase anyone by implying a universal definition. I want to acknowledge the limitations of my personal vocabulary in expressing gender identity, but also note the importance for our narratives, definitions, and vocabularies coexisting and not replacing one another; there are many experiences and identities that exist within womanhood that deserve to be treated with the same level of validity, and my discussion of the female millennial zeitgeist is meant to contextualize, not exclude.

There are so many ways I wish to preface this book; when you have an internet career and become aware of all the eyes and ears, you slowly develop a superpower called The Disclaimer. Even if it's at the expense of the work speaking for itself, you start to prioritize preventative qualifiers that get lengthier and lengthier, usually as a result of the painful experience of people misunderstanding your intentions or requiring your work to cater to their individual needs to be allowed to exist. This is very, very challenging for me, hence this very, very long intro. Like I said, all the Fs. I had to edit down this book by taking out five thousand "this is just my opinion" qualifiers for the sake of word count, so even if I don't always get to say it, I hope these words count.

Please take with a grain of salt the hyperbolic use of my so-called generational truths; my goal is not to exclude others' experiences, rather to share what I know by focusing on my own, and I chose the title to imply that this book represents only one millennial's point of view. My observations, just like the media-fueled stereotypes I shared, will obviously fail to adequately represent how diverse and dynamic people's experiences are within a group of seventy-two million people in the U.S. alone.[4] When I pathologize my experiences, it's for the purposes

---

4. https://www.statista.com/statistics/797321/us-population-by-generation/

of humor, emotional exploration, and cultural analysis, and is meant to serve as entertainment above all else. This is absolutely not self-help; you'll soon learn I can hardly help myself, and I don't want to ever come across as being prescriptive. I hope to take accountability when I need to, include as many of you as possible in the range of things I reminisce about, and will try to navigate this delicate balance of comedy and contemplation the best I can.

I wrote *One in a Millennial* to explore all the ways my experiences feel so poignant and distinct despite also being aware of their common nature and tendency to be labeled as frivolous. Somewhere in between feeling one-in-a-million special, I also know the chances I'm alone in a lot of these feelings are a-million-to-none, as many of us grew up being put in boxes but are now left trying to think outside of the box as we do the work of rebuilding our self-worth. I wrote it to combat how I've felt self-conscious of the superficial nature of my pop-cultural interests, to encourage others to share theirs proudly, and to honor the easily written-off experiences that shaped us as young women. I never want to offend anyone, and I most certainly don't claim to speak for everyone. But like a true member of my generation, I was made to believe I can at least be someone.

And this is just one millennial's experience.

P.S. There are two types of interstitial passages in this book:

Pop-up Biblios are a nod to *Pop-Up Video,* my favorite way to get the scoop during music videos on VH1 that provided context about things that were happening in the scenes. These pop up at the end of chapters and serve as minichapters, elaborating on a topic or pop-culture touchstone that I reference in passing that deserves a closer look. I'll note these topics with bubbles (° O °) so you can refer to the end of the chapter to dive in deeper.

The shorter in-chapter interstitials I'm calling ~*~**SO Random**~*~ in attempts to reclaim this insult that was slung my way many times throughout my youth for having too many tangential thoughts that apparently did not serve to move the conversation forward. Some will be fun facts or miniessays, and not all chapters will have them; that's the beauty of being *so* random. Your interjections don't really make a ton of sense but somehow still feel necessary. You'll see a ~*~ next to a topic to indicate a random related sidenote coming up.

> **P.P.S.** The book is divided into three chronological parts as a nod to my favorite tagline from the radio shock jocks of yesteryear, who would describe their stations as playing the hits from the "eighties, nineties, and today." Although there's some overlap, to share my hits (and misses) throughout the decades, I've separated these essays into the 1990s, 2000s, and today. LYLAS!

Part I

1990s

I see it all, the first day of school, the crisp air of fall
The drop of my mom's hand when I braved the crosswalk
Hid from school supplies and demands in the stall
Find a cubby, pick a buddy, count off in groups
Never trade the fruit snacks that are blue
Don't blow your nose with brown paper towels by the sink
Don't mix the yellow marker with black ink
TV cart rolls in, Lord, hear our prayer
May your milk be chocolate, your pizza be square
Anxiety looks like a game of musical chairs
Take bubblegum medicine straight, no chaser
Resist the urge to chew on the pretty erasers
Pencils number 2, single-file lines led by one
Sticks and stones break bones but crutches look fun
Inside voices, mostly to save the air in your lungs
To live and breathe to impress the teacher
When it comes to people pleasers, start 'em young
Smell the pencil shavings cascading into a trash can
Never step on a skateboard but still wear the Vans
If the words hurt, stack the markers into a lightsaber

Then draw a sun in the top corner of every piece of paper
Stick the star stick-on earrings to your earlobes first
Then collect the star stickers stuck onto your best work
I stay home sick of myself, move a bed pillow to the couch
And wonder where those stickers are now
They fell off, but the need for validation stuck around
How did I get here?
Thirty years, four careers
Five minutes late, several dollars short
I retraced my steps when I laid on the floor
To engage not my abs but who I am at my core
The things I knew by heart but not anymore
Struck a pose with pen to paper, like knee to nose
Relief found in the posture of a child's prose

1

Limited To

In the early nineties, Mattel debuted a short-lived edition of their iconic dolls called Teen Talk Barbie. She was their first talking doll in decades, and finally, young girls could have a more modernized talking Barbie to represent their plight. Each Teen Talk Barbie would say four randomly selected phrases (from the 270 that were preprogrammed) upon pushing a button, including:

"Will we *ever* have enough clothes?"

"I love shopping!"

"Do you have a crush on anyone?"

"I love romantic music."

"Meet me at the mall."

"Let's plan our dream wedding!"

"Wanna have a pizza party?"

"Wouldn't you love to be a lifeguard?"

There were endless combinations of phrases for each doll, but those are a few of my favorites. However, this was not a favorite doll among many parents and activist groups, because depending on the four phrases she rotated through, it was unlikely you'd receive a well-rounded Barbie with a balance of topics related to school, boys, shopping, and hobbies within the random choosing of four out of 270 phrases, though I don't know the exact statistics. In my defense, I wholeheartedly agree with the phrase Teen Talk Barbie said that ultimately got her pulled off shelves:

"Math class is tough!"

In short, she is me. I am her. Math class really was tough for me; the mall was my third place; I loved clothes, boys, love songs, and pizza parties. And I have a pulse and grew up in the nineties, so of course, I've always glamourized lifeguard culture. According to an article from October 1992 in the *Chicago Tribune* titled "Barbie! Say it isn't so!"[5] even though some dolls said, "Let's start a business!" or "I'm studying to be a doctor!," depending on the phrases and the order in which they were said, Teen Talk Barbie's interests could appear problematically narrow for young girls, causing the American Association of University Women and many parents to protest her existence successfully. Initially, the ask was to remove the phrase about math class, but the manufacturer had no way of knowing which Teen Talk Barbies on the shelves said which phrases, so it would've been impossible to recall and reprogram them.

So, what were owners of Teen Talk Barbie allegedly offered as a replacement for the controversial dialogue? A mute model, aka a doll that said nothing.

This has been my experience in life trying to navigate my feminine interests. Early on, I owned my truth and proudly chatted about the hyperfeminine things I liked, before I understood their labeling as superficial, only to be silenced when I was told they aren't things a woman should like in order to be taken seriously. You'll later read how this has impacted me well into my thirties, where I now feel the need to order a pumpkin spice latte (PSL) incognito, so I don't appear too "basic" upon drinking a cozy fall treat. But in the context of "Math class

---

5. https://www.chicagotribune.com/news/ct-xpm-1992–10–13–9204020848-story .html

is tough!" I genuinely understand the backlash; if we want toys to serve as role models, this wasn't exactly helpful in getting more young women engaged with STEM fields that (especially at the time) were marked by our severe underrepresentation. But the doll was developed from a great deal of market research and wasn't designed to be something to aspire to; rather, it was supposed to meet young girls where they were, serving more as one of their peers. And in the nineties, I was less of a woman in STEM and more of a girl who just wanted to have nice stems, happily (if not naïvely) existing with my peers somewhere between "Do you have a crush on anyone?" and "Meet me at the mall!"

As a kid, I was shy, curious, and sensitive, and I surrounded myself with things that dared to be bolder and less plain than I felt. From observing the popular girls with big personalities to the glitter and glamour of pop stars to the self-expression I found in consumerism, literally making my every day a little more glittery with tubs of sparkly body gel. I started by studying my sister, Kelly; we were four years apart, and her world seemed much cooler than mine. From a young age, pop culture served as a unifier, bridging the age gap with our shared love of music, TV, and light crafting. When I think about it, she and her best friend, Monica, were my original influencers, and I remember a lot about elementary school, probably because I was attempting to collect enough data by copying their every move. I'd marvel at the craftsmanship of their oversized sweatshirts with ambiguously sourced iron-on decals outlined with puff paints, studying the effort put into matching the design of a folded-down turtleneck underneath, worn over stirrup leggings sensibly anchored into a pair of Keds. Monica said that her dream car was a Mazda Miata, and for years I'd tell people that my dream car, too, was a Mazda Miata, never having seen one before. I could often be found sporting one of Kelly's Peace Frog T-shirts to school, so everyone knew I was cultured in that mall-kiosk sort of way, and I was green with envy when she was old enough to hit up the Piercing

Pagoda and have some sixteen-year-old probably named Trevor pierce her ears, leaving me in the dust to oversee our collection of clip-on and stick-on earrings.

Our shared love of pop culture started to wear on me when we became fragmented by the entertainment that was considered age-appropriate. But the perk of this age difference was that it was a dream to sneak into her room and get to consume more mature content, stealing her *Romeo + Juliet* soundtrack at every turn so I could giggle at the band name "Butthole Surfers," or unknowingly curse the name of my beloved Uncle Joey via scream-singing "You Oughta Know," which I later found out was rumored to be about *Full House*'s Dave Coulier. Much to the discontent of my ears (but to the delight of my eyes!), Kelly dabbled in floor-to-ceiling nineties door beads in high school, which turned my covert operation of breaking into her room into an obvious criminal cacophony.

While door beads were a stunning interior accent for a teenager (which Limited Too and Britney's *Oops! . . . I Did It Again* cover dreams were made of), they were also profoundly impractical. They get caught in your hair, snag the fibers of your sweater, and make it incredibly difficult to carry things in and out of the room. On top of that, they were also incredibly loud, waking us all up in the middle of the night, like an indoor plastic wind chime nobody asked for. When the noise was brought to her attention, instead of removing the door beads, she decided her best bet was to military-style crawl under them at night every single time she came and went from her room. To this day, I've never witnessed such a commitment to aesthetics at the expense of practicality. For any doubts cast her way about her love of spirited décor, she casts another seasonal throw pillow onto her couch in celebration of her taste, and I have always loved this about her. May we all do more of the same.

My mom, dad, sister, brother (and my dog, Daisy Mae), and I lived in a suburb of Richmond, Virginia, for most of my life. My sister and I spent our days pretending to be the Olympics women's gymnastics team or figure skaters, making it a full family operation, whether tasking my brother as the announcer on an echo mic, having my mom score our routines, or insisting my dad document them on VHS. The early days of our furniture-less family room that my parents would apologize for was a childhood luxury to me; I felt I'd hit the jackpot, having ample carpeted space to perfect my skills, doing cartwheels and round-offs and triple axles for hours worthy of tinfoil medals. We'd make up dances to "Achy Breaky Heart" or "Kokomo" and make sure my dad filmed those, too, with his giant heavy camcorder in case Ed McMahon called and needed the footage for *Star Search*. Most of my early memories of childhood are charmingly disconnected; time was measured between pool parties, Scholastic book fairs, and stapled construction paper ring countdowns to Christmas, followed by Valentine's papier-mâché shoebox making and gumball raking to hold us over until the lightning bugs ushered back in Ghost in the Graveyard season. Making our own fun from scratch was uncomplicated, and I appreciate how it required us to be more creative, but even back then, I knew I had big Ariel "Part of Your World" vibes, and was dying to do as much research as possible for the activities on dry land I was too young to participate in.

If it were up to me, I would have been the most extreme version of a nineties iPad kid, but early on, access to TV, movies, and media was more limited, arguably fueling my obsession. In my house, there were finite windows of TV watching allowed, MPAA guidelines followed for movies, and absolutely no TVs in bedrooms. All of their rules made sense and went along with guidelines for age appropriateness, but I wasn't having it. There were workarounds; for example, it was always a thrill to watch inappropriate programming at other people's houses, and I feel bad for saying this, but I honestly remember hesitating to return to a friend's place upon learning they didn't have cable, as if we had irreconcilable differences. I would take them under my wing, making the rare recommendation to go to my house after school, knowing we could at least soak in some blue rays for thirty minutes to an hour. I feel bad if I was judgmental about this because I didn't understand cable was cost-prohibitive. However, I did understand what it was like to be pop-culturally excluded, so I felt it was my duty to introduce friends to new shows. After all, I couldn't be a snob about it; I felt like a woman of the people because I hadn't reached the zenith of what you could watch on a Zenith: the subscription-based Disney Channel.

At my house, the workaround was to strategically watch certain shows or channels when unsupervised or everyone was asleep, with your finger feverishly glued to the RETURN or BACK button on the remote. In the event of a parent passing by, you could flip from MTV or VH1 to Nickelodeon quickly. But even then, my parents had some hot takes. *Ren & Stimpy* was too crass, but not *Doug*; noted. *Roundhouse* was too mature, but not *All That*; got it. Like Lori Beth Denberg, it was Vital Information for me to understand these preferences, because as badly as I wanted the scoop, there is nothing I ever wanted as badly as staying out of trouble. I'm sure they knew the whole time, but I convinced myself I was outsmarting them by pretending I was watching *Get Smart* on Nick at Nite when I was visibly sweating after switching off *Beavis and Butt-Head* in the nick of time at night, but I felt like it was harmless. Little did my mom know, I was pretty in the loop with mature themes and teenage at-risk behavior. I mean, I watched Fiona Apple's "Criminal" video. I had seen some stuff.

Since my access to TV and movies was limited, the other ideal place for doing R&D about the teenage world was the mall. And like Teen Talk Barbie, it was where I felt like I belonged. I recall discovering my passion for the mall as a preteen at a magical place called Limited Too. One day I was feeling particularly blue, and I walked past an item that read DO YOU LIKE ME? CHECK YES, NO, MAYBE SO. My stomach dropped. I had recently tried to employ this method when I passed a note to my classmate Josh, asking him out, offering these three options: yes, no, maybe. Imagine my delight when he passed it back to me with a promising "maybe," as I spent several days preparing for my yes, with my optimism only mitigated by the ever-present threat of jinxes. I was so excited about my first boyfriend; my thoughts were consumed with girlfriend cosplay as I tried to figure out if I'd be a DJ to his Steve or a Kelly to his Zack. But like Icarus flying too close to The One, I came crashing down when he had a friend tell me in the cafeteria he wanted to change his answer to "no."

On the heels of this "no," I found a sense of home at the mall, likely under a sign in Limited Too that said something like IT'S A GIRL'S WORLD, floating above the racks of clothing, accessories, and sassy sayings inside the store. I remember it being a wonderland of rotating rainbow lights, the curliest fonts, inflatable furniture, funky hair accessories, photo booths, and a personal-care section with gateway tween cosmetics. With multicolored daisies everywhere, flower power appeared to be a domineering authority, but the feminine fanfare solicited overt girl power, too. For me, girl power wasn't new. I was a Spice Girl, after all, from my commitment to their branded Chupa Chups to begging my mom for a platform shoe. My friend crew recently had to ditch our Spice Girls Halloween costumes because the boys in our school seemed to think they weren't hip, so I assume I dodged the shirts that read my favorite Spice name, BABY, to instead rifle through graphic tees that said ANGEL, DIVA, and I DIDN'T ASK TO BE A PRINCESS, BUT IF THE CROWN FITS. Upon fact-checking my memories of Limited Too, I saw other tees from that era that read I ONLY SHOP ON DAYS THAT END IN Y. I wished. I was there to shop 'til I dropped the thought of Josh, a name I thought was hot ever since I saw *Clueless.* I was hoping to buy a fuzzy pen like Cher's to circle tips from a magazine a friend shared about how to shave the fuzz off our legs.

Thinking back to how I felt as a preteen in a suburban mall is a sensory experience. Where else are young people on a leaf-raking budget actively encouraged to take up space? I spent many days there with my girlfriends, subsisting on Auntie Anne's pretzel samples, makeovers from buying one Clinique lip gloss, and gaming the free-gift-with-purchase system like the Groupon queens we'd later become. I loved the sights, the sounds, and the skylights paired with mediocre indoor landscaping that attempts to provide an indoor-outdoor coastal feel in a landlocked state. Despite buying almost nothing, the mall still somehow provided everything. You could further your education at Waldenbooks but spend most of your time browsing the boy-band-calendar section. You could listen to only demos of those boy bands at Sam Goody and pretend you were in the "One Sweet Day" music video when you put on the giant headphones. You could exercise your musical talents further with rain sticks at Natural Wonders, but not before debating if you wanted to buy a single polished rock and place it in a velvet bag (an early sign that millennials would later resort to crystals for self-care). I used to love the wholesome Beatrix Potter energy of Crabtree & Evelyn juxtaposed with the market research one could collect at Spencer Gifts in the key-chain section to learn new curse words. I could then relax and rejuvenate from my guilt toward my expletive enchantment with a chair massage at a Brookstone. If I had been loaded, I would've taken my talents to get a Sharper Image of myself at Glamour Shots, but my mom never seemed interested in sponsoring photos of me at age ten with a smoky-eyed sultry stare and a used showgirl's boa.

I recall being intoxicated by the smell of loose change in a fountain, envious of its riches because I had to find something within my allowance budget to get that shopper's high. Per the canon of the board game Mall Madness, I knew that the only way to lose after a day at the mall is not to buy anything. I found an alternate solution for my under-construction conspicuous consumption and would often take my talents to the barrels at Bath & Body Works, where they sold miniature hand sanitizers that I decided were the perfect timeless, affordable, and fragrant option under five dollars. At the time, Bath & Body Works had an indoor-market feel with barrels of products leading the display, almost like a Cracker Barrel, just without the rocking chairs and with a lot more teenage theft. There were also stunning red gingham awnings that pulled me in like a moth to a flaming redhead because they reminded me of the elegance of Felicity Merriman's canopy bed. I think I speak on behalf of many American Girls° O ° when I say that as a kid, I assumed the ultimate status symbol of wealth was a canopy bed. I grew up circling Felicity's red-checkered linens to remind Santa that my collection would forever feel incomplete without a proper Colonial bedchamber. Underneath the shade of these indoor awnings, I would dig and dig through piles of uninspired Country Apple and Sun-Ripened Raspberry sanitizers, hoping to get my hands (and then sanitize them) on the holy-grail hot-girl scents: Cucumber Melon, Warm Vanilla Sugar, and Sweet Pea. It was the most affordable way I could own an item that held status at school, and most of my memories of going to the mall over the years were no different. I'd acquire popular branded consumer goods to be in good standing with my peers, hoping brands would green-light me as a likable human when I was wading through preteen uncertainty that made it challenging to like myself.

If I went into the lore of a Hot Topic, I'd get way too off-topic, but that was where my sister bought a shiny shirt and pair of butterfly hologram platform sandals with her F.U. babysitting money that would spark my love for high fashion. And by that, I mean the fashions that only look appealing to you when you're likely high from spending too much time sniffing Fierce cologne inside an Abercrombie.

Admittedly, it was always exciting to get slightly asphyxiated by the cologne pumping out of a Hollister or an Abercrombie & Fitch. They were effectively the Subway sandwich shop of the galleria with their forced fragrances that subliminally influenced me to buy more paper-thin layers, or perhaps spend my entire allowance on an age-inappropriate shirt that said MIDNIGHT COWGIRL. The hope was that an employee might notice you, because everyone knew that if you were hot, you got asked to work there. Later I'd come to realize I was likely too young for a part-time job in my peak mall-rat days and maybe that's why I was never asked, but if I'm being honest, it's also fair to say that preorthodontic work, my looks were better suited for a Wet Seal stockroom. But I didn't care. This was the height of nineties makeover-obsessed America; there was hope for everyone, and all the beautiful things and people at the mall made me dream of my potential. However, thinking about the mall serving as a linoleum castle of self-improvement through consumption is precisely why I can't quite figure out if I honor these memories or if I, too, was inappropriately programmed like Teen Talk Barbie.

When I reflect on my immersion in nineties mall culture, I feel confused. Perhaps the most accurate depiction of being in a "girl's world" at Limited Too in my earliest mall days was me seeking a sense of empowerment through clothes or accessories or makeup to modify something about my image in the presence of male rejection. But can't a gal with a deflated ego window-shop for an inflatable sofa, if only to be reminded that the person she loves will one day be seated next to her on an elegant love seat made of 100 percent plastic? On the one hand, it doesn't actually feel that deep. The store did feel like a girl's world, an aesthetic love-bombing that made me feel like—despite my age and broken heart—I could take on the world, Too. But on the other hand, through the lens of Teen Talk Barbie's assumed difficulty with math, these candy-coated memories look disproportionately bleak. In the context of preteen girls trying on in fitting rooms T-shirts that said I LEFT MY BRAIN IN MY LOCKER, the shoe fits. Beyond that fuzzy pen, what Cher and I shared is that they wanted us to believe we were *Clueless*.

I think about the toys and games I loved to play in my childhood, and while gender-neutral or STEM-focused toys for girls were less common in the nineties, I still could have built stuff with LEGO bricks or Lincoln Logs or played Risk with my brother if I wanted to. But I didn't. My parents tried introducing me to more intellectual and cultural pursuits. I couldn't be bothered. Other than being a Francophile in terms of my interest in French manicures or magazine how-tos about French kissing, I didn't have particularly cultured interests. I spent my days willingly and gleefully as the material girl next door, doing a round-robin of neighborhood friends' houses that had the good games, and for me, the more superficial, the better. I loved Pretty Pretty Princess, where you're taught success means simply just collecting more jewelry than the rest of your friends. While it's not exactly virtuous, it's also not *not* true, so I did learn something playing that game. I also loved to dabble in fictitious credit-card debt with the aforementioned game Mall Madness. The goal? To finish your shopping list! How to excel? Score a sale, of course! There were valuable lessons of savviness and task completion amidst the overt cosplaying of consumerism. I guess the devil works hard, but capitalism works harder. But I didn't know better; before we had Lady Gaga to make us feel comfortable in our skin for being "Born This Way," we had Mall Madness ads on Nickelodeon telling young girls in the early nineties we were "BORN to shop!" reinforcing what we already knew from the likes of Teen Talk Barbie and T-shirts that said we only shop on days that end in "y." To be fair, the messaging was everywhere, and I ate it up. With all these cultural touch points reinforcing how I'm a girl and must love to shop, how would I not take it as some sort of a calling?

If I wasn't doing that, I was pretend-calling teenage boys with the board game Dream Phone, whose name says it all. A dream of a game that came with a hot-pink phone, where the entire objective was to call boys who provided minimal, robotic-like responses to narrow down who had a crush on you. Again, it's not *not* accurate for what it's like to date in the modern world. I had to get through countless less-than-charming text responders of the word "k" before I found my prince who took the time to spell out the entire word "ok." The least realistic thing about the game was that all the boys I was interested in would pick up my calls, so if anything, it was aspirational. Another game I spent a lot of time playing was called Girl Talk: A Game of Truth or Dare. It was a board game where you had to pick truth or dare, and if you didn't do an embarrassing dare or admit an equally humiliating truth in front of your friends, you got penalized. But not with something arbitrary like losing points in a game; rather, with a simulation of (a girl's assumed) worst nightmare: getting a zit. Each game came with a sheet of fake red zit stickers to serve as a visible penalty to your beauty if you were uncooperative. The *layers*! I guess long before "chicks before dicks" entered my girl-world lexicon, I learned to put the demands of chicks before zits by participating in games of truth or dare that bordered on bullying in the name of peer pressure and a clear complexion.

A common theme you'll hear throughout this book is how I often struggle with the dichotomy between celebrating the things I grew up with for what they were while also criticizing the way they shaped my worldview. I know that in many ways my interests are a product of the boxes I was placed in, but when you're inside a box and don't know any better, it looks a lot like freedom. So I decorated that box the best I could and had a great time playing games of being at the mall, playing truth or dare, and talking about boys, zit stickers and all. Looking back on my girlhood I'm both charmed by my earnest devotion to semisexist things and horrified that they represented a set of options that seemed so comprehensive of my worldview, I didn't even notice it was narrow. But when I think about the ever-present misogynistic trivializing of women's interests, I also feel frustrated by the hypocrisy and want to defend all of this behavior vehemently. How dare they criticize the way we've chosen to decorate the boxes they've put us in? I find there's great irony in how society aggressively promotes the same things to girls they ultimately shame them for caring about, like growing up surrounded by media that taught us to only care about boys, clothes, and shopping, only to be told you're vapid if you're boy crazy, love fashion, and hang out at the mall. Shows like *Baywatch* were made to pander to straight males, whose gaze is often centered in mass culture, so this trickled down to girls like me developing a fascination with the glamour of lifeguard culture, which likely showed up in the focus groups that influenced Teen Talk Barbie. It's all interconnected. It bothers me to no end that the same world that programmed us to like these things also tells us that we shouldn't tell people they are our interests if we want to be taken seriously. When it comes to women, it often feels like they'd prefer the mute model.

I guess Too things can be true: I found comfort in consumerism at Limited Too on the heels of male rejection, and I look back on this fondly. I had a great time playing Mall Madness, Dream Phone, Girl Talk, etc. But I'm also alarmed that my instincts were no more dimensional than a doll who was comparably programmed to vacillate between mentions of her crush and going shopping. Some days I want to rage against the way I was programmed; some days, I want to be allowed to just exist. Some days I'm not totally convinced that there's enough distance between my hyperfeminine nature and the way stereotypically feminine things nurtured me; maybe they just got the right target audience. But then I become concerned about being brainwashed with some sort of Mars-Venus logic that tells women gender roles are a product of innate preferences and not oppression. Perhaps for me, it was a mixture of both, and I don't know how to feel about it. The older I get, I guess I'm still playing truth or dare in a sense; I'm trying to sit in my truth, but some days I dare to ask if that truth was ever mine to begin with. Like the Facebook relationship status millennials became known for in the aughts or my second-favorite Nancy Meyers film, it's safe to say *It's Complicated.*

It's also complicated that during my more poignant moments, I genuinely do not know how to land a plane without entering into a Carrie Bradshaw "I couldn't help but wonder . . ." cadence (a symptom many of us must work through after spending formative years under Michael Patrick King's verbal reign). But we're talking about the millennial zeitgeist, so I'll channel my seventh-favorite direct-to-VHS Mary-Kate and Ashley film and say, *When in Rome.*

What I'm trying to say is I couldn't help but wonder, all this time, was I empowered by the girl's world I found within the walls of Limited Too? Or did those walls uphold yet another ceiling for what they wanted us to believe we were Limited To?

Decades later, I guess I'm just now starting to put two and Too together.

What can I say, math class is tough.

° ○ ° Pop-up Biblio: American Girls Next Door ° ○ °

In the nineties, across America, many young cereal eaters Honey Smacked the box they had been reading off the breakfast table to make room for the apex of aspirational living through historical consumerism: American Girl catalogs. It was less of a catalog and more a way of life. When people talk about nineties toy hysteria, they usually refer to Beanie Babies, but I think AG catalogs were their own form of Beatlemania. Mostly because I cried a bunch when I realized how out of reach the price points were. I pored over those catalogs; their fearless leader and aesthetics were relentlessly Pleasant; I would dog-ear pages and circle the approved fashions like Miranda Priestly editing the September issue. For a gal with a kindergarten education and not a dime to my name, I sure had some hot takes about antique furniture and sartorial choices. I imagine myself with a mouthful of Waffle Crisp and saying under my breath, "Really, Samantha's birthday story? A pinafore with a flower crown? Florals, for spring . . . groundbreaking."

My grandpa surprised me with Kirsten when I was around five, and it was literally the best day of my life. I was shook to my cottage core upon meeting 1854's hottest frontierswoman. I have a picture of that day framed in my office, and I am now thirty-five years old. I took out those milkmaid braids faster than you can say "depreciation," adoring her crimpy hair that I always attempted to achieve via sleeping in double Dutch braids before picture day, hoping it would finally be the year I'd be less plain and tall. When I really think about it, it's kind of remarkable that Pleasant Company made young women in a Teen Talk Barbie America suddenly enamored with activities like hand-tufting a muslin-border friendship quilt. Being immersed in this world made it seem like Malibu couldn't hold a Saint Lucia candle to the Minnesota frontier. My Barbie wouldn't settle for less than a hot-pink Jeep Wrangler and dream-home McMansion, so I'm sure no one saw it coming that I would audibly gasp upon receiving a doll in a calico dress whose only accessory was a wooden spoon.

Though I grew fatigued of life on the frontier when I flipped the page and the hot accessory for her school collection was a bucket and ladle, aka another wooden spoon. So I set my sights on Samantha Parkington, whose grandmother (named Grandmary) had serious coin and the best grandmother nickname in town. To this day, I find Samantha's winter-story outfit to be unbelievably chic, with a wool cape, white fur accessories, and a tasteful handbag that was somewhat of a Gymboree Birkin of its time. Although I'm not sure I would've gone for the matching rabbit-fur muff and hat to visit my friend at the orphanage; but go off, queen.

Of course, nothing competes with Felicity's red-gingham canopy bed and blue taffeta holiday gown; these girls invented Christmas formalwear in ways that justified my commitment to remarkably itchy velvet dresses with lace collars and candy cane–printed white tights tucked into my Sam & Libbys in hopes I'd have a Merriman Christmas. While Samantha was an aspirational, standoffish Victorian Kate Middleton in the flesh, I never had her. My sister had Molly, whose vibe was more relatable, kind of a World War II geeky fresh. My neighbors had Addy and Felicity, and all the American Girls next door would convene to swap their clothes and accessories to supplement our unfulfilled Christmas wish lists and create the catalog setup of our dreams. To be clear, while I longed for many items in the catalog, I only had one doll, and it was a gift. To this day, I struggle not to pass judgment on people of the whole-bedroom-set persuasion, as if they don't share my same capacity for longing because they got everything I wanted. My mom was so sweet and would get Samantha's or Felicity's dresses for me to put on Kirsten so I could pretend I had all the dolls. For my church confirmation, my parents got me a life-sized replica of Samantha's Victorian school desk, and I can't wait for the day when I can transport it to Chicago. Given that Victorian school desks are full-on cast iron, it hasn't been the most practical item to hang on to for my transient childless millennial apartment-dwelling lifestyle, but hopefully, one day I can give it to my future offspring so they can watch their iPad on it.

These dolls and their accessories were too insanely expensive to justify for most families, to the point where the only time

I didn't find math class to be tough was when I'd do some light mental math eying new school friends' collections when I'd go play at their houses. Devoted catalog flippers knew those price points by heart, and there were certain cues that made me willing to bet that you were also a Horse Girl and you likely had an intercom system where I could call downstairs and inquire if there was a trampoline out back to cement our new BFF status. I knew once I saw a tiny leg cast or doll wheelchair out of the corner of my eye that your parents had the cash to send your doll to the doll hospital. I bet they also loosened the purse strings to mail $17 via check or money order to Mary-Kate + Ashley's Fun Club, a dream!

I wish I could ask my grandpa if he got me Kirsten because she looked like me or if he wanted me to be more in tune with the journey of my ancestors, who started immigrating to the Midwest around the same time as Kirsten did. I wish I had access to the stories of the brave girls who came to America and paved the way for me, and now I realize their invisibility in history books makes these dolls' stories so important. But back then I was pretty much only concerned about the outfits, and I wish I could apologize to my grandpa for being so pretentious about Kirsten's clothing releases. I mean, Samantha's extra outfit was this gorgeous white tea dress she wore to manners class with Grandmary; she *never* missed. Kirsten's extra outfit was a head-to-toe work dress for helping her dad do chores, described in the catalog as "coming with ribbons just the color of the thick cream that filled her bucket when she milked the cows," a caption that maybe bums me out more than her best friend, Marta, dying on that riverboat.

I reread some of the books recently and was honestly amazed at the important stories they told. In history class, it seemed like we only learned about men who held power and leadership roles, and good for Pleasant Rowland for going out of her way to put women in the sequel, if you will, even though it feels sad to applaud a bare-minimum inclusion. I remember borrowing Addy Walker's books from the library, and reading *Meet Addy* for the first time was poignant, heartbreaking, and horrifying in ways that stuck with me. In the beginning, she is enslaved with her family on a Southern plantation, and she eventually escapes with her mother to Philadelphia but is split from the rest of her family. If you looked at the Girls as just dolls, it was easy to focus on who did and did not look like you (and now that I think about it, it feels kind of odd that we played with dolls whose backstories represented very real and traumatizing circumstances). But I think most superfans read the books with a level of respect, like the diary of a friend rather than the frivolity of general fiction, and the beautiful part of each doll having a book series was getting to know who they were beyond their appearance, and learning about the circumstances they were in, the differences we should celebrate, and the similar experiences young girls have spanning generations.

In Addy's case, her historical context was memorable, but more importantly, what stood out were her many other qualities, like her continued resilience, desire to read, and passion for education, along with the main arc of her journey to reunite her family. While my POV isn't the most important in analyzing the impact of her character, I will say reading the books was an informative point of entry for girls like me who were exposed to somewhat selective forms of U.S. history in school. They spoke to young adults with candor, like they were smart, competent, empathetic readers, and shared details of the horrifying realities of slavery and the Civil War that were often glossed over in history class, such as what life actually looked like for families like the Walkers after they were freed. The AG books were a completely different way to understand history, allowing you to experience them through the eyes of a girl your own age. In interacting with the doll, it was like I knew her, and it made the books feel more real, and witnessing the inhumanity had an impact. I worried for her as a peer, unknowingly absorbing the historical accuracy in the process.

The popular choice for AG dolls (at least in my neck of the cul-de-sac) was a doll that looked like you, hence me getting Kirsten. Something about the doll "that looked like you" was exciting, and if we're celebrating and criticizing, you'd think something called "American Girl" would have worked harder on representation when claiming to represent girls in America. Even though I loved the books and dolls, I was a blond-haired, blue-eyed kid who was well represented everywhere; I didn't need more dolls that looked like me. During the brand's first seven years, there were only four dolls: a blonde, two brunettes, and a redhead, and Addy was the only nonwhite doll until Josefina's release in 1997. Following that, Addy was the only Black historical doll for nearly eighteen years, and the brand completely neglected to expand on other storylines that could've highlighted the invaluable role of Black girls in America throughout different eras. I now hypothesize that when they were bought by Mattel, they started promoting the custom-designing of dolls that looked like you so they could cover everybody, rather than focusing on diversifying the backstories. But I'd argue that misses the point; the integrity of the initial collection was rooted in showcasing the less visible contributions of young girls throughout history and sharing the unique elements of their environments and eras. Ideally, girls could find one that looked like them or shared an interest with them, and hopefully, it would help them realize their potential and understand the importance of their contributions, too. It's disappointing to look back and see what a missed opportunity it was to not develop dolls earlier and more often that highlighted the culture and forces of change that existed among young members of historically excluded groups.

While there's a lot I now side-eye about the brand's execution, I genuinely celebrate American Girl's core concept; it's really cool to take a doll that (in the context of a baby doll) represents a toy that once embodied the options women were Limited To and use it to tell stories of young women who, as a result of limitations on women in their time, likely have stories that have been erased from history. Rather than just serving as a shell of a doll to dress up and play with, they had real stories of hardship, triumph, and friendship. Even though they were dealing with things like slavery, being an orphan, experiencing xenophobia, and enduring world wars, those hardships didn't define them as much as they contextualized them. You got to know young women from different eras facing different types of challenges and oppression, not just for their suffering, but for their hobbies, interests, relationships, and, most importantly, humanity.

2

Back in the Daybed

When I think of the mascot of my childhood, I think of my daybed. To me, daybeds are a piece of millennial iconography. While they still exist, something about their style back then was so squeakily specific and something I genuinely miss. Before Pert ever made 2-in-1 seem like a Plus, the daybed was a two-in-one piece of furniture popularized in the eighties and nineties that was undeniably plush. A twin bed masquerading as the world's least-practical couch, a daybed is an upscale futon with big Laura Ashley energy that you'd often spot at your friend Laura or Ashley's house. It was roomy but still only slept one person comfortably; it had two jobs but only did one well, and was supposed to be cozy despite being made of cold hard metal rods. I could never quite figure out how to enjoy the couch feature when three sides of the bed were lined with spaced metal bars that did not make for a comfortable backrest but, to be fair, would've made for a lovely outdoor gate.

All that aside, the fact that I slept in a twin-sized daybed until I was eighteen is kind of fitting; as a person who always had trouble sleeping, nights were more like days for me in terms of my activity level. While I assume most people associate their bed with sleeping, I associate mine with being wide awake. Most nights at home, I would make my own fashion shows, music videos, or fantasies for as long as I could get away with having the lights on. Sometimes I wonder if my love for pop culture comes from always having difficulty falling asleep and therefore needing to occupy myself in my room. I clocked many awake hours in bed, reading, writing, listening to music, or browsing a *J-14* magazine so I could lust after the brothers from *Home Improvement,* who all had three names (Zachery Ty Bryan, Jonathan Taylor Thomas, and Taran Noah Smith—do we think three names were a prerequisite to be on the show?). I also devoted a few too many hours to pretending to be a nineties supermodel, or getting lost in my own movie makeover montages, learning from movies and TV that I could no longer be a "before" if I was to find my happily ever after.~*~ Otherwise, I'd lie awake, balancing a flashlight at the expense of my penmanship, hoping if I drained my head of thoughts, I'd get some rest.

~*~ SO Random: Slay All Daybed ~*~

Writing about how formative entertainment was for me in my childhood is tricky because "pop culture" is much too broad a term relative to what I had access to. To provide an example, my world was a level of insular that resulted in me being introduced to icon/legend RuPaul's body of work via a bargain-bin soundtrack to *The Brady Bunch Movie,* since VH1 was off-limits at first. I lovingly blame RuPaul for why my room was always a mess, with clothes strewn across my bed and floor, playing with outfits in a manner that was fueled by the normalization of the chaotic makeover and fitting-room montages in movies, first simulating the iconic scene in *Clueless* to the tune of "Supermodel." But I found my own "Sunshine Day" after I put the *Brady Bunch* CD into a three-disc changer and heard track nine: "Supermodel (You Better Work)" by RuPaul, *the* premier anthem for pretending to be inside a movie makeover scene. Long before a remake scored *The Lizzie McGuire Movie,* I'd take the trundle out of my daybed to serve as a makeshift bedroom cat-walk and give my best Linda, Naomi, Christy, Cindy, Claudia, and Niki to a flimsy floor-length mirror.

I was enamored with supermodels back in the day, wondering what it would be like to submit photos to esteemed institutions like Barbizon or John Robert Powers. I remember basking in the glow of the limelight when my sister, Kelly, was chosen to model in the Limited Too window at the mall, and I thought it was her big break. We've since learned this gig was more like an early MLM, conning young women into attaining their Niki Taylor dreams by wearing untailored elastic shorts under the guise of girl power to perform free labor for a small discount while drawing all your friends into the store. But what's an aspiring model to do? RuPaul told me I'd better work, and if that meant performing child labor in exchange for a tepid discount, so be it.

I never got asked to model at the mall, or an American Girl fashion show, or ever at all, but I think I look back fondly on make-believe movie makeover montages because I did this before I felt self-conscious about how I looked. I feel grateful there was a time I could joyfully tear through a tornado of outfits for sport and not out of spite. When RuPaul sings, "It don't matter what you do, 'cause everything looks good on you," I believed it. I felt like I could take on the world. Or at least my room. A slay all daybed, if you will. Of course, now I realize that drag terminology didn't belong to girls like me doing a "sashay, shantay" while trying on a twin set at Kohl's, but I also thought RuPaul's start was on the B side of a critically unacclaimed movie soundtrack in a bargain bin at Hollywood Video. I had yet to learn many important lessons.

I also loved daybeds because they were like the nesting dolls of bedroom furniture; many had a twin mattress called a trundle you could pull out from underneath if you had a friend over, and they pretty much served as the guest bedroom of childhood. If the daybed was squeaky, the trundle bed was like the daybed's squeakquel, because it was louder, but still not as loud as the nights of endless laughter had with friends on them, gossiping about classmates, dreaming about our futures, and talking about the meaning of life. I don't have kids yet, so I don't know what the vibe is these days, but I still believe these functions are where life happens, more so than school, church, or activities. I appreciated the company a sleepover with friends provided during these vulnerable years; I felt right at home among preteen girls who were similarly on a fact-finding mission to better understand the mystery of the teenage and adult worlds. We'd acquire intel through a combination of the media and culture we'd consume, e.g., magazines or movies during Blockbuster runs, along with exchanging information we had recently gathered from loose-lipped older siblings. Ideally, about juicy topics like what it was like to lock lips with boys.

Not being able to sleep was a less-charming dilemma when I was at someone else's house. Long before I started *Be There in Five*, I spearheaded my first entrepreneurial venture at childhood slumber parties: The Up All Night Club™ (UANC). I remember a few occasions where I'd recruit friends or acquaintances at slumber parties in elementary school to sign literal back-of-the-napkin contracts with a fresh Ticonderoga in a Mead notebook so they'd feel contractually bound to stay up and talk to me all night. There was nothing like sitting at a suburban kitchen table, negotiating terms with elbows on the slightly damp gauzy disposable tablecloth, like a rebel without a regard for gauze. I knew two things about myself from a young age: I have difficulty falling asleep, and I live for a top-notch heart-to-heart.

I didn't want to stay up to play pranks or be deviant; I just knew the best conversations happened when everyone else went to bed, and if I didn't form these alliances over flat Dr Pepper and extra-cheese pizza, everyone else would snooze. Still, I'd be the one who would lose, lying wide awake against my will in a sleeping bag, overthinking the sounds of the floorboards or ice maker in an unfamiliar home. I noticed the after-midnight hours had yielded some of the most anxious moments of solitude in my life, along with some of the best conversations I've ever had, so it felt right to lock in some quality company via light paperwork. You know, kid stuff. I forged the deepest friendships with the girls I talked to all night. We'd talk about life, death, ghosts, bees (both spelling and killer), boys, our future, the solar system, Mimi-Siku from *Jungle 2 Jungle*; there was never enough time to cover it all, but once we got under the covers, the world felt like ours for the talking.

When I think about the small moments that taught me important life lessons, I often think about how the differences between sleepovers and slumber parties allowed me to pathologize my introversion long before I took a Myers-Briggs test. Even though "sleepover" and "slumber party" are terms often used interchangeably, I believe there are notable differences. My personal definition is that a sleepover is a casual overnight stay with small groups of existing friends for no special occasion, and slumber parties were larger-scale functions for special occasions that had a hodgepodge of the person's friends from their neighborhood, activities, church, and/or classes. If that doesn't sound different enough to you, think of the fun you have drinking wine with your current three best friends versus the fun you have going to the bachelorette party of one of those friends. Group size, friend variety, and focus on casual versus organized fun are three essential variables of a group hang, along with not inviting the friend who does things like analyze variables of a group hang.

By self-identifying as a person who lived for a sleepover (gets energy from small groups where observations are exchanged, likely to sleep on a bed) but not a slumber party (where entertainers thrive, pranks are played, and the invitation tells you to bring a sleeping bag), I was basically figuring out my introversion and an all-consuming desire for plush accommodations. Without knowing that was a thing, I just felt like a loser when I couldn't sleep at big sleepovers because big groups, loud rooms, and pranks made me want to crawl into a hole. That said, I still wouldn't have crawled in a hole if that hole was at the end of a sleeping bag, because I am never interested in involuntary indoor camping. This is the other big difference. At a sleepover, the chances are pretty high that you'll get a bed, trundle, or, at the very least, a semisoft surface to sleep on, but slumber parties never had it in the bag for me when they expected me to sleep in one. My personal "if it doesn't fit, you must acquit" in the nineties was "if I don't get a bed, tears will be shed." But upon getting invited, you didn't want to call dibs or ask in advance like you're Ramona on a *Real Housewives* trip. So at sleepovers, I have many memories of lying awake on the floor, probably experiencing my first signs of anxiety, long before I had the vocabulary to distinguish how it's different from butterflies or tummy aches. Though it could've been worse: I could've been forced to sleep on a Papasan chair. To this day, I find those turtle chairs to be so uncomfortable; sitting on one makes me want to take a long walk off a short Pier 1 Imports where it was bought.

While some of my best times were had at smaller-scale functions, attending large slumber parties at the house of a non-BFF classmate are some of my most vivid memories, even if not always pleasant. Being somewhat nocturnal and staying at someone else's house you hadn't been to before felt incredibly disorienting, almost like going to an away game without your teammates. While these functions were where the entertainers of the world thrived, to be fair, they were a great subject for data collection for observers, too. I've always been hyperaware of details in people's homes and loved seeing a classmate's inner world; their family's general vibe would overtake you alongside a distinct smell upon walking in. Isn't it weird that long before we even got into diffusing signature scents, there was a detectable signature smell everyone's home had and still has (and now yours has!) that is some amalgam of olfactory sensations a group of people's very existence creates, to the point it permeates your clothing (and in my case, my childhood blankie) enough that you can smell it upon leaving, but the people who live there are entirely unaware of it?

I'm not proud of this, but I had the most fun at the following types of households when sleeping over. The kids whose families had: 1. minimal parental supervision, or 2. what I like to call F.U. second-fridge money. These are the places I learned about finer things and subject matters above PG-13, and exposure to these families was formative to my personal development. Gaining access to technology or entertainment you didn't have private access to at home could be life-changing. One of the best parts of sleepovers and slumber parties was going to a person's house who was allowed to have the pinnacle of girlhood independence: a phone in their room. For prank calls, talking to crushes, privacy to gab with BFFs, and just the general mystique that came along with being reachable outside school hours.

I should have seen it coming that my future career would be a form of connecting with people via my phone, because Kelly and I spent a great deal of time in the nineties suspecting that all that was standing between us and booming social lives were phones in our rooms. I have butterflies even talking about the idea of getting your own phone or, God willing, your own line (!!) in your room as a kid. Bells and whistles aside, the apex of the teenage landline experience was reached when Conair came out with a clear phone that showed its bells and whistles inside. Outside of having the hots for Devon Sawa in *Casper,* it wouldn't be until bloggers went hard for Lucite ghost chairs in the 2010s that I revisited my penchant for see-through goods.

The other perk of a home with one of the two ideal setups (rich, low supervision, or both) is that it was the only way to experience the heyday of teen PG-13 movies before I was thirteen. From the qualitative market research I've gathered from my podcast audience, it seems like semiuniversal experiences at sleepovers were watching *Grease, Dirty Dancing,* and/or *Scream.~*~ Grease* and *Dirty Dancing* were early tame sexual awakenings for many young millennials; I started to feel my chills also multiplyin' watching Baby and Patrick Swayze dance. *Scream* was a cult sleepover movie for reasons I do not know; perhaps it was an early pipeline to millennial true-crime fanaticism (and an early diagnosis for sensitive people like me, who find pranks of the "Do you like scary movies?" phone-call persuasion to be grounds for dismissal from the UANC). My lack of interest in true crime and tragedy was cemented by my siblings watching so much *Unsolved Mysteries* and *Rescue 911,* where I mostly learned one of two things were bound to happen to me: if I swam in a hotel pool, my organs would get sucked into the drain and I'd perish, or if I let curiosity get the best of me upon wanting dessert, I'd get my tongue stuck to the freezer and have to call 911.

~*~ SO Random: Rule Breaking = Memory Making ~*~

I think movies like *Dirty Dancing* and *Grease* slipped through the cracks of parental supervision because they're music-forward classics that are so ubiquitous; maybe even parents forget how inappropriate they are for the PG crowd. I was obsessed with *Grease* and couldn't believe I went to an elementary school with a bunch of Bugle Boys when I belonged with a T-Bird. In retrospect, I'm not sure Sandra Dee was the best person to take cues from, as my core takeaway from that movie was that to get a boy's attention, I should fundamentally change as a person, wear all black, experiment with a bold lip, and develop a light nicotine habit. But I'm grateful for the parents who overlooked the ratings to show us the classics; if my kids were interested in my culture, I might do the same. That handful of times you let your kids break the rules, memories are being made. I've heard my brother talk about how one of his core memories is my dad waking him up in 1995 to watch Cal Ripken Jr. break Lou Gehrig's record of 2,130 consecutive games. Even though I hate sports, I have a soft spot for father-son bonding over them.

Similarly, I often warmly recall how my mom let me stay up late and watch *my* World Series finale, the last episode of *Full House,* scheduled to air after my bedtime. She saw my distress from the prior week's episode, a cliffhanger about Michelle's short-lived amnesia following her equine accident, and knew I couldn't miss out. Whenever people use the figure of speech "get back on the horse," I'm assuming their parents didn't let them stay up for this episode. I never got on a horse again. Or I think about when my uncle Bill was babysitting me, and I'm guessing he wasn't up to speed on the age-appropriateness of the latest movies, so he let me watch *Clueless.* I was about to say it was life-changing, but given that *Clueless* has come up four times and we're only on chapter two of this book, I'm sure you could've guessed. I peaked getting to spend time with Valley girls who made me feel understood. I remember thinking to myself, "This is the best day of my life" when he later drove me to the mall in his white Cabriolet, and it was then I took my talents from As and Bs to wanting to chase mostly Cs: California culture, *Clueless,* and convertibles were the life for me. Wind in my hair, I was Cher, I remember it all too well.

Phones and movies were a litmus test for the ideal lower levels of parental supervision that made a person's house a good candidate for a sleepover, but other socioeconomic status symbols made an overnight stay feel like a luxurious getaway. Keep in mind my entire frame of reference is from interacting with my classmates from public schools in middle- and upper-middle-class suburbia, but in my experience, the families of the TV- and phone-in-room persuasion were typically reserved for households that not only had ample AG doll furnishings, but also things like finished basements with big screens and giant sectionals, a pool or trampoline, refrigerators that matched their cabinetry, and my personal favorite: a second fridge downstairs. Something about a second fridge just tells me your parents probably let you watch *The Real World* and you also might have spare Fudgsicles or Luigi's Real Italian Ices lying around.

I loved a freezer filled with loose old Thin Mints and tongue-dyeing desserts and highly processed foods like Kid Cuisines, though I shudder thinking about how it really f'ed with my night watching *TGIF* when the hot pudding would cross-contaminate the corn. Like a yellow marker you accidentally drag over black ink, once they mix, it's never the same. I'm also a person who needs a beverage with me at all times, and at the time, I was partial to a second fridge that was like a Fruitopia of beverages made from 1 percent juice, always tempted to reach for the elegance of a Mistic bottle in the back that made it look like a second-grader was drinking a wine cooler. But maybe the mystique of the second fridge wasn't as tied to socioeconomics or Mistics as I thought; I think a lot of it was also about my anxiety in asking my friends for a drink or a snack, and it was easier to swipe inventory from the fridge less opened. For some reason, *nothing* was more embarrassing to me than someone screaming upstairs, "*Mom*! Katie's hungry!" as I feared they'd stop inviting me over to their house because of the way I housed their Triscuits.

I love (and still love) the experience of being invited to someone else's home, regardless of their socioeconomic status, of course. But I will say I live for a house that's meant to be seen, not lived in. You can tell a lot about a suburban mom by the shape of the tiny soaps in a powder room, the fact that she even calls it a powder room, and if the towels you wipe your hands on have confusingly low absorption. I love how rich people can't seem to bother with terry cloth, they really go hard for a decorative towel. I didn't actually care how much money you had, nor understand money at all—I just was fascinated by things that I saw on TV or in commercials but never used, and it was fun to have friends who brought both Hot Wheels and Power Wheels to the garage. Although being friends with someone with a backyard pool or trampoline was kind of like how it feels now when you become close friends with someone who has a beach house or a boat. Not everyone has the disposable income nor has it in them to take on such a liability in the name of blissful recreation, but if you find someone who does, hold on tight.

The other thing that stands out to me about slumber parties is how weird it was for minors to majorly dabble in paranormal activity or supernatural rituals for kicks. I don't know why anyone is surprised that a generation of young women like things like astrology, crystals, *The Secret,* and manifestation, because we were raised by the guidance of Ouija boards, origami fortune tellers, M.A.S.H., and Magic 8 Balls after spending afternoons at Natural Wonders.

Many of the chants and rituals and games we played at slumber parties were also downright creepy. While most people, including me, blame diet culture for their body-image issues, I also blame how Light as a Feather, Stiff as a Board didn't seem to work as well on tall gals with bigger bones than everyone else. In retrospect, this exercise looked like a high-key pagan levitation ritual, and even though I hated the inadvertent body shaming, I will say I'm here for the preteen witch vibes. I also often think about the lyrics to the weird chants or hand-slapping games we did of the Miss Mary Mack persuasion that started out wholesome but then had an edgy agenda like "Miss Susie Had a Steamboat." It was basically an excuse to say curse words without saying the full word:

Miss Susie had a steamboat,
The steamboat had a bell,
Miss Susie went to heaven,

The steamboat went to
Hell-o operator, give me number nine

So on and so forth. Maybe Miss Susie was also a fan of track nine: "Supermodel (You Better Work)." Songs like this or "there's a place on Mars, where the women smoke cigars, and the men wear bikinis, and the children drink martinis" are interesting to revisit lyrically; my hypothesis is we felt comfortable with creepy chanting in a *Hocus Pocus–* forward America. A culture that was so pervasive, if you head to your nearest apple-cider-donut provider in autumn, you can find a millennial wearing a T-shirt that reads AMUCK AMUCK AMUCK to this day. I'm convinced we liked *Hocus Pocus* so much because it was the only Disney movie that used the word "virgin," and hearing it in a context outside of Mary at church was a real thrill. It added a sexiness to the lore of the black flame candle that I carried into adulthood when I started lusting after sixty-dollar black Diptyque candles to basically light money on fire.

Hocus Pocus may be why we felt comfortable in groups chanting creepily or performing hand-slapping rituals, but since there were more than three of us, it was more like the makings of an amateur choir that specialized in black magic. As if there was a Sanderson *Sister Act 2,* upon nightfall, we, too, would get *Back in the Habit* and perform weird rituals that made Bloody Mary or the Candyman as likely to be in attendance at a classmate's birthday party as someone named Jessica or Amanda. It was as terrifying as it was awesome. Not as awesome were the more dangerous games; my sister used to go to sleepovers where her friends would cross their arms and hold their breath until they briefly passed out. This is why I am comfortable with my children being iPad kids; leaving us to our own devices before we had devices was more of a medical risk than a character-building exercise.

For me, a happy middle ground of spookiness and good feelings was the game Concentrate, where one person closes their eyes and people stand behind them and chant, "Concentrate, concentrate on what I'm saying. People are dying, children are crying. Concentrate." The best part was if you were the person with your eyes closed, it was the nearest thing to a spa-like experience because your friend was behind you and cycled through a series of goose bump–inducing activities, starting with "crack an egg on your head, let the yolk drip down" and escalating to things like "stab a knife in your back, let the blood run down." Graphic lyrics aside, I loved this game because the yolk running down or the fake blood running down your back would be demonstrated by a sort of back-scratching soothing gesture, and I'm nothing if not a slut for a back scratch.

There was a more casual "crack an egg on your head" version that would end on a less bleak note, dare I say a euphoric one, I still think about often: "Tight squeeze, cool breeze, now you've got the shiveries." I have shiveries thinking about the kindness and safety in sisterhood I found in the close friends willing to do a round of egg-cracking shivers while sitting crisscross applesauce at a school assembly or a Girl Scout meeting. I hate sleeping on the floor but love sitting on the floor, and if I can get my hair played with or my back scratched in the process, I'll hang on to your friendship tighter than if you had a second fridge.

There are many versions of these games/rituals/chants; they vary geographically and culturally but typically have the same melody. I miss these simpler times; I spend way too much time now trying to get my ducks in a row and wish I was playing Quack Diddly Oso. What I wouldn't give to be in large groups of women breaking for a snack, my biggest problem trying to avoid a speedy slap after we launch into "and-a-one-two-three . . ." waterfall to our left. It was a slightly more mature, high-octane Duck, Duck, Goose with less jogging. Depending on the regional coven, Quack Diddly Oso had many variations throughout North America, often called Slap Diddly Oso or Stella Ella Ola. I'd say it's one of the hand games with some of the most regional lyrical variability, though it usually starts out "Quack diddly oso, quack quack quack." In my Richmond, Virginia, coven, we sang, "Senorita, rita rita rita," but in the Northeast, for example, some say, "Senorita, your mom smells like pizza," and I've talked to people from the West Coast who say, "San diego, eggo eggo eggo," among other endless variations.

I wish these sweet and/or spooky moments would be more associated with our legacy as millennials because I didn't just learn them at sleepovers: they usually started in places where girls from different schools and backgrounds would convene and exchange information. I first learned most of the hand games and chants in places like YMCA day camps, community after-school programs, and Girl Scouts. Most older millennials didn't have childhoods that were technologically interconnected, and I think this was an essential part of exchanging our own form of folklore. I'm determined to get us all to remember the culture of connection we once cultivated in groups in the absence of speedy communication. Honestly, when I think about some of the darker stuff we were up to, it's a wonder we haven't all gotten together by now and put a mild hex on some of these news outlets that feed into millennial stereotypes, given our witchy ways. Maybe something to keep in mind for the future as we creep toward financial doom we aren't responsible for? If the Up All Night Club™ is good for anything, it's to prepare for when we ride at dawn. You bring the witches and wizards, I'll bring the bead lizards.

In hindsight, the supernatural stuff we did at slumber parties was a little dark, but the bright spot for me was getting older and tightening our coven, when my closest friends and I would solve all the world's problems on daybeds, trundles, basement pull-out sofas, and/or bunk beds in groups of two to six, depending on who was in the neighborhood friend rotation or who wasn't grounded that week, the "find my friends" of yesteryear being a pile of bikes in a cul-de-sac so I'd know

whose house we were sleeping at that night. We'd explore our range as
we rotated between giving each other makeovers and talking about if
we believed in God, then choreographing dances to Spice Girls songs
in basements as much as we'd try to reenact the séance from *Now and
Then* in someone's attic.

I had the most incredible childhood friends I still keep in touch
with; they had big personalities and high energy levels in contrast to
mine, but they always included me. If you asked my friends, they'd
probably tell you I had big "I don't know if this is a good idea, you
guys" energy, often sitting out on pranks that were too much for my
sensitive self, but they never ding-dong-ditched my friendship and loved
me for who I was. Plus, I loved being adjacent to the action and forming
friendships with people who could get me out of my shell. We actually
went through a lot together, navigating some pretty serious stuff as kids,
but our world felt impenetrable in its mutual support and optimism, our
tears dried by paper fortune-teller promises and games of M.A.S.H. that
landed you one day in a mansion, not a shack. My friends Emily, Hilah,
and Morgan were my entire world, along with my best friend down the
street in a different grade, Elise. Between the four of them and other
neighborhood friends who came and went, everything I needed and
everything I learned about life was a bike ride away and likely learned
at a sleepover on a trundle bed.

Speaking of M.A.S.H., before reminiscing, I never really thought
about how our activities at sleepovers and slumber parties orbited a similar theme: trying to predict the future, probably to ease the anxiety
of life's unpredictability. I guess planning your future as a child starts
magically and then evolves to being more formulaic; even before we
looked to the oracle-type games, you start wishing upon stars and blowing out candles, and I dreamed of Jeannie, too, when I started watching
Nick at Nite and it coincided with my *Aladdin* phase. Isn't it funny that
wish-making canon is not to tell anyone your wish, or it won't come

true, only to grow up and be told that our lack of success is because we should've been shouting our wishes at the universe, according to the Law of Attraction? Though I'm willing to bet some of the most prominent playground jinx truthers now sell manifesting courses.

The juice from the game Concentrate was a prediction of how you'd die, a Magic 8 Ball was the authority for yes/no questions, a Ouija board could share messages from the beyond, and M.A.S.H. could predict your fate for whom you'd marry and how many kids you'd have. Although M.A.S.H was somewhat realistic in setting us up for the experience of feeling like our success is often Limited To whom we marry, what house we live in, what car we drive, how many kids we have, and what our job is. Even if the specifics were off, the most telling foreshadowing device of all was that we already felt the pressure of figuring these things out long before we ever needed to, and sought formulas early for how we could be a little more sure we'd fulfill the already high, albeit narrow, expectations the world had for us as young women. And the way it ends was accurate in how it feels to navigate personal milestones, playing the game, or in life: either way, you spiral. The final counting of the rings from your friend drawing a spiral until you told them to stop is similar to the anxiety I'd later feel at restaurants when having cracked pepper or rotary parmesan grated onto my dish. To this day, when someone says, "Tell me when to stop," I think of the M.A.S.H. spiral and the feeling of being one second away from your missed fate. Or overseasoned food.

While reminiscing, I was trying to figure out why my childhood memories are mostly from sleepovers. Beyond my makeshift Myers-Briggs and early feelings of anxiety in a sleeping bag, or my developing taste for finer things I probably wished for during witchy rituals, these gatherings meant so much more to me than that, and I couldn't put my finger on why I wanted to recall them in elaborate detail. But when I mentioned *Now and Then* in passing, I felt a lump in my throat that I tried to ignore, but it keeps coming back. Does even the thought of *Now and Then* make anyone else need to take a forty-minute nap? It makes me so emotional, but it isn't just about being reminded of the hopeful and complex innocence of girlhood scored by bicycle-banana-seat battle cries and "Knock Three Times." My emotional response made it clear to me why I care so much about these gatherings: they were our tree house. Suddenly, how the movie ends hits differently, when Samantha says, "The tree house was supposed to bring us more independence. But what the summer actually brought was independence from each other." When you watched *Now and Then* with friends at a sleepover, your takeaway wasn't the melancholia and inevitability of growing apart; instead, you dug through the final kernels in the popcorn bowl, looking for the last of the buttery pieces while you searched aloud for all the reasons the moral of the movie would never apply to you and your friends. As the VCR played the last of the credits, you tried to give your future selves more credit, and questions of "They grew apart, but we never will, right?" are knocked down three times by your three best friends, quickly achieving consensus. *Now and Then* is a story about them. But that would never be the four of us.

Inevitably, everyone goes their separate ways and hopefully comes back together, if you're lucky. I'm still good friends with these women; their friendship makes me wish there was a word for platonic soulmates. But it couldn't be more true that after you're sleepover-aged, everyone's life goes drastically different ways, and communication ebbs and flows between weeks and months where everyone's independence is the reason being unreachable teeters on the cusp of eventually falling out of touch entirely. But I think the thing that makes me teary-eyed is how female bonding rituals shape-shift over time, and even though they evolve to support one another depending on the life stage, things are never quite the same. The thing you didn't realize Then but do Now is that adults don't have thirty-six free hours between Friday evening and

Sunday morning where they can leave their house and get no sleep and cast spells and tell each other their deepest secrets. And you long for when your attention wasn't divided and time wasn't about how well you could optimize it, when it was a lot more simple. Time spent together was time well spent.

Back in the daybed, we didn't know enough about what could go wrong to indulge in our neuroses; we mostly relished in the joy of possibility or, when in doubt, a little black magic. Even more magical than the spells we tried to cast was the feeling of being at an age when you have nowhere to be, no one telling you who to be, and if ever lost, your confidence could be found again within those four walls. While writing this book, I kept wondering what happened in my head between now and back in the daybed, and it's interesting how much things change when outside forces like technology or church or boys or grades start to slowly poke holes in your inflatable dreams that once made you feel uplifted. But it makes me even more grateful for these shared moments early on, and the luxury of naïveté that allowed us to exist in a state of mutual support that tinted life's unknowns with hopefulness more than helplessness.

Sometimes when we get together now, we laugh about how seriously we took ourselves. But that's the thing about girlhood. You and your friends have to take yourselves seriously, because no one else will. We had to keep our emotional behavior to diary pages and fangirl in private, performing at sleepovers on our trundle stages, because it felt like the rest of the world worked overtime to remind us that girlish things were inherently unserious. But there are few eras of my life that were as seriously impactful as the confidence I found during these nights that bled into mornings, beneath stuffed-animal hammocks and under warm handmade afghans, giggling with every daybed or pull-out sofa creak as we pretended to be asleep. Even though I created the UANC to get people to stay awake, I guess the joke's on me. It didn't matter when we went to bed, we were already living the dream.

3

You've Got Male

One of the unlikely places I learned some of life's greatest lessons was AOL Instant Messenger (AIM). No shade to Mario's side gig (or queen/icon Mavis Beacon), but AIM is where I was taught typing. We may have near-empty 401(k)s, but I personally don't think we talk enough about millennials' impressive WPMs. When AOL came out, I think I was around ten years old, and despite parental controls, the World Wide Web felt like it was at my fingertips. To be more specific, the keyboard was literally at my fingertips, but the process of getting online required a lot of twiddling of the thumbs and a household of pinky promises not to pick up the phone.

Despite our elders thinking we came out of the womb texting, many of us had much more pure and disconnected childhoods. When older generations give us a hard time for our modern conveniences or partake in the "in my day"–type discussions, I think they forget millennials have our own version of the "olden days," just in the form of clunky technology I like to refer to as the "millenniolden days." It's like, yeah, I bet walking miles to school in the snow was hard, but have you ever had to navigate an empty new-release VHS shelf at Blockbuster with a sleepover crew in tow that will never achieve rental consensus? Have you ever spent a night being disinvited to a slumber party in solitude, only to play Solitaire and fail to experience the abundance of flying-card-stacks graphics, an of-its-time "make it rain" you hoped would solve your pain? Have you ever played fast and loose with a LimeWire computer virus that will come to your Windows 95 before your Melissa Etheridge album even finishes downloading? Your skin just gets tougher when a burned CD takes eight hours to buffer, and no one respects millennials for the baby pirates we once were, committing federal crimes on the daily to pay our respects to the arts by not paying anyone in the arts.

With America Online, once you cleared the phone lines, you were forced to withstand the unique audible hazing the internet made us go through before we were allowed to join in on the fun: the sound of dial-up. After nearly five minutes of listening to combinations of beeping, screeching, and scratching, it began to sound like two machines in a catfight. I don't know how best to describe it, other than what I assume it would sound like if a melody of insanity sampled a smoke detector that desperately needed its batteries replaced and then hurled itself into a garbage disposal. Outside of the years when my alarm clock was replaced with my brother's Kenny G phase, dial-up is probably my ears' worst shared memory.

But something about the anticipation made it worth it. There's a reason Nora Ephron's masterpiece *You've Got Mail* is one of the finest films of all time (according to me). Kathleen Kelly was right: you go online, and your breath catches in your chest until you hear three little words: "You've got mail." In my case, I was hopeful my crush would see me online and send me an instant message, allowing me to finally relish in my three-word tweenage dream: "You've got male." Even though I wonder who I'd be if I played with STEM toys, I firmly believe I gained transferable life skills while navigating the early days of the internet by learning how to hold digital conversations. However, at the time, my agenda was not educational. My commitment to being the latest and greatest and up-to-datest in digital savviness was in pursuit of one thing and one thing alone: a boyfriend. These romantic exchanges were not quite *Love Letters of Great Men,* they were more like instant messages from okay dudes, but I feel nostalgic for how assembling keyboard characters developed my character all the same. In retrospect, I see so much benefit to practicing wordsmithing in remote interactions, but I also feel sad about how I genuinely thought these people were into me and they were obviously using me for emotional support and platonic company. More on that l8r.

We're now so deep in the worlds of Instagram, Facebook, and TikTok that I think we forget about the social-networking stairsteps that were far from blips on the radar. From 1997 to 2009, twelve years of my life, AIM was my watercooler. As I've come to appreciate in retrospect, it was also kind of a safe space for trying on different versions of myself at an age where I lacked a strong sense of identity. Although from the screen names we chose, it was already pretty clear we were all hanging by a thread. Unbeknownst to us, these questionable choices would represent our digital identities for years to come.

Choosing a screen name (SN) sounds like it would be a pretty straightforward task to the tune of picking a name in combination with some variation of initials and/or notable numbers. But nope, not for me. Not many millennials. We didn't have the foresight to understand their potential longevity, nor did we grasp the brand equity that's potentially built with one, making the switching costs feel too high when you go to college as xxBaByLuvChrisK or ThrdBaseGirlie12. You'd be faced with the painstaking process of deciding between forgoing your social clout or going to college openly advertising Chris Kirkpatrick as your favorite member of NSYNC (risky!!). With the latter name, you'd be forced to figure out how to deal with the hand you've been dealt when your SN sounds like you're super into doing hand stuff, despite that it was from eight years ago when you just wanted everyone to know your softball-field position.

Since SNs would get taken, you had to innovate around the root word of your ideal username with terms of endearment. In hindsight, these did less to differentiate you than they did to make it KrYStaL clear to internet predators you were, like, an actual infant. But that didn't break our spirits! For example, if you took creative liberties with the spelling and alternating caps of terms of endearment like "QT," "baby," "girl/gurl/girly," "love/luv," "chick/chica," you were usually in the clear. If it's taken? Easy: bookend it with "xx" or "xo" or "x0" and/or add "LiL" to the beginning and you're "xxG00dAsg0Ldxx." When push came to shuv, we would abandon letters and replace "o"s with "0"s, "L"s with "1"s, and/or just drop vowels altogether until your screen name appears to have been created the moment you chose to clean your keyboard due to the volume of characters chosen that do not belong side by side. Though I guess trying to have people guess if "HrSeGrL610" means "horse girl" or "hearse girl" keeps things interesting! One's a Felicity Merriman, the other a Vada Sultenfuss. Win-win!

One of my screen names was so bottom-of-the-barrel for word combinations, what I wanted was "CrazyAndCool," but what I got was "KrAzEnKewL." I don't know what a Krazenkewl is, but I think I saw it at Ikea next to an Ektorp sofa. I had so many, the first being "Love-Plum1," a nickname from my dad; "BluEyez878"; "Katiemae87"; and the list goes on. One strange weekend I soft-launched "WaFFeL77" in honor of the amount of Waffle Crisp cereal I was eating at the time, which was a mistake. Or rather, a sticky situation I should've seen coming, not just because I was starting to perspire that faux syrupy glaze, but also because it would solicit randoms in chat rooms to ask me about my nooks 'n' crannies.

I have a vague memory of being with a friend when she started an account, and it was supposed to be something like "IDuNNo4048." She could only get "iDoNnA4048," which completely changed the integrity of the brand, and I don't know why I still find this so funny. But *I,*

Tonya's got nothing on I, Donna because that same friend—we'll call her . . . Vanessica—hacked into my other friend's AOL account and IM'd me, then proceeded to suspiciously jump right into "Vanessica is so annoying, let's not walk home from school with her tomorrow." Suspicious (and fresh off my peak *Harriet the Spy* days when I didn't understand that it wasn't normal to bring a fresh notepad and trespass on your neighbor's property), I had the sleuthing wherewithal to sign off and call the friend's house who was allegedly IMing me, and lo and behold, the signal wasn't busy, therefore I knew she wasn't online. It was obviously Vanessica trying to trap me into talking badly about her so she could use it against me. Did someone put tariffs on imports? I am *spilling* this tea.

I wish I could tell you about a dramatic callout or falling-out, but I responded by being like, "I love Vanessica! She's such a great friend and I'd never want to leave her out!" If she was trying to trick me before I had done anything wrong, I couldn't imagine what she'd pull if I made her feel called out or embarrassed. I was less focused on her doing something mean and more focused on the fact that she was doing something mean to me, because it meant that she probably didn't like me. I was always less concerned with justice or being right and more interested in doing everything in my power to get people to like me. This is terribly unhealthy behavior; it's almost like I heard the phrase "keep your friends close, keep your enemies closer" and I Amelia Bedelia'ed that shit and took it literally, maintaining friendships with people who were mean to me in the absence of personal benefit. While I've gotten better at this, to this day I find it remarkable that anyone can eat, sleep, or, like, breathe knowing someone else is mad at them.

The other big AIM drama from the early days is when my friend, I'll call her Elizabecca, made *so* much fun of me because I allegedly put up the wrong lyrics to Sisqó's "Thong Song" on my away message. I put "She had dumps like a truck, truck, truck" and she told me it was "*drums* like a truck," and proceeded to laugh maniacally in multiple IMs, ridicule me, and bring it up *again* at school that I had messed up the lyrics, and the whole time, I was right!!! Isn't it weird that this still bothers me? There are a million things you can make fun of me for, but when your talents are few and far between, it stings to be ridiculed for something you actually know you're good at. I'm nothing if not a vault of nineties top-forty lyrics, and it felt unkewl for my lyrical integrity to be put in question. With parental controls (I think mine were on "young teen"), you could instant message, but you couldn't get on the World Wide Web. Without Ask Jeeves or Alta presenting me the lyrics from its Vista, I had no way of knowing I was being so aggressively gaslit by Elizabecca in real time.

Lord knows I didn't have the album leaflet; the "Thong Song" single CD would've never been allowed in my house. When we would cruise around in my mom's Ford Windstar, one of the features was the ability to mute the radio from the back. Among my siblings, one of our favorite songs was "Torn" by Natalie Imbruglia, and we'd take turns hitting MUTE when she'd sing in the chorus "lying naked on the floor." In retrospect, my mom's not a weirdo, she wouldn't have cared, it's not like I grew up in that *Footloose* town. I get her not wanting me to scream-sing in fifth grade, "IS SHE PERVERTED LIKE ME? WOULD SHE GO DOWN ON YOU IN A THEATER?" per the Alanis of it all. In fact, I was so committed to sexy song lyrics, one time my parents found the lyrics to Shaggy's "It Wasn't Me" in the printer tray, and I'm 99 percent sure it was me who printed them out. I have to laugh thinking about my mom and dad reading a Word document printed out with lines like "picture this we were both butt-naked bangin' on the bathroom floor" without melody or context. They called a family meeting, and in an impressive moral loophole, we all denied it, but never lied, saying "It wasn't me" when they asked what it was, having no idea it was the song title and not a formal alibi.

Anyway, back to e-males. One option for digital seduction was to create an SN involving a hobby or interest you did not possess in hopes of impressing your crush. While I was in the throes of tween orthodontia and didn't have many options for a boyfriend at school, I set my sights on a far more elusive creature: a vacation boyfriend.~*~ Ideally, we would keep in touch via AIM throughout the school year, and I could pretend I was spoken for to look cool while also keeping my options open (in case I found a boyfriend at school who could do things, like, iDoNnA, hang out in person). I had always heard girls in my class mention "hot guys" they "met on the beach," and I wanted in on the action. I had also been watching a lot of Mary-Kate and Ashley movies, and I simply couldn't move forward in life without recruiting a local hottie named something like Blake or Riley for a three-day whirlwind romance that would culminate in a Jet Ski montage. To this day, one of my core goals in life is to vacation at Atlantis in the Bahamas and get myself romantically entangled in a ring of stolen antiquities wearing a Fendi bucket hat like in *Holiday in the Sun*.

A few years ago, I did a podcast episode about screen names, which made me realize that my experiences truly aren't that unique, as fellow millennials echoed their similar desires to digitally rebrand due to their annual trip to the beach. A common experience was to toy around with screen names like "OBXSuRfChiCkA" and "R0xYquiCk-slLvRbAbe007" (give or take some digits) so you could have an SN locked and loaded to give your hypothetical surfer boyfriend, allowing you to maintain an AIM relationship after tearfully parting ways. I did this multiple times and was shocked it didn't work. Did I surf? Nope. Skateboard? Not-a-once. Own meaningful amounts of Roxy and/or Quiksilver garments in my wardrobe? No and no. I just thought the only way I could get a boy to like me was to strip myself of my identity and only represent things he likes. It is a little sad that I thought I had nothing to bring to the table when I first got on AIM, though I suppose all the rebranding did set me up well to take on a vague marketing job later. Now that I think about it, creating an SN about a hobby I didn't have so I could impress a boy I hadn't met yet to maintain a relationship that did not exist is truly delusional girl-boss behavior, and I love that for me.

~*~ SO Random: Vacation Boyfriends ~*~

The key to achieving a vacation boyfriend is to spot hot guys in the wild, then do the most while never speaking to them in the least, hoping they notice you in your natural state out of the corner of their eye. But in order to be spotted in your natural state, you have to first change everything about yourself. The screen name was just step one. Once I was in Touristy Beach Town, U.S.A., I would have to embody the laid-back, sun-kissed lifestyle through newly purchased beachy accessories from souvenir shops so I could get noticed. To do this, you tell your parents you are going to get shaved ice, then take a detour at the Ron Jon Surf Shop or Super Wings and blow your entire allowance on the local landfill's hottest items. Buy a puka-shell necklace and a shirt that says LIFEGUARD, or maybe get your name written on a tiny piece of rice if the airbrushed hat is too pricey. Be sure to save room for a license-plate key chain that says SURF DIVA on Myrtle Beach plates. You can give it to your daughter someday. Even though the Roxy and Quiksilver goods are too expensive, as long as you start wearing anklets, he won't know the difference. Then, just park yourself in the sand, partake in the conspiracy theory of an Irish girl needing a base tan, and commit to leaving it all behind. You changed your screen name, started wearing toe rings, bought a skimboard, and all there's left to do is wait until you become indiscernible from Kate Bosworth in *Blue Crush*.

Full disclosure, this never actually worked for me: I was too scared to talk to boys. Regardless, unlike an MK&A movie, my parents weren't superinterested in letting me drive off into the sunset on a Vespa with a townie. But I still tried every year. Main-charactering hard while listening to Dashboard Confessional, watching the waves crash upon the sand, dreaming of a hot summer night on the boardwalk where I'd meet a "real man," unlike the immature seventh-grade boys at my school. I'd have my first kiss and get to tell all my friends, and before we parted ways I'd say, "Hey, thanks, thanks for that summer." Even though it never worked out for me, I have no regrets. A wise woman (me, age twelve) once put on her away message "the tans may fade, but the memories will last forever." Do they ever.

Beyond a watercooler and third place, for me, AIM was also a safe space. It was a place that allowed me to transcend my social awkwardness in pursuing friendships and flirting with boys, where I could wow people with what I knew to be my strength, even at a young age: words. For all the ways people criticize social media for its drafting of keyboard warriors who take advantage of anonymity to spread cruelty, it also can eliminate a person's self-consciousness in ways that are empowering, depending on how you use it. In my case, once I could remove the awkwardness I exhibited in my social interactions, I felt like I was able to be measured by something other than the shallow metrics of teenage socialization. I wasn't worried about the way that I looked or the food in my teeth or wondering if my Xhilaration V-neck would make my Christian brothers stumble. It relieved me of the exhausting mechanics I felt at school trying to appear naturally cool. So while I waited for coolness to manifest in my reflexes, I could rely on AIM to proofread and finesse my way into social acceptance. Somewhere beneath the stale glow of a nineties Gateway 2000 desktop computer, despite every time adults told me I was rotting my brain, I found a great deal of confidence in my personality on the internet.

Even for a tycoon, the art of AIM flirtation was a real roller coaster, and I don't mean to brag, but it was both a gift and a burden to electronically shine so bright in the blue light of America Online. Finding a way for my personality to stand out would come back to megabyte me eventually, but for many years, I treated AIM flirtation like a part-time job. I remember having multiple chat windows open at once, hedging my bets on which hottie would see me as his model girlfriend when I'd strike my prose. When I started to get emotionally invested, I'd position myself at a specific angle on the couch so the reflection of the desktop in the TV entertainment center could let me down easily if I wasn't receiving a response. First, I'd minimize the windows so I'd see their blinking status in the glass, notifying me someone had replied so I could manage my anticipation prior to seeing the text. They say when God closes a door, he opens a window. But on AIM, when you hear a closed door, you log off Windows. The door-slamming sound reverberated through my very soul if my crush signed offline without a proper goodbye. Like the personalized ringtones of days to come, you could adorn your crushes with custom sounds like a "moo" or "cha-ching!" when they signed on, putting out a playroom Bat-Signal telling me to make myself available. I vividly remember the rush that went through my body seeing my crush sign on, the anticipation of hoping he would IM me first, while I waited with bated breath that I'd use as my muse for a future away message about life "not being about the breaths you take, but the moments that take your breath away (~*HiTcH*~)."

After one too many nights clogging up the phone line waiting for a crush's return, I had to rethink my strategy. Nowadays, it's popular to say, "If he wanted to, he would," but in my world, I was very accepting of "He probs wants to but, like, what if his mom picked up the phone and he got kicked off or he has homework or his internet isn't working or he's playing hard to get? What if he wants to so badly but he just can't right now???" Once you realize none of those things are happening, and he's not interested, you have to regain your power. This is where away messages and idle statuses come into play. An away message was a beautiful thing; it was like an out-of-office message for teenagers who never actually left the office but wanted to appear as busy and interesting as possible. Now that I think about it, we were glamorizing turmoil and prepping ourselves for hustle culture from a young age with our "packed" schedules.

One way to get noticed was to publish your daily calendar for attention, where you have the sexiness of scarcity, given your back-to-back day, but by sharing it in detail, it's an open invitation for how to reach you, e.g., "crazy day today! school, vball, CPK, Emily's house, homework, more homework. hit the cell!" so your crush knew you were way too swamped to be thinking about him, but you were still *very* reachable in person or by phone. A common form of subtle seduction was to indicate you were in the shower or bath in some way, with "shower power" giving your crush an opening to reply with something suggestive, like "Wish I could join ;)." If you were feeling like your physique wasn't quite where you wanted it, alerting the masses with a "working on my fitness" from "Fergalicious" was a way to brag that you're physically active, while also reminding love interests that Phil Vassar won't be the only one showing up to summer with a six-pack. I had a period where I shared a lot of aggressive Vince Lombardi quotes about victory, sports, and athleticism. In retrospect it's like, relax, you're playing freshman volleyball, I'm not sure you need to be projecting onto peers your new "no guts, no glory" lifestyle.

There was a point where I would pick the default options just to be chill and ironic, assuming boys would think it was hot that I wasn't like all these other try-hards. You could pick "I am away from my computer right now," but I found options like "I am unavailable because I am playing a computer game that takes up my entire screen" to be spicier. But sometimes away messages were simply there to inspire, to be the change you wished to see in the world. Maybe you were having a good day or a moment of clarity and thought it would be important for your peers to remember that "iT's NoT AbOuT wAiTiNg 4 ThA StOrM 2 PaSs, iT's AbOuT LeArNiNg 2 DaNce In ThA RaiN." Unfortunately, you probably made a person's tough day measurably worse by choosing to write it with a migraine-inducing combo of radioactive fuchsia on a lime-green background, but the intentions were there.

Away messages also were a great opportunity to turn passive aggression into an art form. Instead of telling people how you felt or (God forbid) telling people what happened, it was far better to communicate your torment, sorrow, or frustration via an away message, so everyone thought it could possibly be directed at them despite having no idea what was going on. This phenomenon was adopted by Facebook users in later years and is best known as "vaguebooking," where people would put things like "Send prayers!" on their status, then proceed to get an unbelievable amount of attention. Mostly because no one knew if their thoughts and/or prayers were being directed to the Big Guy because of a terminal illness or because your Toyota Camry is in the shop.

If a boy was making you cry, you could put up something like "~*I <3 WaLkInG iN ThE rAiN cUz No1 Can SeE My TeArS*~" to alert everyone that you're crying, but not make it clear why, which is great because you'd return home from your emo walk to a digital Rolodex of concern. If you wanted a boy to know you're crying because of him, "No man is worth your tears, the one who is won't make you cry" was always pretty reliable. It's straightforward, but hopeful, providing an opportunity for the boy who made you cry to feel bad about it, while also suggesting another suitor could slide right in since you're open to crying less.

I liked to exhibit my top-forty taste in music along with my troubling low self-esteem with quotes from bands like Train, attempting to solicit male attention with things that weren't so much song lyrics as they were cries for help, like "You see her confidence is tragic, but her intuition magic." Sometimes, when trying to appeal to dudes of the stoner persuasion, I'd pretend to be into Phish or the Grateful Dead, once quoting Phish as the artists behind "Gin & Juice" because of an attribution error on LimeWire when I illegally downloaded the song. Dave Matthews Band and O.A.R. were also a safe bet, so putting up something like "Celebrate we will, 'cause life is short but sweet for certain" was a slam dunk if you wanted to get attention by reminding a frat star in training who wears his sunglasses on Croakies that you could croak any minute.

Above all else, romantic passive aggression was perhaps best illustrated with emo lyrics from bands like Dashboard Confessional or Taking Back Sunday. Any emo kid knows that *the* angsty away message was from a Taking Back Sunday song called "You're So Last Summer." In retrospect, it is *incredibly alarming.* I'm going to have to paraphrase here because I don't have the usage license for relaying lengthy lyrics, but it was something along the lines of saying that a person could cut your neck, and while you are dying and about to breathe for the last time, you would still say you are sorry for bleeding on the person's blouse. Without the context of knowing that's a song from Taking Back Sunday, I'm shocked parents weren't taking us in Monday to go see a therapist. But the real pièce de résistance of sexy scarcity was having your status go idle. It was such a power move. I'd park my mouse in the bottom corner of the screen, demand nobody else in my household touch the computer, and soar like I stepped on a Mario Kart star while I imagined my crush pining for me to rise from the ash-colored grayout of a person who went idle on their buddy list. Long before we diluted and muted our homes with gray (or greige) in the 2010s, it was *the* hottest color you could wear online.

I had to do everything in my power to not be myself in this era, because the only way to get a guy according to my sources (friends and *YM* magazine) was to play hard to get and I was, *como se dice, very* easy to get. I was always detailed, verbose, emotionally available, and quite literally, available. I'd get excited about a boy, talk a little too much, say hi first one too many times, and inevitably watch them lose interest, swearing I'd show up to my next interaction as more of a mute model. Even though I was still shy, once I got going, it was hard for me not to be quite rambly, excitable, and curious, and to this day, I still feel embarrassed leaving interactions, wondering if I came on too strong. Since I couldn't ever remember to lead with a more chill/disinterested disposition, when the ability to go idle came along, it was the only way I could both manufacture and imply apathy, and it was effective. The ultimate power move was to come back from idle but *not* away, which showed your crush that you saw his message while you were away, virtually shrugged, decided to not return it, and go idle again. What an ice queen!!! I have goose bumps.

Upon reflection, obsessing over if I should have been active, away, idle, or go invisible was an early lesson in feeling the need to overhaul my instincts in favor of what's appealing to boys. I guarantee you teenage boys were just existing while we meticulously curated our away messages, buddy info, and online behavior, using it as a billboard for our states of contentment and eligibility. Via AIM, I was learning at a young age that as a woman, I couldn't be too excited, available, or emotional. I had to take the guy's lead and mimic his level of interest, otherwise, I'd appear to be "crazy." If I messaged them too fast upon signing on, I'd get called a "stalker." The same dance applies to texting or dating apps; it's very hard to convey tone and to clearly communicate electronically. It's especially interesting to think I was experiencing this for the first time at ten to twelve years old. I would take a lack of response or a boy not saying hi when we were both active so incredibly personally that I developed habits to keep myself busy and allow myself to go idle. Not even in the pursuit of genuine hobbies and interests, just because I needed to kill time in between hits of male validation. I would go out of my way to find stuff to do around the house, keeping the computer screen in the corner of my eye, so I could keep my mind off not being IM'ed back, while still being around enough to respond quickly if they did.~*~

~*~ SO Random: Notification Parkour ~*~

I still have a lot of weird anticipatory behaviors when I'm waiting for news via text, call, or email to this day. It's crazy to think of how long I've been performing this communication-based parkour, mostly from trying to mitigate my anxiety about unresponsiveness. From AIM to Gchat to texts, I'd develop full routines to keep myself busy but semiaware of electronic notifications, minimizing the opportunity for disappointment by limiting proximity, while still optimizing the chance for response speed with visibility. If I'm waiting for news or a text or a call, I will put my phone faceup but far away from me, breaking up the process of receiving news into two steps: 1. the phone glowing from afar with a notification, and 2. the mental preparation performed on my journey while walking to the other side of the room to see what it is. In the days of BlackBerry/ BBM, I had just started dating my now-husband, and the subtle red light blinking in the distance was my North Star. My days were strung together like constellations following those lights; I mapped out my romance with the contents of these notifications because I, for the first time, was experiencing the magic of being courted by someone who, get this, *responded*. When we were dating, and there were times when I didn't know where he stood, I'd go to the movies to occupy myself while waiting for a reply. Even though I had other things going on, I always resented how consuming I found moments of romantic tension, but I'd feel better about it if I distracted myself in the meantime by supporting the arts. So I'd go see movies like *Katy Perry: Part of Me 3D,* and sit through the whole movie watching the small part of my phone visible from my purse on the floor, especially on days when it was being ever-so-stingy with the warmth of its notificational glow. That's the great part about killing time in between texts with the silver screen: the darker the activity, the more obvious the illumination will be out of the corner of your eye, all while you can pretend to be doing something else. Yes, it's exhausting to be me.

See also: activities where you can't use your hands that physically withhold you from texting too much. I swear to God, I got a lot more manicures when I was single because I needed activity-based straitjackets to curb my tendencies for highly calculated breezy follow-ups in the absence of a text response. There's an episode of the sitcom *Happy Endings* where the main characters take a fictitious industrial-grade sleep aid called "NocheTussin" to literally induce themselves into slumber for the sole purpose of appearing too busy or apathetic to engage in communication with their significant other. I remember watching this highly exaggerated scene and being alarmed that I had never felt so seen. I'd be lying if I said I didn't knock myself out in the name of romance on more than one occasion in my youth. This is so troubling and unhealthy and not something you should ever do! But I thought it was normal; in fact, my roommates and I called it being "on the 'quil" and would pass around a bottle at night sometimes so we could get a whole night's sleep despite a broken heart.

For years, I would get into these incredibly involved AIM-only friends-with-conversational-benefits situations where I was having daily flirtatious heart-to-hearts with members of the opposite sex, yet we almost never interacted face-to-face. It's so odd to even try to explain this without it sounding more pathetic or catfish-like than it was. I have a distinct memory of having an AIM-only rapport with a football player at my high school. He was hot, he was intimidating, and he was way easier to talk to from behind a screen. I remember mapping out my route in between classes to pass him in the hall, planning my outfit and salutation with a level of effort in direct contrast to the breeziness I tried to exhibit. Sometimes he would smirk in my direction or pretend like he didn't see me. I never knew if he was embarrassed by me or shy, and it's probably for the best that I never found out.

This happened quite often; I'd be too nervous to talk to a boy at school, but we'd develop a connection on AIM, talking near daily about our hopes and dreams. It was flirtatious and mutual and fun, and I'd grow meaningfully attached to them, praying that one day at school they'd make a move or formally ask me out. I would really, genuinely fall hard and be absolutely crushed when almost always, I'd find out these people asked out somebody else they barely knew. I'd have full Taylor Swift "You Belong With Me"–style spirals, comparing myself to her, cursing her name, wondering why he'd pick a girl who didn't know him like I did, who didn't listen to music as cool as I did, who didn't get his humor like I did. They would always tell me that I misunderstood and we were just friends or that I read too much into it or that I was overreacting. They'd say they wanted to keep me as a friend and they just didn't see me "like that." Many times, they'd have other girlfriends and still IM me late at night wanting emotional support, like a teenage work wife for boys who don't want to make it work with me.

The *worst* was when they would tell me that they loved my personality but weren't attracted to me. My personality??? Ugh! The audacity! "How rude!," to bring up the Olsen twins for the third time in one essay. I hate admitting this, but I knew the second a male complimented my personality, it was a relationship death wish. It endlessly confused me for years to come why I would always get such positive feedback on how great I was, yet no one I liked wanted me to be their girlfriend. Can I also say I'm mortified to have just said that I'm "great," but hopefully you know what I mean. People almost overcompliment you in the process of letting you down, and those are the words you're left with to excavate once they've withheld further communication with you.

But yes, not to brag, all things considered, I was very good at digital flirtation. The key word here is "digital"; I was so painfully uncomfortable in person, but I had fun getting to be a version of me that felt closer to who I was than I was able to access at the time in hallway conversations. In the moment, I always thought I was crushing it with saucy discourse, and I'd be surprised over and over again when they'd pick someone else, and I'd then spiral wondering if I talked too much, said something stupid, or got carried away. I'd often copy and paste conversations into Word documents, printing them out with my Shaggy lyrics to investigate where I went wrong because the males seemed to always claim "It wasn't me!" when I suggested they led me on. People who tell you that you "read too much" into things don't take into consideration that some of us literally read them back, print them out, and study them closely to try to talk ourselves out of hurt feelings. Even though I wanted to be KrAzEnKewL, I knew I wasn't crazy, and I felt taken advantage of.

I don't mean to sound like one of those "But I'm a nice guy!" types who treat acts of human decency as transactions for personal gain; I would've been cool establishing a friendship if that was the vibe, but it wasn't. Bottom line, I think that I was being used online for a soft place to land, for emotional connection, and for friendship with people I genuinely had a lot in common with, but I wasn't their type or at their level in real life. They wanted to take advantage of the company of a person they shared things in common with but didn't want the appearance of dating, especially in the event of me being not as popular or cool or hot as the people they typically dated.

As I detail this, I have no idea if this is at all relatable to anyone else in the context of AIM, but I do think that this can happen in life, where people will lead you on because they are drawn to you and feel safe with you, but they also weaponize that sense of comfort as the reason for why they aren't sexually attracted to you. To be fair, I'm sure I've done this to people, too, but the heartbreaks are far more formative experiences, and they are the things you remember most. When I read back my journals, it made me really sad that I expressed having everything they seemed to need except for how I looked. I mostly felt okay about my appearance, outside of feeling kind of plain, and I had plenty of friends. But in high school, college, and my first years of early adulthood, I felt like I didn't get the same treatment as other girls who were courted, romanced, and asked out all the time. That's the thing about self-esteem; it's not about what's actually happening or how anybody objectively looks. It's about how you feel, and it's often a function of how you're treated by other people.

While I now see there were other forces at play that I had yet to notice, the pattern of men saying they weren't sexually attracted to me eroded my confidence in ways that made me feel unrecognizable to myself after several years. I had a long way to go; I'd be obsessed with the way that I looked and dressed, and would use male validation as a barometer for my self-esteem for years to come, and this was just the

Gateway 2000 for the role technology would continue to play in my teens and twenties, navigating the politics of screens intersecting with matters of the heart. And my tense peer interactions weren't the only times online I got dumped like a truck, truck, truck.

Despite the dim angles of the screen, for the most part, I learned a lot from being so committed to AOL Instant Messenger. As much as I resented the ways that digital communication didn't make me feel like I ever could say, "I've got male!" I genuinely think it helped me cultivate my personality, sense of humor, and social skills. At the time, this was the social-networking equivalent of scrolling TikTok or mindlessly tapping through stories. It was a powerful tool for remote connectivity, and at the very least, it required real dialogue instead of parasocial content consumption. All things considered, I don't think those long nights of meaningful conversations (after long days pretending I was away) were a waste of time. AIM is where I safely navigated the social politics of middle school, high school, and college, and no matter how dull a boy made me feel, I knew that I was sharp when it came to words.

Even if these online relationships never materialized, looking back, there's something sweet about me getting the chance to build social confidence while I grew out of my awkwardness. This was a very early stage of digital communication, and little did I know I'd have my whole life ahead of me where I needed to constantly do things like curate an online presence, carefully draft typed messages, and work through how to convey humor in the absence of tone, not to mention navigate the fine lines between quick and desperate, leisurely and disinterested.

I genuinely think so few things we do are a waste of time; it's what you do with it that counts. Eventually, I'd move on to being a Facebook wall climber, then a Gchatterbox, until I found my footing on Instagram stories and in podcasting, and my love for the internet social club is still alive and well. Sometimes I still feel guilty, like I'm conning people through a screen to think I'm much more interesting than I am in real life, but at the same time, who I am in real life is a person who is able to come to life virtually. When you're a creative whose livelihood subsists of cultivating a digital audience, that becomes a skill in and of itself.

I had to get myself out from behind a screen to get started, but I think I knew deep down there was someone out there who would think I was interesting in person, whose presence didn't make me feel like I needed to say I was in the shower or fake a surfing hobby to solicit their interest. Did I stop seeking validation? Of course not, I just set my sights away from the ocean and said, "Take me to the lakes!" There was a summer camp that I heard had waterskiing—what could go wrong? I figured learning an actual water sport could only help. I may have lacked confidence, but I've always been resourceful. And if at first I don't succeed, I just AIM somewhere else.

4

God Must've Spent a Little Less Time on Me

Feeling a sense of disapproval for loving pop culture was always challenging to deal with, but it took on a new afterlife during my religious phase, when I was told the church was at war with "the culture" and my participation in worldly interests would impact my salvation. This confused me, because I'm pretty sure we had other wars to worry about besides J. Lo's Versace dress at the Grammys in the early 2000s, but okey-doke. Like most fear- and shame-based tactics, they don't inspire change, just encourage you to hide. And I wonder if around the same time I was hiding behind a screen, I also hid that a big reason I stuck around the church despite the doomsday vibes was because I heard heaven was a gated community. If M.A.S.H. couldn't get me a mansion, who knows, maybe I was destined for one in the skies.

Jokes aside, I've always been keenly aware of how my love for surface-level things feels at odds with my deep longing for purpose and meaning. I can hardly remember a version of myself who wasn't incredibly distracted by my own existential curiosity, and from a young age, I was interested in how religion could fill that void. I grew up going to a more low-key Methodist church with my family, or mass with my relatives, and my early experience with faith was much more about love and light than fire and brimstone, unlike the evangelical-adjacent

churches and camps I later attended with friends. I liked having someone I trusted when I was afraid, someone I could ask to keep my family
safe, and someone to talk to when my friends breached the no-sleeping
clause of the Up All Night Club™ contract. Nowadays, I find I mostly
become born-again on airplanes, often defaulting to my old conversations with the Big Guy when I feel turbulence or right before landing,
which kind of warms my heart. It's interesting how you can intellectualize a situation all you want, but still don't lose your reflexes where the
Spirit (Airlines) meets the bone.

Religion is a hard topic to breach; I understand and respect its sanc-
tity, but I also think the taboo nature can absolve religious organizations of well-intentioned criticism that creates space for improvement
and accountability. I'm a big believer in talking and joking about it,
though admittedly, I have a level of comfort toward speaking about
faith casually because I have the privilege of being part of a family
who will support me regardless of my religious beliefs. I know that's an
incredibly difficult factor for many people when they begin to doubt or
push back; the community-related elements of religion make it hard to
ask questions or find a safe space. I'm not here to talk anyone out of anything; I'd rather make a case for the importance of being discerning toward the figures of authority, mentors, and influences that teach young
people about their hearts, bodies, and souls. I'm not against religion,
I'm against how people with spiritual authority use religion to control,
ostracize, and oppress, and how Christian doctrine can be conveniently
interpreted to further a time period's social or political agenda.

Given its existence across, well, millenniums, Christianity is the
farthest thing from being specific to millennials. However, in my experience, I'd argue there was something about nineties and aughts
Christian-youth-group culture in the U.S. that uncharacteristically
permeated popular culture. From WWJD bracelets to worship music
from bands like Relient K and DC Talk to the evangelical funding of

abstinence-only public school sex-education programs on the heels of the True Love Waits~*~ phenomenon, these influences were very present in both secular and nonsecular spaces. So when the opportunity arose in the late nineties to attend a Southern Baptist church camp, I didn't even flinch. Going to a summer camp with a vaguely religious agenda wasn't the exception; in my reference group, it was just what you did.

I can see now that I have nothing to blame for how I started down this path other than my tendency to be quite taken with two things: 1. the glamour of water sports, and 2. my love for live music. In the nineties, I started going to said religious camp because it was hard to pass up the appeal of waterskiing as an activity. While it's alarming that I was ready to trade my soul for some recreational boating on a manmade lake, I'm sure I'm not alone in my childhood intrigue of wealthy friends with waterfront homes, whose summers were steeped in the mystique and joie de vivre of tubing culture. Ultimately, my pursuit of water sports wasn't entirely in vain; one summer I made my mark and was given a superlative at the end of the week: "Most Christlike at Waterskiing." On the back of the award, my camp counselor wrote, "Katie— Remember, waterskiing is nothing, and Jesus is everything." To this day I cannot figure out what this award is supposed to mean. Was it my middle part and shoulder-length hair, a What Would Jesus Hairdo, if you will? Was I so bad they gave it to me out of pity? I guess we'll never know. But a mediocre child does not take the receiving of an accolade lightly, and I probably chose to believe it meant I was *so* good it was like I was walking on water, so I have it hung in my office to this day next to my other less-than-honorable mentions.

This award was part of a broader era during middle school and parts of high school where I made my rounds through various friends' church youth groups, camps, lock-ins, small groups, retreats, and Bible studies. All of these places had one thing in common that really lured me in, even more than the water sports: top-notch live music. If you think I'm talking about run-of-the-mill hymns in a cathedral, it's not quite the same. No offense to mass, but I've found Catholic services to lack in the goose bumps department. Historians say King Henry VIII's divorce was a major turning point of the Protestant Reformation, but I'm willing to bet the marital dissolution was a cover for a pursuit of the real solution in getting people engaged with the Holy Spirit: chord progressions. Author and linguist Amanda Montell pointed out to me the power of these progressions when she came on my podcast, and it completely changed how I look back on my religious experiences. Had I known this, it would've saved me a lot of time when I felt stuck trying to reconcile the vibes inside and outside of worship-music venues. Apparently, goose bumps aren't necessarily a product of the Spirit moving through you, they can also be a product of "collective effervescence," another way I've heard this phenomenon categorized, where harmonious energy and good feelings are exchanged when engaging with a shared purpose. Some Protestant churches have services that are basically like concerts, and in my experience, they can be delightful and transcendental frisson fests, especially at megachurches. You know, the kind where the hype-beast youth pastor's mouth is saying he is "wholly surrendered to Christ" but his sneakers are saying, "I slept outside of a Nike store all night."

When you're amid a large group of people singing lengthy, slow-building ballads about love and life and salvation, and it's led by people who seem cool and modern as if it's a rock concert, it feels hypnotizing. It becomes easy to imagine the Holy Spirit is moving through you when you're listening to bangers like "I Can Only Imagine," and between the music and activities, I was having such a good time, I didn't even know I was being evangelized to, which is exactly why it was so effective. To get roped into this, all it took was one invitation to a ropes course or an amusement park, and like the Jesus-fish necklace you came home with, you likely took the bait. When you think about it, the formula for these youth programs makes sense; we started going at an age when we weren't old enough to drive, we were too broke for the mall, and we needed something to do that parents would approve of. It would have been hard for my parents to know it was anything other than good old-fashioned wholesome teenage fun because honestly, it was fun. Fun is a classic form of sneaky evangelizing. Who was I to say no to things like extra-cheese pizza, laser-tag lock-ins, water sports, and shiveries-inducing music with booming choruses amidst an ideally coed group hang?

~*~ SO Random: True Love Traits ~*~

True Love Waits (TLW) was the brand name at the forefront of a massive abstinence initiative created by the Southern Baptist Convention in 1993, and it basically turned into an anti–premarital sex marketing campaign designed to incentivize young people to save themselves for marriage, almost treating one's virginity as a commodity worthy of heavy ad spend like it's a subsidiary brand of Procter & Gamble. The idea was to simulate a contractual obligation utilizing purity pledges or purity rings to publicly hold people accountable to not having premarital sex. And in the mid-aughts, purity rings became a Disney star's hottest accessory, arguably surpassing that magic wand they drew Mickey ears with during commercial interstitials. At one point, purity rings were spotted on the Jonas Brothers, Miley Cyrus, Demi Lovato, Selena Gomez, and Hilary Duff, and even before that, mainstream MTV pop stars like Jessica Simpson.

Now I find the marketing push for TLW and the Disney-star trend alarming; adults were the ones sexualizing the minors they were claiming to keep safe. In my opinion, regardless of how virtuous you want to pretend an abstinence message is, the fundamental conversation surrounding the sexuality of minors is the thing that's responsible for sexualizing them. I have to assume companies like Disney just found a way to capitalize on "sex sells" by realizing no sex sells just as well, and found a way for this to benefit their bottom line in the event parents only wanted to support a network and merch machine of "pure" talent.

I'm not sure if I was more influenced by celebs wearing purity rings in popular culture or the popular girls in the town I grew up in, but I remember thinking it was almost trendy to be this wholesome/mysterious hybrid of hot-girl devout. I was fascinated by how my religious peers performed their verbal and emotional enthusiasm for the Lord. There was a specific type of religious teenage girl I longed to be; they were often popular but not necessarily cool, and had mastered the evangelical-prayer lexicon, complete with frequent and unnecessary direct addressing of the Lord by name when leading a group prayer. Perhaps they had a strong collection of Beth Moore Bible studies and Vera Bradley duffels, an ample sterling-silver-cross-necklace collection, and maybe even a tendency to experiment with hair accessories like scarves, bandanas, or headbands. I can't quite explain this, but many of these lovely devout young women or camp counselors I envied often had beautiful curly hair that somehow seemed to thrive regardless of humidity, as evidenced by the Facebook album of their most recent mission trip. I, unfortunately, wasn't aware of the concept of white saviorism and/or performative philanthropy at this time, but I was well versed in studying how a person could look cute as a button in church-mandated modesty board shorts, so there's that. Best of all, my church idols would often serve as examples of young ladies living out my dream scenario: landing a Godly boyfriend with youth-pastor good looks who was willing to talk about the prospect of marriage at age sixteen. It's wild to think about these teenage boys getting onstage with their girlfriends in the audience and condescendingly telling us about how they've established boundaries to reduce temptation, when I'm 99 percent sure all of them were doin' it in the back of their parent's sensible sedans.

This idea of scoring a Godly boyfriend made me do the same attention-seeking things at church I would do at school, hoping to live out my John 3:16–age dream. This is sad to admit, but I used to obsessively watch what other girls did with their hands during worship music because I was curious to figure out the cutest way to be superdevout while also vaguely DTFK (down to French kiss; F wasn't on my radar). I usually settled on an unassuming palms-up, eyes-closed pose every now and again so the boys knew this megahottie was megaholy, but it didn't really work. Regardless, I was swept away by pandering lyrics, booming choruses, long instrumental cliffhangers, and most of all, the elaborate hand choreography that made me feel like I could really school my nonchurch friends who only knew Michael Jackson's "Heal the World" from our fifth-grade chorus concert. You can imagine the sheer envy on their faces when I showed them I knew how to sign the words "awesome," "God," and once again, "awesome." I must have genuinely thought I was fluent in American Sign Language, but it was more like I only knew parochial hand choreography with a few proper ASL words peppered in that were generally a huge bummer. You can only get so far having a conversation in sign language when the only words you know are things like "death," "grave," and "blood."

There was a believability and intensity to the type of religious peer I looked up to, and I wanted to experience what they were experiencing, but I always felt like something was wrong with me. I started to feel especially self-conscious within the jargon when people said things like God spoke to them or called them to do something. I was like, *Damn, He calls you?* I probably told my parents this was another reason I needed my own line in my room: my eternal life literally depended on it. I wanted to have God talk to me. I wanted to be called to do something or be able to say things like "the Lord put it on my heart" and pretend it wasn't a clear means to absolve myself of accountability for my harsh words. But I never heard from Him on the other end; the vacant dial tone scored my assumed inadequacy that I somehow deserved the cold shoulder, even though I worked hard to build a wardrobe of non–spaghetti strap tanks because I was told I couldn't expose my shoulders.~*~

~*~ SO Random: Fingertip Lengthy ~*~

Growing up, it wasn't just camp or youth groups that were strict about clothing; my public-school code of conduct also made it seem like there was nothing more scintillating than shoulders, and belly buttons were effectively a private part. I'm sure I'm not the only millennial who feels confused by the clothes of today's teens, because if TikTok is a microcosm for the modern-day teenager, their options now seem like the cream-of-the-crop top, and I'm glad they have more freedom. I'm all for looser guidelines if it means kids no longer have to be publicly shamed by being made to change into their gym uniform for violating a subjectively enforced rule. I ran into this a few times; one was in the era of high school that I Expressed myself with cowl-neck blouses and got in trouble for the draping being too low-cut. Which is crazy, now that I think about it. I just thought it was cute; on what planet does a person put on a cowl-neck to make a sexy statement? Last I checked, they're like the crumb catchers of blouses. My other run-ins were usually due to not meeting the "fingertip length" rule for shorts and skirts. The joke is, I wasn't trying to be a temptress, I simply had long legs, and not all femurs are created equal. But enforcement of the dress code rarely examined intentions; it just sexualized you by subjectively policing (and thus often discriminating against) the way clothes fit people's bodies, disproportionately affecting some students more than others.

Dress codes are another secular manifestation of purity culture, where young women are taught that they're expected to control other people's behavior through how they dress. Yet in my experience, no one policed the staring or inappropriate comments or touching with the same intensity, if at all. Looking back on this, the audacity of school officials to pull a young woman out of class due to how a garment fits her body is some puritanical patriarchal nonsense that we should all find truly horrifying. Essentially, it's prioritizing the education of the male student, who gets to stay in class, and compromising the class time of the female student, who is pulled out and forced to change, just *in case* she might distract someone, rather than punishing the person who is choosing to be distracted. At the time I felt ashamed, but this now makes me so enraged, I wish I had the vocabulary to push back when it was happening.

I recall a few moments where I started to side-eye things, like when I heard one of the girls pray before something pretty low-stakes, like a rec-soccer scrimmage, saying in a team huddle we should play like we're "on fire for the Lord" and are "covered in the blood of Jesus." Again, for a scrimmage? The take-home test of athletics? How was I to be covered in the blood of Jesus when I was covered in a musty gym-class pinny that was already interfering with my MK&A *Switching Goals* aesthetic? As a teenager simply trying to not be covered in the blood of period stains on my off-duty double-rolled Soffes; not unlike my flow, it all felt very heavy for a person simply trying to survive adolescence. But if I was told it was right and true, and I wasn't experiencing what everyone else was, it was further proof that something had to be wrong with me, not them.

When my "God Squad" (as we were often teased) tried out different youth programs and Bible studies throughout the school year, I noticed patterns from camp that landed differently when you heard the concepts more regularly. There were denominational differences between megachurches and Southern Baptist camps that I was new to versus the churches I was raised going to. Specifically, more of a focus on God's wrath than God's love, and I started to feel an enormous amount of guilt and shame for very normal tweenaged thoughts and desires. Entering my formal teen years, youth leaders and camp speakers began to endlessly proselytize about how we're all broken and unworthy, while shifting their sermons to topics like modesty, purity culture, and the dangers of sexual immorality almost exclusively. Suddenly, it was all so negative, heavy, and shame-inducing. The messaging was designed to scare us into behaving the way they wanted us to, by making sure we felt guilty enough by simply existing, and it worked. I started to adopt a cause-and-effect mentality to every microscopic action and passing thought, labeling good or bad things that happened to me as direct rewards or punishments from God.

In general, there was a lot of mixed messaging that made me paranoid about sinning. For example, it was incredibly confusing to be told we shouldn't think about boys, but then have group activities that centered on creating lists of the qualities we wanted our future husbands to have as early as sixth or seventh grade. I got in trouble because the first quality I listed was "wears a watch," when apparently it was supposed to be "Godly." Frankly, I'm charmed by my early self-awareness of my problems with punctuality, and I find this manifestation proactive. But similar to making a list of qualities you want, only to be told it's about what God wants, almost everything they told us to do directly contradicted itself. At the time, I felt confused and couldn't pinpoint the hypocrisy. Now, I think it's incredibly odd I was told to dream about and save myself and make lists for my future husband, but not lust after him; I was to know that sex after marriage is awesome, but not allowed to think about it beforehand whatsoever, and told that men are in control while simultaneously being told that through my attire, I must control how they react to my body.

These contradictions would send me into spirals of guilt, causing me to short-circuit at boy-girl functions where I was torn between this new directive of sexual morality and my desire for some good old-fashioned attention. A memorable example of this was in middle school, at a rare coed function off school grounds, when *all* I wanted was to be asked to dance. I wanted to have a first *something*, to find the Kevin to my Winnie, and I can still taste the Styrofoam cup I nervously chewed on the sidelines, cursing the crooked indent my teeth left that meant my braces weren't coming off just yet. Even though I was to withhold lustful thoughts, perhaps I saw some gray area because no one ever specified if some light grinding to "Back That Azz Up" would cause you to backslide. Too nervous to engage in pelvic thrusts, I remember deciding to set my sights on an arms-out, elbows-locked, leave-room-for-Jesus-style slow song, as I waited with bated breath for my chance at romance. As I watched my classmates live out my dream of getting to sway with a love interest to *the* nineties hits, like K-Ci and JoJo's "All My Life" and Backstreet Boys' "All I Have to Give," I then heard the opening chords to the holy grail of complimenting a holy female: "(God Must Have Spent) A Little More Time on You" by NSYNC. As the song began to wrap up, it seemed like all of my peers got asked to dance under the magical oppressive overhead lighting of this suburban neighborhood clubhouse for rent by the hour. But not me.

Since an observer heals through analysis, this was one of my first memories of starting to assign a divine explanation to everything that happened to me. Was I being punished for wanting my future spouse to wear a watch, and God was using a song about time to remind me He only spends time with people who put "Godly" at the top of their list? Was it because during my devotionals at camp, I spent less time thinking about Him and a little more time thinking about the abs on display at free swim? The way the song merged a woman's perceived Godliness with the male attention it would yield was a little too on the nose for what I wanted in life (megaholy megahottie), and I remember thinking to myself, "I guess God must have spent a little less time on me" because I did something that made me unworthy of others' affection. It became an inside joke with myself I'd sing in my head over the years, and when I really think about it, it represents how this place that was supposed to be all about love and light dimmed a lot of my girlish innocence and wonder.

I was starting to feel the weight of it all. The burden of my thoughts, the burden of controlling others' responses to my appearance, the burden of having to think about all of that while I wasn't supposed to think about it, and the burden of thinking there was something wrong with me for feeling at odds with it reinforcing my alleged brokenness. I'm quite alarmed when I think about the dangers of telling young people they are fundamentally broken, incomplete sinners who aren't worthy of God's grace and mercy during some of the most formative years of self-esteem development. I know this disposition is doctrinal and sacred to many Christian churches, but to use this preaching style with young women present is something I now think resembles an abusive dynamic more than a loving relationship with a well-meaning higher power.

I struggle with how subtly (and not so subtly) the Gospel reinforced submissive gender roles by using male pronouns for God, who is allegedly supposed to be genderless. So why isn't He? I know there's a theological response to this, but not the point; it's kind of a baseless argument when the choice is to both use and punctuate male pronouns as identifiers. It embeds a default reverence, gratitude, and sense of not be-ing "enough" toward a male figure at all times. I can't speak to how all Christians are taught, but from my experience, we were told to worship a figure with male pronouns blindly, told we're worthless and broken without him, and although we can never question the standards we're held to, we must constantly repent for all the ways we'll inevitably fall short of them. And the only solution for the looming threat of wrath or punishment from this alleged father figure was to praise, worship, and obey harder. In any worldly context, no healthy person would endorse to young people a one-sided emotionally abusive relationship that glori-fies a power imbalance through a fear-based dynamic.

I didn't have this experience with the men in my life at home, at school, or on sports teams, only at church. Yet I've found something is uniquely pervasive about this religious mentality, given how much they integrated our spirit with our sexuality, resulting in a weird relationship with men in a romantic context that would take me years to unpack. I hate the term "daddy issues," but I sometimes wonder if I developed a form of "sky daddy" issues during this time, navigating the constant whiplash I felt between love and rejection while desperately hoping for the approval of an omnipotent force in the skies. It was confusing to worship a figure who loved me unconditionally with countless condi-tions, it was hard to believe my suffering at his hands was in my best interest, and it felt manipulative to threaten to take the keys to my ce-lestial new construction in the afterlife every time I made a mistake.

While I am willing to acknowledge many cultural forces contrib-uted to the mainstream success of things like True Love Waits (and the era's obsession with virginity), when it comes to sex and relationships, I unequivocally blame my issues on the church way more than the "raun-chy" pop culture we were told to avoid. The hypersexualized media they spoke of was labeled as the handiwork of Satan, but in my opinion, it didn't hold a pitchfork to the damage done by the evangelical church's shame-based approach to discussing premarital sex. My sister and I are kind of the ultimate controlled/exposed experiment in this hypothesis; we grew up in all the same ways: same household, same parents, same school, same neighborhood, same shows and movies, etc. My parents were reserved and they never pushed these conversations onto us unless prompted, which was honestly what I wanted as a teenager, so we weren't spoken to about family life and sex-ed stuff at home in a way that stood out to either of us. However, I attended evangelical camps and youth groups in middle and high school, and she did not. Guess who came out of their adolescence with a confusing lifelong battle with this topic? Yes, 'twas Most Christlike at Waterskiing, in all her aquatic glory. Or defeat. Still unclear.

"Purity culture" is a term frequently used to describe the movement that involves promoting biblical purity to young people, mostly prevalent within white evangelical Christian, Mormon, and Southern Baptist communities. From a young age, many leaders in these communities will teach girls their sexual desires outside of marriage are impure, they need to cover up so they do not tempt others, and they must abstain from not only sexual activity outside of marriage but also sexual thoughts and urges. Your virginity is positioned as a gift for your husband and the conversation is usually void of nuance regarding personal autonomy and sexual identification, assuming a young woman 1. wants to get married, and 2. will marry a man. Many times I've groaned at how my celebrations of girlhood fail the Bechdel Test, but church-related activities placed so much focus on this majestic creature, my *future husband,* it's like I was conditioned to think about him all the time, and I remember worrying if he'd approve of my actions from before we met.

It wasn't until years later that I understood how this language was part of a broader social purity movement, because it didn't seem odd; in fact, it felt familiar because it aligned with the abstinence messaging we were hearing in public-school sex-education in the nineties and aughts. The legislation that outlined requirements for sex-ed programs to receive federal funding was influenced by grassroots (mostly Protestant) Christian single-issue abstinence or "profamily" groups. Many of these groups supported and strengthened the agenda for abstinence-only programs in United States public schools and gained political leverage in the nineties, successfully influencing the Title V abstinence-only-until-marriage program in 1996 as a part of the Welfare Reform Act, followed by the even more restrictive Community-Based Abstinence Education (CBAE) program in 2000. A full *History of Sex Education* (and where I fact-checked myself) was documented by the nonprofit SIECUS (Sexuality Information and Education Council of the United States), an organization dedicated to advancing sex education through advocacy, policy, and coalition building. These programs were central to millennial sex education until 2010, when Obama eliminated most federal funding for abstinence-only sex-ed programs in favor of science-based programs.[6]

In talking to my millennial podcast listeners about this topic, it's interesting how many of their recollections of sex ed, regardless of their religious background, mirror what I was taught in youth group, with the same conservative scare-tactic-riddled rhetoric at the forefront. This makes sense when you consider the timing of legislation: in 1996, the oldest millennials were around sixteen; in 2010, the youngest millennials were around fourteen; so very few publicly educated millennials were spared a curriculum influenced by religious propaganda masquerading as health care.

~*~ SO Random: What's the Damage? ~*~

Popular conversations about purity in my day often involved some sort of symbolic representation of a woman's virtue as a prop,

6. https://siecus.org/wp-content/uploads/2021/03/2021-SIECUS-History-of-Sex-Ed_Final.pdf

serving as a dubious show-and-tell that truly left a generation un-well in understanding their self-worth outside of virginity. For example, a youth leader might ask someone to chew gum, then ask them to spit it out and hand it to the person next to them and ask them to chew it. Upon being disgusted and refusing, since no one wants germ-filled flavorless gum, the adult informs the minor they are like gum and having sex is like being chewed, and if they let someone "chew them" before their husband, that is how disgusted he will be by you on your wedding night. There were ones that involved a piece of tape, where a girl was repre-sented by the tape, which would be stuck to a boy in the class to represent the bond that is created when you have sex. When the tape was removed and attempted to stick on other boys, it wouldn't stick; the lesson was that when you have multiple part-ners, you've already given away your opportunity to bond.

Whether it was chewed gum, spit-out water, crumpled pa-per, a heart torn in pieces, or petals off a flower, the message was clear: if you were intimate with another person before marriage, you'd be perceived as used, washed-up, broken, damaged goods to be met with disgust, thus compromising your eligibility to be a bride. Yet I have no memory of learning men would be met by their brides with the same disapproval if they were promiscu-ous. Purity culture often positions women as objects or gateways to male transgressions, centering their value as a human not on what they can provide, but what they can withhold, and thus control. Ironically, purity culture is all about male control. The desire to control women, control their bodies, and control the narrative that men cannot control themselves.

I think one of the reasons I'm embarrassed for this time is because when you're told you're part of an elite club, and you know people who aren't in it, it makes you worry their salvation is at risk, and it causes you to say some weird shit. One of the reasons I never told my parents the details of these places was because at the Southern Baptist camp, someone told me my mom would probably go to hell for being Catholic. I assumed she'd find this offensive, and naturally, I feared I wouldn't be allowed to go back to waterskiing. So I kept it to myself because, well, priorities. But I probably believed it and tried to subtly save her soul in the meantime, which is insane because she is the kindest angel walking on this earth and the faith she introduced me to was always kind, loving, and forgiving. But this fear ran so deep it made me question what I knew about my own mother.

At one point, I cornered my sister in the bathroom and scream-cried to her that she was going to hell for drinking alcohol. I'm sure you can imagine this was not well received. But that's what I was told, and I was genuinely, deeply scared that Captain Morgan was steering her right into the devil's air fryer and she must be stopped. I also wept when I found out a guy friend had smoked weed, and now want to crawl into a hole and die thinking about how I asked him to pray with me about it. I had a crush on him and am mortified I was too high on my own supply as Christ's warrior to see the situation for the boner killer it was.

I knew I was a hypocrite because I'd be a judgmental member of the God Squad for things I hadn't done yet, like drinking or drugs, but I was still actively participating behind the scenes in the culture the church was allegedly at "war" with, like the pop stars I was told were raunchy, or the lusting after boy bands who were apparently sinful. I remember one of the worship leaders at camp referring to fans of boy bands as being lustful and airheaded, accusing them of acting like "basket cases" when they should be on fire for the Lord. This was concerning because "pop-cultural basket case" was one of the core ways I self-identified. I remember eating a Handi-Snack at the canteen one day, spreading my radioactive orange cheese on a cracker, wondering what's so wrong with being a superfan of the sights and scenes and socializing and screens that surrounded us. If experiencing pleasure was Satan's doing, and experiencing hardship and sacrifice was God's, deep down I was worried I felt more inclined to go to hell as a handbasket case and enjoy my life rather than spend my existence being allergic to fun.

One memory that genuinely makes me shudder is when some friends and I called out one of our classmates for her "sexual immorality" because she went to second base with a boy in middle school. I vaguely remember us confronting her about how this was an impure, sinful act, and grossly offering our unsolicited, manufactured forgiveness. Understandably, our friendship was never the same, and now I cannot comprehend how a version of me could have ever existed that was so comfortable projecting such overt judgment onto someone. It's so disturbing that "accountability" in the form of shaming our peers was encouraged. But I learned this judgmental behavior (disguised as righteousness) from sitting in circles with camp counselors or small-group leaders whom I looked up to, where they'd talk about purity and the importance of keeping our virginity for our future husbands. And without fail, people would for some reason start to feel obligated to confess their sexual sins to the group, one by one. I remember my peers hanging their heads while crying and feeling forced to confess that they participated in run-of-the-mill teenage intimacy and suddenly feeling relieved I didn't have a juicier testimony because I'd obviously have to admit to anything sexual.

Sexual transgressions were often a focal point of my peers' public testimonies, and I'd be lying if I said I didn't live for the kind that seemed intentional in sharing their spicy stumbles. I guess I can only speak for myself, and maybe I'm the worst, but I sure as hell could not be trusted with this kind of tea. I'd remember every damn detail of a random person's strangely specific tale of heavy petting, recreational drug use, or routine pornography habits. I'd try to figure out which girl/ guy in the room they'd hooked up with, which drug they were talking about based on the descriptions I learned in D.A.R.E., and wondered if occasionally glancing at a body part every now and then in between the TV static on Skinemax was something I could position as an edgy trip wire in my walk with Christ.

In retrospect, it's beyond horrible to treat this as casual fodder, and I shouldn't even joke about it, but it was the adults in the room who would comfortably allow minors to feel ashamed and dirty for their consensual curiosities by feigning a safe space for them to confess their private lives to the group as a form of testimony. It wasn't a safe space at all, and their private details were made into a needlessly shameful centerpiece so their peers could dine on their despair.

Obviously, this still goes on and is not limited to church; I've seen this type of forced public sharing under the guise of a "safe space" in all sorts of environments that benefit from shared trauma and groupthink, from self-help large-format trainings to MLM conferences to sorority pledge retreats. Hot tip: if you notice senior leadership manufacturing connection among strangers via confessions, run. It's not community-building, it's trauma-bonding.

Sometimes I still lie awake at night worrying (and deep-down knowing) there must have been young women in those circles who weren't provided the distinction of how this concept of their purity was completely and utterly inapplicable to situations that were nonconsensual or involving sexual assault. I never remember anyone making that distinction, which is shocking, because it seems like consent is the single most important thing you could clarify to a group of young women and men. I am horrified by the thought that they'd believe they did something wrong or that something was taken from them. I'm horrified that any well-meaning adult would allow a person to feel at fault for something that has nothing to do with matters that are spiritual and everything to do with behavior that is criminal. I'm horrified if I ever sat in a circle and let a young woman cry in shame about perfectly normal and healthy exploration. And I'm horrified thinking about not noticing a young person struggling with their sexuality or gender identity and how it must have felt being at an age where you are just getting to know yourself as a person while simultaneously hearing messaging reinforcing how you will never be accepted as that person. Now I see the irony in going to youth group one day after another, and we all looked like each other and talked about loving one another while making people who weren't like us feel not loved but othered.

The way I understood sex and related acts had nothing to do with a loving interaction, mutual pleasure, or a deeper connection. It was a weapon, a pawn, a shameful act, or a first-class ticket to the devil's tanning bed. The alleged uncontrollable nature of a male's desire and my responsibility as a woman to control it rooted my understanding in avoidance or secrecy, and completely overlooked any education or information about what would happen if I wanted to participate safely somewhere in the middle. I'm not sure why I internalized this so intensely; I've found it depends on the person. I know people who attended these places with me and didn't take it that seriously, and I have friends who are in therapy to this day talking about how purity culture infiltrates their healthy marriages. And I don't even know where to place these thoughts, because I'm the one who elected to go and to keep going, and I'm not sure I fully understood how this impacted me until more recent years, when I thought back on why I had a hard time adjusting to sex and relationships as an adult.

But it being my choice to participate in the organized group fun doesn't mean as a woman I need to just accept the lifelong discomfort and disgust I've often felt toward my curves, the anxiety I still feel in a low-cut top, the blame I placed on myself because I wore one when I was aggressively sexually assaulted by a bouncer at a bar a few years ago, then couldn't report him, because he literally was the security you report to. It doesn't mean I needed to be objectified in a way that subliminally taught me to seek male validation instead of romantic love or the internalized deep-seated beliefs that took me years to shake about sex being inherently bad or dirty. It doesn't mean that I needed to weather years of toxic and reckless casual hookups I didn't even want, but without a sense of what is normal, I had to find out through experience. Looking back, it's not that I wish I had more sexual experiences; my issue is I worry I missed out on accurate information that would have empowered me as a young woman to pursue intimacy safely, with self-respect, boundaries, and standards for my own pleasure.

While this is how I reflect on it decades later, it's hard to explain that at the time these conversations felt normal. You get used to this style of speech that alludes to you being a broken sinner in need of saving; it wears you down and makes you crave being built back up, creating an illusion of netting positive. It's a tried-and-true formula for preying on the vulnerable. When you're told by a critical mass of allegedly divine adults that this is what is right, at a time when you have no real life experience, there aren't red flags waving. You're told there are pearly gates opening. And if anyone says otherwise, we were told we should feel sorry for their soul, not listen to their well-meaning criticism. My friends and I didn't talk about how weird it all was until recent years when we gained life experience outside of our previously homogeneous environments and took inventory of some of the undeniable baggage, though we mostly agree it's a both/and situation. It was fun *and* it was problematic, a confusing spectrum for your memories to operate within, and I've learned what someone takes away will fall anywhere on that spectrum depending on their perspective.

Despite all of these things I just detailed, they aren't what inspired me to leave. My disengagement with church-related activities has to do with an event called See You at the Pole (SYATP). At the megachurch I admittedly only dabbled in, there was a lot of talk about religious persecution, and SYATP was spoken about as everyone's big chance to witness to their peers and be loud and proud about their walk with Christ in ways they'd potentially be ridiculed for at school. I don't deny that there can be embarrassment and harassment involved with being vocal about your beliefs; we got called the "prudies" on a regular basis for our lack of sexual activity, but even back then I think I knew better than to believe I was doing something noble or brave by outing myself as a Christian in central Virginia. But attending this event was positioned as a big deal in proving your commitment to Christ was real, and I knew it would be used as a barometer for endless judgment by peers and youth leaders, so I had to go.

The morning of SYATP, my mom turned on my lamp in my room while it was still dark out, and as I lay curled up in the corner of my daybed, I realized I'd had enough. I went back to sleep. It felt like an out-of-body moment of confidence, as if I was someone else, but looking back, this was the moment I was being the most myself. That was the authentic me in the corner, that was me in the lamplight, losing my religion. Not because I had a spiritual epiphany, but because SYATP started at 7:00 A.M., and that was simply too much to ask of me. You can take my self-worth, my faith, my salvation, my dignity. You can cruelly dangle me forty-five feet in the air from a rock-climbing wall until I recite Scripture verbatim (true story). You can even take my watch-wearing future spouse or my slow dance to one of NSYNC's finest, but for the love of God, you cannot ask me to wake up early, too. That is where I draw the line.

And just like that, I pulled a fiber that ended up unraveling the whole operation, though I'm not sure I realized that at the time. It was the first time I placed my needs over the pressure I felt to be a good Christian, and it just so happens I physiologically lack interest in an early rise in ways my body finally prioritized above my spirit. After that, I started attending things less, getting comfortable disappointing people, and realizing the things that didn't line up with my instincts weren't existential crises or panic attacks; they were my gut trying to take the wheel away from Jesus (who can't even drive, by the way?). I also quit my serious volleyball team, put Sun In in my hair, and got a job at California Pizza Kitchen to afford flammable fast fashions. My new free time allowed me to make new friends and party with boys and dabble in less-wholesome teenage activities.

Sadly, the church's influence didn't stop there. The things I internalized during this time would creep back into my mind anytime I was in a vulnerable position, and its deep roots in my psyche would continue to be a source of tension throughout life. It surprises me how these internalized beliefs pop up to this day, and it reminds me of a common phrase I often heard back then that I've always had an issue with, "We plan, and God laughs." With all due, wouldn't that make Sky Daddy kinda rude? Best case, it makes God a fellow subscriber of Amelia Bedelia–core, misunderstanding our requests and making the opposite happen for comedic effect. But it applies here, because I planned to leave this era of my life behind, but God continued to be like, "LOL, you'll be unpacking this camp duffel for decades." The point is when you're taught to tie your actions, appearance, or sexuality to your self-worth or the fate of your soul at a young age, even when you're past intellectually believing in it, you don't lose the shelving that holds on to guilt and shame. Who would've thought that when I felt the wind in my hair on the lake, decades later I'd still be dealing with what this life phase left in its wake?

After all of these words I've shared, I suppose it's pretty anticlimactic that I lost my religion because I wanted to sleep in, but it tracks with how easily it started with water sports and then was sustained by live music and my curiosity for pulling off the megaholy megahottie persona. I think the broader metaphor of sleeping in is that I was simply exhausted, and many things had led me up to that point, but I appreciated that it ended with as little depth as it started, skiing the surface of my shallow needs. As troubling as a lot of my memories are, the high points remind me that despite all the manipulation, guilt, fear, and confusion, I was always true to my core self. I love getting invited onto boats, I love live music, and I love to sleep in. This is my trinity, welcome to my church.

It's incredibly hard to criticize something that seems so pleasant on the outside, and it's difficult to get through to people when they believe they are doing the right thing. I behaved the same way when I held it as truth; I get it. I genuinely have empathy for how people can be both victims and perpetrators of harmful beliefs in these circumstances, and there's a spectrum of helpful to harmful. I'm glad I stayed out of trouble, but I'm not sure I needed to be tricked into making good decisions. The impressionability of youth is one of the reasons I am so hung up on this period of time in my life, because in many ways I feel robbed of the opportunity to nurture my own instincts prior to the interception of religious moralism by a handful of random adults who weren't even my parents or trusted mentors; they were people like my nineteen-year-old water-ski instructor or my twenty-one-year-old counselor in the girl's cabin. It's wild to have your frontal lobe be developed by the contents of other people's, who are still so underdeveloped that their narrow perspective is the very thing giving them the false entitlement to do so. Sources of influence matter, and in my experience, they need to be examined closely no matter how unassuming or benevolent they appear. And nothing seems more well-meaning than church-adjacent activities that keep teenagers out of trouble.

While I still continue to struggle with how to process and talk about my religious experiences in productive ways, the most important thing to me is being loud about the subtle ways religious groups can manipulate people into believing they have the right to deny other people their basic rights or personal autonomy. Over their reproductive choices, over who they marry, and over the dismantling of systems embedded in racial- or gender-based oppression, to name a few. Theocratic values sneakily infiltrate our lawmakers' actions often, and it's important to know what to look out for, because, like camp, it can appear subtle and seem well-meaning in theory but actually be designed to oppress and control people at every turn.

At my church of snoozin', boats, and live music, we believe God spent an equal amount of time on all of us, we don't claim He hates the same people He creates, and we trust people to know what's best for them because they know themselves better than our judgments ever will. I won't ask you to come to meet me at the pole, but I do hope we can continue to support people, policies, and institutions that promote true mutual religious freedom, the kind that protects your right to worship and your religion as much as it protects others from being oppressed by it. I may never see you at the pole, but these experiences will forever make you see me at the polls, voting out people who have the audacity to think their religious beliefs should impede upon people's rights and autonomy.

Eventually, I tried to stop asking questions about all the ways I wasn't worth the time in God's eyes and asked myself what would happen if I spent a little less time on God and a little more time on myself. Not to spite or disobey Him; rather, to exercise my own version of faith that I think has a lot more to do with *this* life, and finding a source of confidence, connection, and self-expression in the image of a creator (or whatever you want to call it, God, the universe, etc.) that is inclusive, compassionate, and empathetic. Because you're not a broken, flawed, undeserving human in need of saving. You're not just a body. You're a heart and soul and spirit so much bigger than whatever this is. And while I don't have the answers nor the sneaker budget to be preachy, that's honestly what I believe, however lofty it sounds. I'll likely forever be seeking instead of settling into one way of thinking, but I maintain that spirituality has a lot more to do with the mutually understood contents of our soul between us and our creator than it does with controlling our earthly behaviors to appease any one modern leader's quest for control. The Christianity I was introduced to in my early days was about love and light and watching out for you, and I'll forever hold on to the part that gives me peace with the Spirit. The kind that cares about leading with love and acceptance, and makes me trust that a higher power is looking out for me, at least enough to continue flying Spirit.

Part II

2000s

I could never fall asleep on the floor
But it was my favorite spot to dream
Still the space where I write late at night
Creating a whole new world behind closed doors
Over, sideways, and under covers
On a magic wall-to-wall carpet ride through my soul
Learned to navigate my dark places and moods
I came out of my Shel, where my Sidewalk began
My poems turned into a punch line at school
I let them cut me in line for punch at the dance
Before Words With Friends, words were friends
I danced to my own mental Melody without resting
My favorite character on *Hey Dude*
Wanted to live on a ranch for the dressing
It's a little wild and a little strange, too
The ground once used to explore my interests
Now a parking lot of pedestals for other opinions
Grounds for sit-ups and breakdowns, unbroken ceilings
Windows boarded up with mirrors so disorienting
Can I call myself skinny if I'm stretched too thin?

Before I got drafted to war with a tyrant dysmorphic
Version of me trapped in a mirror
I used to run and jump and swim and play,
And row and go on trips, play sports
Did I just plagiarize *Salute Your Shorts?*
The theme song these days I keep on humming
It feels coincidental as hell, especially now
Life feels like a salute to my shortcomings
I once felt strong and befriended, life felt open-ended
When you're young they assume you know nothing
But they didn't tell me I already knew who I was
The person deep down wasn't the one who grew up
Sing to me, Paolo, show them what you're afraid of
Hey now, this isn't what dreams are made of.

5

Popular-Girl Handwriting

I'll never forget the first time I saw it. It was right after a girl in my grade sat down next to me at a lab table, and I caught a glimpse of its clean, cartoonish essence when she opened up the Cadillac of notebooks: a Mead Five Star, five-subject. As an avid doodler, I've always had hot takes about school supplies, and the Five Star lived up to its name. When it came to note-taking, it was a knockout, with sturdy pocketed subject dividers, great ink-bleed prevention, and ideal perforations for a clean tear. I'm sure I was like, *Great, is this girl going to keep peacocking and bust out a Pilot G-2 .5mm?* Is humility dead? But I was relieved when she pulled out a more modest Pentel R.S.V.P., a surprising twist that forced me to retract my assumptions about her only using higher-end retractable gel pens if I wanted the chance to R.S.V.P. to boy-girl parties in her basement.

In middle school, we had moved on from Spacemakers, funky erasers, Yikes! pencils, and colorful JanSports that showcased self-expression to make space for more serious school supplies, even though I swore to my mom I'd use the more expensive Lisa Frank backpack *forever.* At Walmart one year during back-to-school shopping, I spotted one of her backpacks that stood out in a sea of unicorns, golden retrievers eating sundaes, and kittens playing in shoes: a leopard-spotted seal.

It seemed different, edgy. At the time, if you weren't a Horse Girl, you were a Dolphin Girl, or at the very least an Orca Girl, likely with a well-known ambition to pursue the official cool-girl answer to "What do you want to be when you grow up?" in elementary school: a marine biologist.

But I was still navigating the multitudes in me, like a leopard-spotted seal hiding behind rainbow coral in the sea, and I could not *believe* my mom splurged on that b-pack. It was stunning. But by the time middle school came around, you wanted people to know you got the memo that we were now doing more uniform school supplies, and nothing proved you had L.L.Bean there, done that like a double-compartment monogrammed backpack with a reflector stripe in the tasteful shades of cobalt or feldspar. Before I became overly aware of brand names on clothes or jewelry, I kept tabs on school supplies as a status symbol, noting things like who opted for brown-paper-bag text-book covers and who splurged on the spandex bike shorts of textbooks, Book Sox. Like the backbreaking work of many later-in-life multilevel marketers selling LuLaRoe leggings, Book Sox also damaged spines, came in countless highly questionable patterns, easily tore holes, and were constantly pushed on us as a more gaudy and expensive solution to a problem we never even had.

Anyway, when this popular classmate opened her Five Star note-book, I marveled at the style of handwriting that filled the pages. The opposite of a cursive flow's elegant chaos, it was choppy but neatly spaced, often had hearts or stars dotting the "i"s, and boldly experi-mented with line-to-curve ratios of ascending letters in ways I found shockingly disproportionate, though somehow still delighting the eyes.~*~ A popular girl's way of writing the letter "b" would have a stubby line with a circle as large and bubbly as her beloved personality; her lowercase "d"s would be almost indiscernible from "a"s; if only the teacher had made the same penmanship error on my math grades versus hers. The "y"s often had a deliciously voluminous descending tail, sometimes a rowdy convex scoop, turning a hook into the chaise lounge of glyphs. It was a new take on the art of handwriting (of which I considered myself an expert), but I was mesmerized. The sight was what I imagined it would be like to snort Pixy Stix; it was sugary and sweet and whimsical on the inside, with clean, straight strokes on the outside, often with color-coded lines and consistency more like a font. Like the popular Christina Aguilera song at the time (but before we were graced with the Bynes–Firth classic film), to me, it represented "What a Girl Wants" in personal branding.

When I've brought up this type of decorative print on the podcast, the consensus seems to be that it's colloquially referred to as "cool-girl handwriting" or "popular-girl handwriting," so I'll abbreviate it to PGH. The reason I obsessed over PGH was not only because it was a form of popular-girl hieroglyphics that penetrated the student body faster than I could put pen to paper, but it also impeded upon one of my only offerings at school up until that point. Everybody needs a "thing," and I had established residency as one of the go-to people in my grade with good handwriting following our required pivot to cursive in third grade. I was a savant at slightly messier script styles with swirly-curly letters, elaborate drop caps, flair, and swashes, and was usually your right-handed gal for the latest and greatest in hand-lettering, from locker signs to binder covers and more. However, when it came to clean print, I was suddenly out of my league.

~*~ SO Random: So Ransom ~*~

The fun part about observing so many kinds of PGH is that you'd start to notice patterns that can correlate to character traits. Naturally, I started creeping on people's writing to pick up on stylistic tips, and like a detective studying a ransom note, I also started to draw sweeping generalizations about their personality as a result of their upstrokes, line weights, and/or throwing of caution to the Wingdings regarding kerning. I was a regular gumshoe, judging books by their binder covers, determining that boys probably thought you were a cutie by the way you opted for more acute angles in the curvature of an "s," maybe drawing it from the bottom up, causing it to tilt sideways. I could also discern popular girls who were friendly from popular girls who were mean, not through our interactions, but through the way they drew their lowercase "e"s. In my research, I noticed there was something about an overextended crossbar of a lowercase "e" that screams, "Don't cross me," and I literally took note. Similarly, if the bottom curve of your "e"'s tail was more of a narrow point, there was a high likelihood you called me "SO random" behind my back after I commented on the bubble-to-tail ratio of your lowercase "g"s while attempting some light bonding over penmanship. It's like, I get it; I came on too strong, but so did your downstrokes, so sue me for wanting to talk shop.

Why was my penmanship's reputation prior to PGH so important to me? Because many millennials experienced the opposite of being told they were special in elementary school, thanks to the prevalence of "talented and gifted" programs (or some variation of the phrase) in public schools in the eighties and nineties, and I'm proud to be here today on behalf of the normals. Perfecting cursive was a big deal for me developmentally because following our grade being divided between "talented and gifted" (most of my friends) and then "not talented and gifted" (me), I realized being graded on my ability to write sentences and essays in curly, swirly, chaotically beautiful streams of ink was a gift and one of the only spaces where I felt talented. I'd lose track of time watching my words elegantly dance in between the loose-leaf lines, wondering if the high they described in D.A.R.E. was the feeling of mastering the flair of an uppercase cursive "L" or perhaps the danger you felt in the air committing to a cursive uppercase "Q" that looks like a two. Whether writing the word "antidisestablishmentarianism" (a favorite tail-free spelling-bee flex) or "the quick brown fox jumped over the lazy dog" so I could experience every letter in the alphabet, I was obsessed.

Once I got to middle school a few years later, and popularity became more of a thing, I realized I needed to trade on some sort of social currency that defined me if I couldn't hang my bucket hat on the most valuable traits of the time, like being hot or smart or athletic. I think this was the first time I learned a lesson I'd carry with me in life: whenever I was looking for where I belonged, it wasn't all that complicated; I always felt the most myself not during the times when I counted the minutes but during the minutes when I lost track of time. And doodling, like consuming pop culture, was another thing many considered a waste of time. But I didn't care, so I got lost in doodling and lettering for years, signing my name's double "K"s and debating the optics of "HAGS" versus "KIT," so by the end of the year, the way my pen glided would make me shine on a yearbook's backside like the top of the Chrysler Building.

As the groups started to settle into cliques, something finally clicked; I noticed that one of the only things I ever got complimented on was my handwriting, so I ran with it. For a while, good/fancy handwriting wasn't popular, it was rare, and it made me feel valuable, artistic, and proud at an awkward stage when positive reinforcement was everything. I had a routine; I'd ask my mom for lunch money, buy French fries only, then spend the rest on overpriced milky pens and one canister of orange Tic Tacs at the school store. Something about the candy's pocket rattle reverberating off the linoleum floors gave a middle school Tic Tac–er the audible authority of an Elias-Clarke clacker years before I learned of their legacy in *The Devil Wears Prada*. Milky pens in hand,

I felt finally in command, marching toward a future where I could provide something of value to my classmates and feel less invisible.

Speaking of invisible, have you ever spent all your money on milky pens, only to realize you cannot see them on white paper? If I used black paper, the teacher would know I wasn't paying attention, so I found a more subtle canvas for my designs: the back of my hand. The "put a ring on it" of middle school was to doodle "I <3 so-and-so" on your hand to indicate your relationship status, so I made it clear the doodling could be outsourced to me, a gal with a ton of time on her hands to practice the artwork I could draw on theirs, and people started to take me up on it. Suddenly the cool girls I felt inferior to were entrusting me like a Limited Tattoo artist inking their skin with whimsical pastels. I'd experiment while drawing their names, their boyfriend or crush's name, and/or their BFF's names in swirly letters with milky pens, trying to be more creative than an uninspired neighborhood-carnival face painter but less risk-oriented than a caricature artist at Paramount's Kings Dominion. While it started with writing names or relationship statuses with mostly milky pens, I eventually became more skilled in decorative script and curly lettering styles with markers, which widened my offerings immensely. In my spare time, I was making people all sorts of signs and banners for birthdays, Bible studies, and sports games, even taking my talents to writing names on dark notebook covers with white-out pens, maybe followed by a makeshift Bic Wite-Out Shake 'N Squeeze French manicure for some homeroom bonding. Not for a job or reward of any kind; I simply appreciated the classmate bonding and the sense of belonging.

But approaching seventh grade, popular-girl print handwriting (like I saw in that Five Star notebook) became the premier style, and it was clear cursive was out. I feared becoming obsolete, so I spent all my time attempting to copy PGH despite having to hit reset on my stylistic instincts. I remember a few times I'd "accidentally" take an artwork request from class home with me, which I'm sure a real popular girl could've completed swiftly, but I needed time overnight to perfect it and didn't want to disappoint a potential new friend. I practiced in school, out of school, skipping the occasional sleepover with pals to spend weekends with a girl's other best friend. Diamonds are cool, but have you ever come home to a fresh pack of midrange office pens?

Eventually, I found this perfectionist print unnatural for me, and it simply took too long. I can write in well-formed cursive letters quickly, but I found emulating the spacing, bubbles, and ratios of PGH to be tedious and counterintuitive, kind of like me right now trying to explain how letters look with words. Feeling the need to write in such a clean manner felt like having a new Molly or Kirsten American Girl doll and leaving the braids in or an anniversary-edition Barbie and being forced to keep it in the plastic. I've always struggled with things that are obsessively neat or organized; if it must be pristine to hold value, is there any point in having it? I like things that are relaxed and lived-in, and this type of handwriting was marked by its meticulousness as much as its magic; mine always came out too messy. I could fake it, but it never felt organic and was no longer fun.

An inability to execute print with as much skill as script may speak to an artist's minimal range, but some people (me) would argue they're simply different mediums, like an artist who is skilled in painting with oils but not acrylics. And visually, it's a different vibe. Socially, it seemed make-or-break. Imagine existing on the internet, and everyone else's font reads as Helvetica, but yours shows up to the world as Curlz MT. People would be like, *"Are you okay? It was cool once, but not anymore!!!"* I may tell this tale dramatically in tone for effect, but to be clear, I'm no Jokerman ITC or IRL regarding fonts. If your personal brand is on the line, it's best not to F with needlessly whimsical typefaces.

Because this is tough to articulate without a visual, for reference, unless you're in the future far, far away, you can likely find a video online I made about this type of handwriting (@bethereinfive on Tik-Tok and Instagram) from August 2020 that shows small examples of its progression, like how it evolved from bubbles and sticklike letters to what it is now, a blog-tastic combo of print and script, like if Bradley Hand ITC grew up and bought a Hamptons home. For the book cover, I tried to stick to canon for how sticklike the handwriting was back in 2003, which was the apex of my CD-R decorating career and the most stressful handwriting gig of all. After a full day of buffering, the stakes were high, and like the new Eminem track I illegally downloaded for it, I knew I'd only get one shot, and I could not miss my chance to show my community the skills that once were my lifeline. Upon searching popular-girl handwriting on Twitter, I found some threads where people shared their definitions of PGH or teenage-girl handwriting, which was fascinating. Everyone's explanation is a little different, but it made me feel validated in the experience; these kinds of observations are the small things we share despite our different upbringings, and they shed light on the psyche and desires of our younger selves. I can only assume that so many people making this connection of handwriting style to perceived social status speaks to what many of us hoped our middle- and high-school experiences would look like on paper: that we'd be popular.

It's almost embarrassing to admit popularity is something I valued when I was younger, but I'd be lying if I said otherwise. I wanted to belong, as most kids do, and since I don't think I got a ton of rein-forcement in social settings entering puberty, it really did a lot for my confidence to have a skill that made me feel liked and aligned with the interests of the in crowd. But beyond that, popular girls have always interested me regardless of their handwriting. I love a celebrity of any kind, however local or niche, and I enjoy observing those who have found it's their time to shine, whether onstage performing at the VMAs or underneath the harsh and ephemeral glow of the fluorescent lime-light of a public-school hallway.

When you're in middle or high school, popularity can feel like everything, but once you're out of it, it's a weird thing to pathologize, and no one really talks about it unless it's in the context of being an irrelevant metric. As inconsequential as this label seems in adulthood, when you think about it, the idea of popularity isn't limited to K–12; the same themes of status, networking, and visibility become increasingly important as you age, especially in moving through your career or when taking on leadership roles. I think about this construct all the time in my job; it's safe to say subjective popularity is alive and well with the proliferation of influencers, who are effectively the popular kids of the internet. So, whether it was to make friends and get a boyfriend back then, or sell books and attract podcast listeners now, I think popularity is fascinating to analyze. But admittedly, something about the word "popular" is off-putting, because you immediately feel like you're psychologically putting yourself back in detention with *The Breakfast Club,* where your existence is unfairly flattened to things like "a brain, an athlete, a basket case, a princess, and a criminal." Obviously, in life and in Mario Kart, I always chose the princess, but the homecoming princess never chose me, and maybe that's why I'm still talking about it.

Obviously, this wasn't *everybody's* goal; I don't want to project my quest for sameness onto all millennials, especially those of you who had the confidence not to care, or the wisdom to understand something I'd realize later, how oppressive this pursuit can be to individual circumstances that separate people from the status quo. I know this goal was far from noble, but honestly, I didn't want to stand out as much as I wanted to appear "normal," and in my experience, a handful of people dictated how that was defined.

When I think of how the observer in me prescribed the best practices for popularity, I almost have to separate it between my firsthand experience in school versus the tropes I studied in pop culture that, despite certain elements trickling down to the zeitgeist, mostly misrepresented a lot of the teenage experience. While it started with me attempting to mimic attainable similar behaviors like handwriting or school supplies, as you get older, it gets more complicated, and what makes a person popular becomes stratified across multiple variables that commingle for optimal effectiveness. In my experience, there was a type of popularity that you could attain through status symbols, behavior, and/or physical appearance, and a style some people naturally garnered by way of their friendliness, charisma, and involvement with the school. In my head, this divide is the difference between "cool" and "popular," which I think have a square-rectangle relationship, where cool kids are usually popular, but popular kids aren't necessarily cool. "Cool" is all about someone possessing something that solicits peers' fascination, admiration, or, on occasion, fear, whereas "popular" is a metric more about the kind of involvement and likability that makes you well-known among your peers. It's a reputation- versus relatability-based strategy to build recognition with a group.

Relationship-building is the transferable type of popularity that serves you in life; having the ability to network and make friends (to the point where many people know who you are) is always a helpful skill. This is the one I wish I had spent more time on. The reputation/admiration kind is mostly useless long-term, however, because it's entirely dependent on status symbols and appearances, and even if your natural state meets the current gaze, everyone eventually becomes a victim of trend turnover that can appreciate or depreciate your social capital without your consent. But experimenting with your appearance, clothes, persona, and partying habits often felt like a faster way to achieve status than the painful process of trying to make friends and find acceptance through your true self, and that's definitely what I tried first. Like many people, my awkward years weren't marked by my raw social or sexual magnetism, so I spent a lot of time studying the standards and symbols that made a person "cool" in attempts to see what I could acquire to rig the system while I waited for a miracle or movie makeover montage to make me feel considerably less dull.

Common depictions of popular kids mostly focused on "queen bee" types in my media repertoire, meaning the kind that gained status by being mean (and therefore feared/admired), being a cheerleader (and having built-in status), being reckless party animals, being sexually active, and/or just being rich. Pop culture terrified me of entering high school, fearing the queen-bee trope would be as pervasive in real life as TV and movies made it seem. As a nonconfrontational seal girl with a love of school supplies and a paper-thin skin being held together by paper reinforcers and positive reinforcement, I could not imagine how I'd handle the popular girls who were competitive, conniving, and catty whom I saw on-screen.

This type of character ruled the schools in nineties and early-aughts entertainment, making it easy to convince yourself that cruelty for sport and psychological warfare were core to the female condition, and these traits were eventually parodied by the ultimate queen bee, Regina George in *Mean Girls*. Regardless of their wholesome or R-rated presentation, I was terrified of these people, finding Angelica Pickles from *Rugrats* and Helga Pataki from *Hey Arnold!* just as intimidating as the mean queens I met in PG TV and movies, even when I was well into high school and knew better, like Lana from *The Princess Diaries*, Brianna Wallace (as in the Wallace department-store Wallace) from *Holiday in the Sun*, Libby from *Sabrina the Teenage Witch*, or Kate from *Lizzie McGuire*. Don't even get me started on PG-13 and beyond; I still have nightmares about Big Red from *Bring It On*, *She's All That*'s Taylor Vaughan, or Kathryn from *Cruel Intentions*, along with the cult classics that made the blueprint, like the *Heathers* who inspired The Plastics, eventually inking the Sharpay in *High School Musical*. I'm sure I was too young to pick up on the layers these women had that semijustified their bullying, but honestly, I didn't care if it meant I'd get pranked in front of the entire student body. I know we all know this type of trope, but to me, it doesn't accurately represent real life, where popularity is at the very least rooted in a level of friendliness that makes you well-liked in addition to the status that gives you visibility.

Unfortunately, in many cases, the popular girls in media who were more friendly were often positioned as the ditzy "Valley girl" type for their lack of brains, despite their status, but they were usually at least kind and often had storylines designed to prove you wrong. This was more my sweet spot. My homecoming queens were shallow but secretly savvy, like Cher and Dionne from *Clueless,* Kelly or Lisa from *Saved by the Bell,* Tiffani from *California Dreams,* or Hilary from *The Fresh Prince of Bel-Air.*

Speaking of *Saved by the Bell,* I have to say, rewatching episodes now is a truly shocking experience in terms of problematic messaging. [o0o] But a Kapowski can't be bothered with gender equality! I had bigger fish to fry, like winning the proverbial title of Miss Bayside. I was drawn to the breezy, unbothered, somewhat airheaded gals. On-screen, I loved this arc; it represented the plight of a fellow untalented and ungifted person who ended up being smart against all odds. Now, I hate how this type of popular girl often reinforces stereotypes in the context of being surprisingly sharp despite their appearance, not regardless of it.

~*~ SO Random: My Girls ~*~

Once I was exposed to the glory of watching television, I quickly migrated my interests from playing with blocks and learning ABCs to prioritizing a packed parasocial calendar of TV programming blocks on ABC, NBC, and Nickelodeon. It's a wonder I made time for sleepovers because I was already pretty swamped spending time with my best gals on TGIF on Friday, TNBC on Saturday morning, and SNICK on Saturday night. Even though they weren't always the token "popular girl" stereotype, many girls on TV appeared popular to people like me because they were relatable in a life phase where you desperately seek representation in the discomfort of girlhood.

I loved to spend my weekends with D.J., Stephanie, Michelle, and Kimmy on *Full House,* which I watched religiously, thus hitching my wagon to Dualstar Entertainment for years to come. I loved the snarky perfectionist cheerleader vibes of Laura Winslow from *Family Matters* and Topanga's big personality and bigger hair on *Boy Meets World,* and I was obsessed with the stepsisters on *Step by Step* and the separated-at-birth storyline for the Mowry sisters on *Sister, Sister,* which debuted on TGIF. Growing up, I wasn't as privy to women's empowerment, but given my very Roald Dahl–forward childhood, I was interested in women with supernatural powers, and thankfully *Sabrina the Teenage Witch* on TGIF and *The Secret World of Alex Mack* on SNICK held me over until I could get my hands on the *Matilda* VHS to get my fix of adolescent telekinesis. While I loved Clarissa on SNICK because she taught me the importance of computer programming, clashing interior patterns, and sporting globe earrings, she didn't Explain It All regarding safety and privacy, because that show convinced me it was chill for men to BYO ladder to your window and surprise you any time of day in your private space. See also: Zack's window-climbing tendencies to visit Jessie on *Saved by the Bell.* What a confusing time, not knowing if being welcoming to intruders would land me a boyfriend or land my face on a milk carton, turning a young Katie into a *Whatever Happened to Janie.*

When I think about my direct experience trying to be popular in middle and high school, it's funny to think of how I thought the key was acquiring cool things more than being friendly and networking, but I guess I don't regret it, because I had a great time wading in my shallow pursuits while hiding them from my waterskiing instructors. The more profound point I could be making here is that I think there *are* transferable principles of social politics that transcend school, but honestly, it's way more fun to talk about the things we chased that ended up having the shortest shelf life. Ironically, those are the freshest memories in my mind, even though I worried they were brain-rotting subjects.

Regarding the now-expired status symbols I remember most, my observations are limited to a pretty homogenous suburban Virginia public-school experience with mostly middle- and upper-middle-class families. Although I'm not sure my former financial framing is reliable, it's all relative when you're young. At the time, I thought I was among the Upper East Side's elite, assuming people at my high school were loaded because they shopped at Cache, but I also thought drinking a Frappuccino would make me seem more European. Regardless, I recall my high school had a decent amount of affluence, not in a Range Rover way, but in a pays-Lifetouch-for-Package-A-on-picture-day sort of way, if that makes sense. Like, if your parents bought a mouse pad with your face on it *every year* with twelve eight-by-tens and eighteen wallet-sized photos, they must really love you and have cash, you know?

The concept of popularity and its related artifacts are entirely subjective and impossible to universally define; its variables depend on things like time period, location, school size, demographics, the school's public, private, or parochial nature, etc. To me, there's an ick factor in hearing a person describe brands, products, and price points with a sentiment implying normalcy or high or low quality. When I see people make videos about this stuff in a serious tone, it oozes with socioeconomic subjectivity; that's why I can't emphasize enough that this chapter is meant to be taken more lightly than the candy-coated bubble letters I once superficially scribed.

At first, I didn't rule the school, call the shots, or set the trends, but I did follow the rules, eventually take the Jell-O shots, and attempt to mimic the trends so I could pull off what I call popular-adjacent. Trying to be popular-adjacent was mostly about having a delusional level of self-pity for not meeting whatever appearance- or class-based social standards defined popularity at the time, not realizing that your endless pursuit is underscored by your proximity to them, which is a privilege in and of itself. Instead of exercising self-awareness, you channel your energy into finding resourceful ways to attain material things to get as close as possible to the in crowd. Getting crafty to participate in unaffordable trends felt similar to practicing handwriting to fit in; I would always find hobbies and gain new skills as a part of my quest to belong.

The people who were popular and most eligible for necking often lived in more affluent necks of the woods, and could be spotted wearing the latest and greatest in sterling-silver neckwear or bracelets, never missing a charm, adorned with Pandora's latest or stacked Yurman bracelets that people would have the audacity to position as a stocking stuffer. While some kids dabbled in fine jewelry, I couldn't splurge nor be trusted with it, so before I was introduced to Canal Street, I nickel-and-dimed by wearing the latest nickel finds masquerading as silver, eventually making my own jewelry that honestly looked pretty close to the real thing. I didn't graduate to sterling silver until I got a part-time job, mostly just to shop; working for that 925 stamp, just trying to make a living.

Silver-ball-chain necklaces and large silver-ball-stud earrings were all the rage in high school before we got into giant pearls, and I assume the former was a trickle-down effect of Tiffany's silver-ball necklace. I remember wondering if I got ripped off when my dad showed me how to fix the toilet flapper, and I spotted a ball chain under the lid that was suspiciously identical to the one I wore around my neck purchased at a local boutique. So, I started to DIY them with a needle, ribbon, and beads I bought from the local Ben Franklin Crafts, made cuter replicas of silver-beaded and ginormous-pearl necklaces, and would tie them with a preppy colored bow to wear under polos. When making these necklaces, I made the unfortunate choice to pull the needle through the beads with my teeth, chipping my front tooth in the process, and I still haven't fixed it. I think of those damn necklaces every time I brush my teeth; it reminds me how far I've come since my days in the mines of elective low-stakes manual labor in the name of social acceptance.

Speaking of polos, when we started doing polo shirts with jean skirts and ribbon belts, I didn't want just any polo; it had to be one with a preapproved tiny mascot on the left chest. I was open to possible contenders, whether a real Polo, a tiny gator from Lacoste, a pink whale from Vineyard Vines, or, best-case scenario, a cartoonishly giant moose from Abercrombie. I once described on the podcast the sense of urgency I felt toward acquiring 2000s moosewear as feeling like I needed "a bigger motherfucking moose on this motherfucking shirt," and while it's not every day I make a *Snakes on a Plane* reference, I still stand by this statement. I felt like I hit the jackpot when I noticed in an old coat closet my dad's outerwear from the seventies and eighties when Lacoste was previously popular. I found a green windbreaker with the famed green gator and, despite it being a men's XL, wore it constantly, thinking I was passing it off like it was off-the-rack from Saks. Which is fitting because it fit me like a potato sack, but I didn't care if the label was there.

After that, later in high school, I realized a workaround was to go on this new website I found called eBay.com where, in between sultry AIM seductions, I'd buy old men's Lacoste sporty outerwear items that could be worn oversized and try to pull them off as new, though I think when I saw *Mean Girls* and Regina George said, "Vintage, so adorable,"

I formally rebranded my digital-garage-sale finds as being vintage. But all that mattered was chasing the high of a deal and reaching the summit of a savvy solution, and despite being ill-fitting or old, I felt like a million bucks. More specifically, around eighty bucks, which I think is around how much Lacoste polos cost at the time. But that was so much money for one shirt, and worse, at one point, the popular girls upped the ante and started stacking polos, pricing me out of their tier.

So I had to get creative; one option was to put a no-name brand from Target or Walmart on the bottom layer and just hope I wouldn't also experience a sense of Faded Glory if I was found out. But you couldn't tell if you put the name-brand polo on top, stacking them to round out your look, ironically making you look like a literal human square. To this day, something about preppy clothing tends to have a real reverse–Jessica Rabbit effect on me that turns my curves into boxy, bulky edges that I just cannot get behind. When I started developing, it was clear not all ample racks were friendly to heavy knit weaves that insisted on being stacked, but I forged ahead with the trends anyway. Maybe it was just a shock to the system after prioritizing paper-thin lace tanks and Henleys from places like Hollister that would disintegrate in front of your eyes after all those years.

But the problem wasn't just that; it was also the tailoring, because my workaround for Ralph Lauren Polos was to buy the actual name-brand shirts at Stein Mart, but in the little boys' husky section. They were cheaper than women's, allowing me to acquire more variety. I had to seam-rip and restitch the sleeves on a few, and they were definitely shorter and higher-risk for midriff dress-code violations, but otherwise, I thought this was a life hack for the ages. In photos, these polos looked absolutely terrible and were way too small, but for some reason, these status symbols gave me the confidence I couldn't consistently manufacture. Now, I think it's crazy that I chose to either drown in fabric wearing my dad's clothes or squeeze into children's clothes simply for the sake of repping a label, but I guess not caring at all about the fit wasn't nearly as important as fitting in.

I find my preppy phase to be funny because it's a metaphor for me beginning a process where I was drifting so far from who I actually was; the self-expressive days of leading with my cursive had left the classroom, and I was sartorially printing those tedious, predictable bubble letters one by one with polished preppy looks even after I had retired my Spacemaker. But abandoning my taste in favor of what was popular is perhaps best exemplified by my fixation on Vera Bradley bags in late high school. Her designs are lovely and still popular, and I'd never want to jilt enthusiasts of the floral and quilted, but I don't fully understand how I justified the whiplash from appreciating aesthetics that were more *Coyote Ugly* to suddenly insisting that my vibe was more French Provençal between the ages of fourteen and seventeen. Many patterns were beautiful, but they were mature for a teenager. Yet there I was, frothing at the mouth for fabrics busier than I was pretending to be on AIM, like coffee-colored paisley duffels with blue accents or a blindingly bright-sherbet toile wallet that would clash with every single one of my possessions. Even though I worked at California Pizza Kitchen, I was suddenly better suited for the tropics or the Cape, dreaming of summering with a handbag in Bermuda-pink or Nantucket-navy prints. I'm unsure if I actually loved it or convinced myself I did, but there's something powerful about power-clashing hyperfeminine prints, and I regret nothing.

Well, except for the first Vera Bradley bag I bought and spent my whole paycheck on, which was a huge creative risk that I didn't see coming. I picked it out at a store near my grandma's house that was the type of store with the most random assortment of housewares that I loved to peruse. It had the type of nonfunctional items that rich people buy as hostess gifts, where the recipient overlooks their impersonal nature due to being flattered by the price point. I love these stores because they're where my mom would say something to me about markup under her breath, and we'd talk about how we could save money by making everything ourselves at home. Moms sure are good at warning you of the perils of markup; no excess margin was safe around mine, from movie theaters to minibars to Scholastic book fairs. Her skills were remarkable, like a walking game of *The Price Is Right* specializing in pointing out retailer wrongs.

Some of the most fun memories I have with my mom are from the times we pulled off a coupon-combining deal at the mall or scored at the outlets in such an epic way, the discussion of our savings lasted the whole forty-five-minute ride back from Colonial Williamsburg. In hindsight, moments like that, where material things were acquired not with ease but with effort, are much more valuable to me than the items themselves. In putting in the effort to score a deal, I didn't just save money; more importantly, I gained quality time. And the Michael Kors watches from the outlets wouldn't stand the test of timepieces, but hanging out with my mom while chasing low prices and relishing in the high of a discount was one of my favorite things we did together when I was a teenager.

At the boutique with the Vera Bradley bags, past the porcelain-rabbit tealight holders, hand-painted Lolita glasses, and Maxine cards, they had a unique selection of her patterns in the back if you took a left at the magnets with nuns saying unsavory things. This shop was in another school district and had a lot of prints I hadn't seen my classmates sport, so this was my chance to make a statement. I went and looked at these bags probably four or five times just to imagine having one, which I don't say wistfully and nostalgically, but with a level of sadness, as I was becoming a little too attached to external status symbols, and I probably went so many times because I didn't like any of them, not because I couldn't choose. But like I mentioned, once I got a part-time job, having money was exhilarating, and picking out and paying for this

Vera Bradley set was one of my first big purchases. I remember it more vividly than my high-school graduation.

After a great deal of thought and deliberation regarding my selected pattern, I made a shocking last-minute decision to double down on a nonreturnable matching bumblebee-and-yellow-rose-patterned purse and wallet. I knew right away it was a *big mistake, huge.* There was likely a reason my classmates didn't sport this pattern, and I'm not sure why I chose that moment to try and do something different when my individuality had gone out the window the moment I started lusting after octogenarian-targeted prints called things like Piccadilly Plum. The thing is, I'm scared of bees. And I think the postpurchase dissonance paired with it being a purse covered in bugs just gave me anxiety. I also hypothesize that it likely triggered my deep-seated millennial fear of bees, thanks to Thomas J.'s fate in the movie *My Girl.* I gather people want society to band together and save the bees, but I don't think the movement is going to get the support it needs from millennials, who never asked to be exposed to a "He can't see without his glasses" level of despair, only to be rivaled by 1995's *A Little Princess.* Whoever thought it was a good idea to show me a movie about a young girl forced into servitude after her father dies, only to realize he's still alive (and have him not recognize her during the most intense police chase in a thunderstorm you can imagine), was out of their goddamn mind. That movie, and *The Secret Garden,* destroyed me to the point where I almost got their plots confused. Come to find out, they're written by the same author, and everything makes sense. Thanks for the trauma-bonding session; back to popular kids.

It wasn't just about material things; I also paid close attention to popular-girl behaviors that were free, dabbling in becoming a school-desk majorette with a particular type of pen twirling, made possible by the friction from my PGH callus on my middle finger that I still haven't gotten rid of. Or better, use a pen to master the art of rocking a writing-utensil French twist in the absence of a hair tie, so you could look adorably down-to-earth with a more off-duty-model look. And this is so specific, but I remember watching the way cool girls turned their wheels in driver's ed when I was learning how to drive, putting one hand underneath the top of the steering wheel, palm out, the sun glaring off their latest sterling-silver stack, and operating their vehicle with reckless abandon away from ten and two, so I did this to try and look like a ten. So casually cool. Another car-related example of a minor, inexpensive thing I thought was *so* fierce to have was a long lanyard, ideally with the college you wanted to go to, that you'd twirl on the way to or from school, showing that you had wheels.

I'm worried if I go on a detour about cars, I'll never get back on track, but wow, what an exciting injection of a costly and privileged status symbol that enters the equation when you can get your driver's license. The topics were hot when it came to politics over parking passes and special spots and the dreaded overfill in the senior lot, and every day was a winding road for ole Be There in Five here, because I literally never got there early enough for a spot, causing a further unexpected twenty-minute delay. My lifestyle has always been a HomeGoods hand towel that says RUNNING LATE IS MY CARDIO. I'm a time optimist who genuinely thinks that every delay represents circumstances of an unavoidable one-off situation.

When I think about cars as status symbols, that's a whole other can of worms as it relates to the subjective socioeconomic situations of schools. And I feel like this is a space where my opinions don't belong because I use Uber and public transit and never even think about getting a car. Yet it doesn't prevent me from still having hot takes about cars that I saw fifteen years ago (the last time I regularly drove one), and when it comes to my taste, unfortunately, it's still parked in the senior lot. People seem surprised when in passing I highlight the sexual magnetism of a VW Cabrio or Toyota Solara like it's a Ferrari, but I'd be open to a Pontiac Sunfire, too!

I feel bad now; it's pretty rude of us to judge the cars of our classmates as if what they drove was a function of their personal choice. Did we honestly think Jason C. had his pick of the litter at the luxury-car lot but opted for the classifieds because he couldn't keep his mitts off a 1992 Grand Marquis? It was probably passed down or what he could afford. Or I don't know, maybe he likes the unwieldy handsomeness of a six-seater from the George H. W. administration; let him live!!

I was lucky to have any wheels at all; when I got my license, I drove a gold 1990 Honda Civic passed down through my siblings. It was a great car until I crashed it into my friend's brand-new red Jetta on the way to the pool, like a deer in the brake lights, likely stunned by the elegance of a private Jetta lifestyle. But I guess it's remarkable that anyone that age was fortunate enough to have a car that, like Kristin, we just hoped wouldn't be dunzo.

The most popular girl at my school had a yellow Toyota Celica, and I loved that for her. What an iconic popular-girl car; I don't know how you could drive that and not be a star? I also loved scoping out the parking lot for those who drove Mitsubishi Eclipses, Jeeps, 4Runners, and two-door Honda Civics with spoilers. I still salivate at the sight of a wood-paneled Wagoneer. I steered clear of outdoorsier cars that looked like they'd get chosen for cow tipping or off-roading, and I feel like most schools in my area had at least one kid peacocking with a yellow Nissan Xterra. Like the Nextel phone of cars, it was needlessly brawny and durable relative to most exteriors, but served as a fixture in being the senior-lot show pony. My dream car to this day is a Geo Tracker, like the one Torrance's mean boyfriend in the ribbed turtleneck drove in *Bring It On,* ideally with a white soft top, purple exterior, and a teal racing stripe like a 1993 Sea-Doo.

I wanted to choose a few memorable moments of my mimicking popular behavior that continued far beyond pen and paper throughout my teen years, but countless other elements of sartorial millennial iconography also come to mind. I don't remember high school being at all like the movies or millennial nostalgic memes I see, even though I tried on certain elements for size. I think many of us are familiar with the popularly held image of a Y2K queen, but I think that's more of a SoCal starlet than a homecoming queen from 2000s high-school Americana. You know the gal; she's likely in a Juicy tracksuit, wearing Uggs, maybe in a low-rise pocketless denim with a tiny purse, a Playboy Bunny–sticker tan line peeking out from the lower left hip, a bedazzled flip phone in her pocket so she won't miss her "ride or die"'s texts. This is definitely accurate to the imagery from the era that I aspired to, and unfortunately, the Playboy Bunny sticker I eventually acquired, too.

But when I really think about it, the clothes the popular girls wore in real life were more business casual than Y2Kcore. At my high school, I don't remember the upperclasswomen being super into trends; I remember them being into looking "nice," if that makes sense, almost like a form of conditioning for future sorority-pin attire. I'm not sure exactly when, but there was a shift in my style that's best represented by footwear, when my friends and I stepped away from casual shoes like Rainbows or Reefs or Birkenstock Boston clogs and started wearing heels with jeans, an unfortunate trend we'd carry well into our college years when many of us would need to be carried home due to the inflexible realities of patent leather on a dance floor. The style was kind of like if Express and Talbots had a love child, creating a look that said, "Class officer, but make it sexy," where the silhouettes were classic and predictable, but there was an occasional modern accessory, texture, or neckline that would surprise you, like when a teacher had a cowl over my unavoidable light cleavage in a drapey blouse. I wasn't after cutouts and mesh; I lusted after tailored three-quarter-length sleeves and boatnecks, and thought small details like keyholes were innovative must-haves.

Speaking of keyholes, we really got down with a button-up during this time, but I suffered from the inadvertent keyhole boob gap that had to be remedied with a cami or vest. My friend (and talented writer/podcaster) Caroline Moss refers to this era of millennial dressing as when we all looked like "cater waiters," and that pretty much hits the nail on the head. For example, I don't remember feeling my best in revealing clothing, but I do remember feeling like a goddamn smokeshow walking down the halls in a crisp turtleneck with a first-day blow-dry and a pair of dress pants that could double as a vague choir bottom. In my head, I call it JBC, short for Juniors Business Casual, primarily because I was eating a lot of Wendy's JBCs off the dollar menu in between shopping sprees in the juniors' section at the time. JBC was all about nice tops, pretty sweaters, polos, cardigans, and tailored boot-cut jeans cascading over pointed-toe pumps and peacoats whose dousing of Estée Lauder Beyond Paradise or Clinique Happy you could smell from a mile away.

Eventually, you learn none of these things were ever an appropriate means to judge people. I think longing after consumer goods to look like popular girls was never "about what it's about," so to speak. It was about the idea of becoming the people with adoration and decoding the formula for how they got there, but it was also about the butterflies I'd feel in my stomach, hoping the movie makeover scenes were true: that minor modifications to my appearance could make me show up to school one day and things would never be the same. It's a similar anticipatory feeling to situations like returning to school with tan lines after spring break, maybe with a singular threaded piece of hair, getting face-framing layers or your braces off, or basking beneath the glow of your new waterproof purple digital watch's Indiglo. Like a human iOS update, these features felt like major opportunities for minor improvements to keep you up-to-date and fresh until you could build up the capital to constitute a formal rebrand over summer break.

If I may generalize, pursuing status or material things was a shallow quest, but in practice, it was more of a side effect of seeking social acceptance for survival, which I think is a very millennial trait. Different currencies hold value within and across generations, and in my experience, uniqueness was not valued when I was growing up the way it is now. As I mentioned in the introduction, one trait I've observed about Gen Z online is their celebration and prioritization of identity and individuality, which I applaud. We're now in the era of the personal brand. But before we could curate personal brands, we just had name brands, and as weird as it sounds, a huge-ass moose or a Vera Bradley hanging loose from my arm felt like armor in a sense.

But I appreciate the memories; I always tell my parents the material things I wanted and never got don't make me feel like I missed out, but lucked out in a way, because that's why I remember them well enough to articulate it here. Longing implies a sense of absence, but for me, it was mental real estate that I used for dreaming of the "new me." While I find this mentality exhausting, and now see how capitalism subsists off convincing you the "new you" is just around the corner, at the time, I really believed it was. To this day, it's still nice to believe sometimes.

When people say you don't want to peak in high school, I wonder if they mean the type of fleeting coolness that doesn't really hold up with age, becomes normalized, or dissipates when high school ends. Like hedging all your bets on your looks, partying, your relationship, or the admiration of your peers, especially because relying too heavily on them can make your decisions shortsighted at the expense of your potential. I started dabbling in a more party-girl phase later in high school, and it was arguably the most fun I had, but it is also the time I probably regret most because I wasn't myself. I had the rest of my life to do that stuff, but it felt so exciting at the time to do things adults totally do, like drink a glass of Malibu rum neat so you'll be warm enough at a party in someone's heatless garage.

It's interesting that once I started hanging out with a group that got invited to the parties I always wanted to attend, I have no memories of paying attention to what or who was popular at that point; maybe it's because I almost finally was. Or maybe it was because the upperclassmen were gone so there were no more out-of-reach local celebrities. Regardless, I had the time of my life watching those two summers fade to fall junior and senior year, killing time between oversized-sunglasses gossip sessions at the mall, long drives listening to burned CDs we made for each other, healing our broken hearts with "Since U Been Gone" and trying to take "1, 2 Step"s forward, but listening to "I Go Back" and similarly wishing time would stop right in its tracks. Like "Strawberry Wine," we were seventeen, and the hot July moon saw everything, like the time I threw up fettuccine alfredo on my friend's back deck after being too empowered by a power hour, or the time I made a grave amateur drinking mistake and got coerced into doing a keg stand but forgot I was wearing a dress.

In reality, the *actual* cool kids weren't the ones doing the most to try and appear cool, they were the ones who already were in some way and who weren't defined by any metrics the high school provided at all, and it took me too long to realize the coolest thing I could've done is not care so much about achieving social status. To this day, as much as I resent it, an appearance of effortlessness appears to rise to the top in popularity, and that is simply not a trait I possess. I'm fascinated by people who seem carefree, take on social situations breezily, and/ or possess a level of natural beauty that makes me assume they don't require a twelve-step shower/shave/self-tan routine to go out of town for a wedding in hopes to appear presentable as a human woman. I call this a "dolphin shower," because I leave this venture squeaky clean and hairless, making me eligible for all the fish in the sea and for people to take pictures with me, not unlike a Discovery Cove (maybe I am a Dolphin Girl!).

Whether it was the clothes, parties, or involvement with the student body, by the end of high school, I finally felt a level of acceptance that I genuinely appreciated. Not like senior-superlative or homecoming-princess levels of formal recognition (outside of something called "prom court," where you do a dance with thirty classmates at prom and wear a red dress, something I still struggle to understand, but it was exciting nonetheless). But when I graduated, I realized I felt proximity to popularity, and it had a lot less to do with how cool I seemed to other people and a lot more to do with finally feeling like I belonged.

It was an exceptional experience forging meaningful new friendships toward the end of high school; I still feel misty remembering my friend and I sobbing to Coldplay's "Fix You" when we said goodbye before going off to college. We were sad to be apart, but I think we also knew everything was about to change and could easily fall apart, and we were right. I don't keep in touch with everyone, but still think about them often. Weirdly, I always dream about my high-school friends; there's something so important about the people you first experience teenage rites of passage with, and I think my subconscious feels safe with them. Ultimately, I'm grateful that in seeking the status I wanted, I eventually got what I needed: support. I genuinely loved the overall community I grew up with in high school. Maybe I overromanticize this time, because college was a different, much darker time for me. Anecdotally speaking, I find that people often describe having thrived in a maximum of two out of three of the following scenarios: high school, college, and/or early adult years in the workforce. It seems like a lot of people who liked high school hated college or vice versa, or if you went straight to the working world, it had a similar inverse relationship to high school. After college, the same thing applies; if college represented freedom and fun, the working world felt restrictive, but some people (me) benefited from the structure over a fancy-free existence. You can't win 'em all, and I had to learn the hard way that it's okay to not be having the time of your life when everyone else is.

Teenage popularity was the start of a quest to endlessly try and fit in, even when it felt like a stretch. But focusing on proximity to popularity has its limits; it convinces you that you can repeat the formula, and your classmates in college or the real world will value the same things, the same brands you splurged on, the same bumblebee bag you wear so little it stings. But the personal brand you established through wearing brands and making friends in the same pool of people K–12 doesn't carry over. You finally found your identity in the friendships you made and the goods you could attain, but you are now expected to know who you are without them.

This was one of the early signs of a pattern I'd repeat throughout my life, where I obsessively searched for a style I could copy instead of creating my own, seeking a formula I could follow to find the secret solution everyone else had, without realizing that my believing there was one was the problem. I spent more time copying everyone else than getting to know myself, ultimately drifting further and further away from the scrappy school-supply-loving gal who was as full of life as the swirly-curly letters she once drew. This was just the start of a lesson I'd have to learn, time and time again: in life, you can't let obsessing over how the letters look be at the expense of discovering what you would've written on the page.

° ○ ° Pop-up Biblio: Saved by the Bell Jar ° ○ °

For most of my youth, "feminism" was not a word most girls I knew wanted to be associated with. There are likely many reasons for this, from the nineties zeitgeist to my being raised in the South in a fairly homogenous environment. However, there's another element I hadn't thought of until recently: how some self-identified "feminist" characters in teen-targeted entertainment were portrayed. Within my friend group, before we understood how this completely missed the point and centered our fragility, we were too scared of being typecast as what we saw on-screen; you know the tropes, the sometimes-unpleasant, angry, "bra-burning," allegedly humorless people who can't take a joke because they're so worried about women's rights that they can't be bothered to giggle at innocuous male wrongs to validate them. I found the idea of not laughing at a misogynistic joke to be rude, somehow, and assumed my reacting to it negatively was a choice, when I could choose to "lighten up." While the mainstream adult world in the nineties had plenty of media influences that reinforced these stereotypes, likely as a form of backlash to second-wave feminism (like Rush Limbaugh's coining and calcifying of the term "feminazi"), I wasn't really aware of that cultural conversation, so I have to imagine the themes I picked up were embedded into the programming I was watching.

While writing this book, I rewatched some of my old favorite pop-culture fixtures to get back in the headspace of a younger version of me, and one of the shows I revisited in more detail was *Saved by the Bell* (*SBTB*). It felt like seeing old friends; the Bayside crew was canonical to my understanding of the American high-school experience before I was old enough to have proximity to it, serving as my PG Saturday morning Brat Pack when I was too young for the John Hughes multiverse and wasn't allowed to spend time at the Peach Pit watching *Beverly Hills, 90210*. Following this rewatch, I am convinced *SBTB* is partially responsible for my negative association with the word "feminism" for most of my youth. In terms of the cafeteria archetypes provided by this show, I remember thinking Kelly Kapowski was the breezy, naïve, sometimes ditzy cheerleader short on cash, and Lisa Turtle was the rich fashionista whom Screech was in love with and who always had the best comebacks. And I turned into my own form of a macho pig while watching, thinking Jessie Spano was too serious, studious, and needed to relax, while perceiving her pushback to sexist behavior as disruptive and difficult relative to her laid-back counterparts. When the show got picked up on streaming sites recently, I was seeing her character be celebrated on the internet for being groundbreaking, but I remembered it differently, like it shattered my interest in sharing her beliefs. Fortunately, I saw a *Jezebel* article from 2009 that supported my theory called "Jessie Spano: Friend or Foe?" and it made me feel like maybe this deserved more exploration.

Part of my goal in rewatching the show was to see if the younger me was a built-in baby misogynist or if Jessie's peers positioned her personality as undesirable in some way that taught me not to like her. Turns out, it wasn't Jessie's character's fault; it was due to how her male counterparts responded to her, informing me that her feminist principles weren't good points, they were punch lines. To be clear, I take accountability for being a garbage feminist in how I consumed a lot of pop culture, whether it was the things I took away from Bayside to taking Justin Timberlake's side in the Britney breakup and beyond, but I think it's interesting to examine where seeds of influence were planted that inspired this mentality. And in the world of stereotypical chauvinist pigs, there was no influence greater than A. C. Slater, and no matter how hard I've tried to forget him, I can't. Mostly because I had to see him in literally every hotel room I checked into while writing this book, and all I could do was shake my fist in a *very* intimidating "why I oughta" fashion, while I tried not to succumb to the impulse of renting one of the movies he shared via his iconic dimples on the *Extra at the Movies* Welcome Channel screen.

A. C. Slater's behavior was pretty cliché and PG in terms of chauvinistic humor, and he did things like almost exclusively referring to women as "chicks" or "babes," referring to Jessie as "mama" and calling her a "cute little feminist." When she calls him out for being a sexist pig after he mocks the ballet, he responds with, "Oink, oink, baby, and if you don't like it, go steady with some other pig." The crowd loves it. At one point, in a marriage simulation, Jessie tells Slater that since they both work, they should share the household chores, to which he says, "Fine, you cook, I'll eat," and the audience laughs. She then asks him if he's heard of the women's movement, to which he responds, "Sure, put on something cute and move it into the kitchen." The audience laughs a little harder.

Zack Morris was just as guilty, but I mostly took note of Slater's active mocking in response to times when words like "sexism" and "feminism" were explicitly used, trying to figure out why I internalized the dismissal of these specific topics. In another scene, Jessie states that women, in addition to men, can go alone to parties without a date and it's perfectly acceptable, and Slater says, "When you do that feminist thing, your nose scrunches up and you look so cute," and the audience is in a flood of "awwwwwww" noises. For every good point she makes, he minimizes it, gets rewarded for doing so with sound effects, and Jessie then melts back into his arms, her steadfast statements offset by her never-ceasing softness to his infantilizing charm.

But the most shocking realization of my rewatch was that

perhaps the most manipulative aspect of all was the laugh track. Even though the show was filmed in front of a live studio audience, in television, there can be something called "sweetening," where audience laughter is punched up or replaced entirely with a laugh track or other sound effect, so the audience's live reaction can be edited, enhanced, or removed to communicate to the viewer what's supposed to be funny or solicit some sort of emotional response. *Saved by the Bell* seemed to have a lot of canned laughter, as well as other sounds that were nearly identical episode to episode, and in my opinion, they were undeniably biased in favor of the male characters. I saw enough examples where her legitimate points were met with silence more often than she gets a cheer, and it's clear her feminist views are mostly used as an object for comedy. The cadence was usually that she makes a decent point, then someone makes fun of her, and the audience laughs at her being the butt of the joke, or she's in a scenario where everyone else is having fun, but she can't see past something that's sexist or unfair, so she's told to lighten up. Rinse, repeat. Maybe my monkey bars–aged misogyny actually wasn't the problem; I didn't have to put much thought or judgment into how I felt about the characters' stereotypes—the sound effects and dialogue completely engineered how they wanted me to feel about them. The laugh track is a key part of how our perceptions are formed about people whose experiences we're new to, and especially for older millennials; most sitcoms we grew up with used it. These sound effects told you who is funny and who is to be made fun of, and as a young, impressionable audience member not yet marching to the b-b-b-beat of my own drum, it was effective.

Because of this, I understood it was best to go with the flow when responding to behavior that's degrading and macho, and to be more like a Kelly or Lisa if I wanted to be like Hot Sundae and "put my mind to it, go for it" when it came to being well-liked. Watching back, Jessie's my favorite character, and even though her feminism is flawed, she attempts to stand up for herself, but it's maddening how her friends (whom I idolized) rarely supported her. For me to find Spano whiny is terrible when she was having such a tough go; she honestly should've complained more. Her boyfriend openly degraded her, her friends seemed to find her annoying, and despite her best efforts to make salient points about sexism, her legacy is led by a lyrical nod to The Pointer Sisters, in an iconic scene where her packed planner and penchant for perfectionism pushes her into a downward spiral that culminates in a caffeine-pill addiction, causing her to incoherently scream-sing sans eye contact the words "I'M SO EXCITED. I'M SO EXCITED. I'M SO . . . scared." Bless her fast-beating heart.

In general, rewatching nineties teen shows with laugh tracks is a fascinating activity; I noticed in several shows I revisited that the young men were in control of their comedy, while the young women were used as material for comedy. Even rewatching *Boy Meets World,* I felt this way, which is a show I'd argue tackled a lot of issues pretty well for its time (my favorite is when Shawn joins a cult!). In one scene, Topanga talks about how people shouldn't be forced to do traditions they don't understand or that make them unhappy, and Cory says back, "Can you spell 'peculiar'?" and the audience cracks up at him making fun of her for an earnest statement that isn't peculiar at all. In another scene, Topanga tells Cory, "When people laugh at you, they're depleting their own karmic reservoir," and the crowd laughs (not because she told a joke, but I assume at her precociousness), and Cory replies, "You're going to be one of those girls that doesn't shave her legs, aren't you?" and the crowd *roars,* thus losing Topanga's point entirely. Based on dialogue alone, these shows had good lessons, but combined with other ways they set the tone; the points the female characters attempt to get across seem to vanish in the wake of consistent male mockery.

Just like the handwriting of popular girls of yesteryear that stylistically represented the time we were in, popular tropes in screenwriting can tell you a lot about society's widely held beliefs in a given era, especially those held by individuals in the writers' room, which in *SBTB*'s case (with the exception of two episodes, according to IMDb) were males. Although the eighties and nineties contained notable progress in successful network shows led by female showrunners, like *The Golden Girls, Murphy Brown,* and *Designing Women,* or the first primetime series developed by a Black female, *Living Single,* the representation in the writers' room didn't seem to infiltrate teen-targeted programming in the same way. Clicking through most of my favorite shows back then, it's wild to think about how the storytellers teaching the masses about our experiences in girlhood were mostly adult men, and it makes so much sense why these shows manipulated us into not taking young females and/or feminists seriously. They probably were people who didn't do that in real life, either.

While I know it's meant to be a lighthearted show about high school, it actually could have had serious implications on how people were taught to tolerate sexism in an educational environment who weren't yet in high school. Rewatching it, it wasn't funny or well crafted; it felt more like a product of male writers venting about their sexist perceptions of second-wave-feminist stereotypes, something I sadly wouldn't even have known how to identify until my twenties and thirties when

I started reading literature from the women I ignored who were actually doing the work in representing feminism. I wish I had spent less time with *Saved by the Bell* and more time with *The Bell Jar* and authors/activists like bell hooks. While my own privileges and obtuse adolescent approach to gender studies are undoubtedly to blame for my lack of pursuit of a more well-rounded understanding of feminism, I stand by that for me personally, these pop-cultural tactics were influential in how I internalized that feminists possessed traits like being un-likeable, difficult, or annoying as young as elementary school. I think it's sad this messaging was distilled to a young audience who couldn't calibrate it with their own wisdom or experience, mostly because this show's time slot targeted kids who weren't old enough to have it, airing on Saturday mornings alongside other networks airing cartoons.

Another reason I decided to rewatch some of my former faves like *SBTB* or *10 Things I Hate About You* was because of a podcast episode I recorded with my friend and former coworker Charlene Corley, who does brilliant work in an area of media research designed to inform audiences, advertisers, and creators of programming about the importance of representation. Not just in terms of being diverse in front of the camera with casting, but also behind the scenes, because the backgrounds and creeds of showrunners, editors, producers, etc., will ultimately in-form how decisions are made and then mediated to the masses. In our conversation, she shared a particular finding from her research that stuck out to me: when an experience on-screen is being represented that a viewer self-identifies with, they are more likely to cite its inaccuracy. However, when an experience or community is being represented that's outside of the viewer's identity, they are more likely to perceive it as being accurate. If

I'm making an argument in this book for how pop culture matters, it's important to clarify how this can be for better or worse in this context. While one of the best ways it can be influential is to help us learn about other people's experiences or better understand our own, one of the worst ways it can influence us is by reinforcing stereotypes or creating harmful biases.

This made me think a lot differently about how media and entertainment informed my understanding of communities I had never been a part of, and now I want to rewatch everything I've ever loved that influenced me and deep-dive into the cast, crew, and creators. With shows that involved storylines that tackled sexuality or race, it's interesting to see if it was at all informed by the lived experiences of people of color or LGBTQ+ individuals. If not, you can see how stereotypes take shape to create a predictable mold instead of real experiences that explore the contours of the human existence. To quote another, far more inimitable bell I mentioned earlier, bell hooks, "Stereotypes abound when there is distance."[7] And while I knew this about who was on the screen, it didn't click for me until recent years how a lack of diversity behind the screen likely played a profound role in a lot of my development of biases along the way.

Now, it makes sense to me why writers would portray the aforementioned feminist characters as people who seemed difficult, frustrated, or annoyed. Their response to misogyny wasn't the problem; either my age or how showrunners chose to contextualize it was. I caveat my age at the time of viewing because when I first watched *10 Things I Hate About You,* I was young, and I completely misread Kat's personality, which was positioned

---

7. Atul Gawande, Black Looks: Race and Representation (New York: Routledge, 2014), 170.

by her teacher as a "heinous bitch." This descriptor being assigned to a person who was standing up for women's rights scared me, but I totally missed the fact that Kat smiled at this descriptor in the movie. She was actually making an important point about it being revelatory for a young woman to uncharacteristically not care about her own likability amidst the teen-movie boom of the late nineties. Even better, *10 Things* has a scene where Kat is called out by a teacher on how her white feminism lacks intersectionality, and I beelined to IMDb to see who wrote this movie that seemed ahead of its time relative to others in my time. Unsurprisingly, it was two women: Karen McCullah and Kirsten Smith, who would go on to write a movie that was less of a moment for me and more of a millennial moon landing, *Legally Blonde*. The underestimated eighties and nineties Valley girls walked so Elle Woods could teach us about ammonium thioglycolate.

We could argue for taking all this at face value, and for lots of media and entertainment, I did. I rarely put thought into the things I watched or read that served as a getaway car for escapism, but now in hindsight, I see how traveling through those experiences left me with cursory impressions along the way of circumstances I didn't know firsthand, and I think it's interesting to take inventory of what I internalized about people unlike me at the time, self-identified "feminists" or otherwise. Even though I question the accuracy of the "bra-burning" feminist stereotype, I'm not even sure it's entirely off base, because I grew up to become a person who is so angry and frustrated with the many issues women and girls are still facing, I feel like burning things near daily. Probably not my bra, because that's what makes it easier for me to run away from the arson, but the point is, I get the rage. Since the 2016 election, I don't know how to exist without being in a state of feeling heated, with my general disposition at a light simmer, usually dialing up to a rolling boil by the time I pass Mario Lopez on channel 00 to get to the news. Even then, I'm further triggered by the name of a network that reminds me of my life-Spano of bad feminism, making me wonder if girls like me had been more vocal and understanding of this plight for equality all along, we wouldn't be sitting here day after day, witnessing a regressive dystopia on C-SPAN. I wish it hadn't taken me until my twenties to understand feminists better; maybe I wouldn't have needed to be saved by *The Bell Jar* if *Saved by the Bell* had contextualized Jessie's disposition more accurately. Who knows what would have happened if from a young age I had viewed her traits as desirable and strong; maybe I would have stood up for myself more or tolerated less of the misogyny that I detail in upcoming chapters that profoundly impacted me.

Representation in storytelling is something I've thought about constantly while in the writing process, and, as I mentioned earlier, is the reason I chose this book's title. Similar to how many writers of my favorite works only wrote what they knew, for better or worse, as much as I can criticize it, I'm writing what I know in this book, which comes along with a great deal of not knowing what I don't know, too. By default, I'm not capturing endless other millennials' experiences while co-opting the generational moniker.

In conclusion, part of why I say all this is because what's popular in history books and the mainstream media hasn't always been written in girls' handwriting (or regular writing or screenwriting). There's a long history of women being written out of the narrative (or of different groups of women being incorrectly written into it from an oppressor's perspective), and what matters going forward is who is doing the writing, who dictates the variety of stories told and the perspectives considered. What's important is that all girls (not just the "popular" ones) keep writing if it interests them, whether working on their handwriting or writing their stories in a way that will allow them to be shared with the world, because they deserve to be heard and better understood.

My argument isn't that there's a way to do this perfectly; no one can represent everyone. Revisiting this show reminded me of the importance of paying attention to representation in entertainment as viewers in what we support (and also as a writer, in what I help move forward) to accurately portray experiences as well as support and inform audiences to be accepting of themselves and others. Ultimately, this makes pop culture both entertaining and productive. We should be the ones representing the details of our existence to the masses; when they're written from the perspective of how someone on the outside responds to us instead of the person who is living it, it often manifests onscreen in the form of reinforcing harmful stereotypes.

And those stereotypes totally aren't true; while I'm a newfound Spano-apologist, I'm not excitedly/nervously melting down while writing every page of this book because I'm overwhelmed, neurotic, and have a caffeine-pill addiction. It's because I'm overwhelmed, neurotic, and have a general caffeine addiction, likely because our daily millennial preamble became "But first, coffee" in the 2010s.

The thought of opportunities and platforms continuing to open up for girls and women of all different backgrounds in office, leadership positions, and, for the purposes of this essay, creating stories and shows, inviting us into worlds we may never otherwise experience, is exactly why I love pop culture and am hopeful for the future of the female zeitgeist. I have a feeling many of you are school-supply-loving milky-pen savants who love to draft fantasies on paper as much as you love to watch them develop on-screen, and for the love, keep writing them into existence.

Because when I think about what's ahead, imagining a world where I can relive a life of pop-cultural education through the eyes of (hopefully) my future children, but with a more broad and balanced set of experiences than I had access to, is what honestly makes me want to shout from my coffee fumes that for the future, I'M SO EXCITED.

And so much less . . . scared.

6

Are We Going Out? Or Out-Out?

There's something magical about a group of women getting ready to hit the town. So magical, most towns will never live up to their own hype. But in college, week after week, night after night, somehow our frail spirits were renewed once our rail spirits were consumed, as my girlfriends and I regularly convened for our favorite midaughts bonding ritual: the pregame.

There are a few core components of this ritual. First, to achieve full harmony, not unlike feng shui, you must balance your Chi. In a spiritual sense, sure, but no 2000s pregame was complete without a Chi straightener balancing precariously on a porcelain sink while playing fast and loose with a security deposit. To spot one in the wild, first you must pinpoint the roommate who perhaps got straight As and shopped at Arden B., and then proceed to complete your full hair routine in their home while benefiting from the finer-things habits of someone else's dome. I spent so many nights panfrying my hair with a flat iron at different women's houses that my noticing how often they were hazardously left on is quite literally the pillar upon which my entire career stands.

There was nothing quite like the Louboutin-esque velvety red-bottomed luxury of a two-inch Chi flat iron that was locked, loaded, and ready to slowly incinerate your hair until it was fashionably lifeless. Part of me blames the cast of *Laguna Beach,* their fried side bangs and spiky ponytails serving as our teenage Alfalfas, normalizing gravity-defying breakage. But another part of me has no one else to blame but myself for my general proximity to high heat in the name of beauty throughout my adolescence. From flat irons to tanning beds, it's like I slowly spit-roasted the youth out of myself to be more appealing, only to emerge in a society that told me they preferred the vegetarian option.

There's something so contagious about the energy contained within the walls before you venture out to face the world. For tonight, we aren't regular girls, we are *party girls.* We aren't just going out, we're going *out-out.* These are different things; we never waste a chandelier earring when there's not a second location, ladies. You see, going out, you might wear jeans and a top. But going out-out, you'd wear . . . jeans and *a different top.* For a casual apartment hang, you might straighten your side bang, but to go out-out to a bar after, you may feel like teasing it straight back into what we called a "pouf," which was basically one-eighth of an updo. It was all about elevating your look with metallic accents, and in college, we departed from sterling silver and started to mix metals in an attempt to Get Male with various vermeils, whether going for the gold braided belt, a silver stack of bangles, or caking bronze makeup on your face. Unlike the Olympics, all three metals worn meant you were qualified for going out-out to a first, second, and/or third place.

Once it was determined we were hitting the town, everybody piled into someone's off-campus housing, turned the iPod on shuffle, and I'd wait until I no longer felt like myself while I imbibed liquor from the lowest of the bottom shelf, though I want to be clear I do not endorse nor celebrate the binge-drinking part of nights like this. It was weirdly part of the collegiate culture and seemed normal, but the alcohol was mostly a downer for me, and, as we'll discuss, a symptom of a larger problem.~*~

~*~ SO Random: Jesus, Take the Banana Peel ~*~

When I first started drinking, I had to learn some lessons the hard-liquor way, and one of the worst was after that night I mentioned in chapter five when did a keg stand in a dress. I was so hungover the next day I lied to my parents for one of the first times, saying I ate a rogue smokehouse turkey sandwich at Panera Bread. I can't believe I would throw a good friend under the bus like that; Panera deserved better. Thankfully, they left to go somewhere for the day, and I rethought my life decisions as I sat on my playroom couch, feeling like my "Grace Is Gone," like the DMB song I'd just downloaded on LimeWire, especially after I threw up on myself after seeing a commercial for the show *Bananas in Pyjamas.* I realized at that moment why I was so sick, and the very sight of dancing bananas made the contents of my stomach want to split. It was because the night before, I had been introduced to a beverage called 99 Bananas, the official drink of people who don't know better and will never do it again. That shit *was* bananas.

When you first start going to parties and people are underage, you don't realize the booze choices aren't normal; your beverage options are a who's who of things stolen from liquor cabinets, and I'm not sure we understood the difference between liquor and liqueur. I'm guessing I thought it was a matter of personal preference based on how rich you wanted to sound, like how some people pronounce Ralph Lauren like they're addressing their friend Lauren or say Lau*ren* and emphasize the last syllable. To this day, I'm not sure which is correct, but I know we were wrong to believe mixed drinks meant you just like, mixed drinks together. Any of them, all of them, not a ratio in sight. Shockingly, as an adult, I rarely come home after a long day and mix myself a lovely peach schnapps–Goldschläger on the rocks at cocktail hour. Though Goldie Schnapps is a darling name for a drink.

In hindsight, I appreciate the pregame ritual that was a round-robin of reassurance of how great we all looked. I love this about women; I live for an enthusiastic salutation with a hug or an air-kiss, followed by the "That's *so* cute!" "Such a fun top!" "Oh my God, where did you get this?" It meant the world to me during a time when I was really struggling with my appearance. For every Luke who wouldn't warm up to me, there were eight sorority sisters who would tell me I looked *so hot*. The affirmation was probably obligatory. But I'm not sure I cared? Support in any form was what I needed at this vulnerable phase; I wasn't in the market for someone being Contempo Casually cruel (in the name of being honest) about my outfit. This is why I actually loved these gatherings more than any other collegiate function; the hopefulness found within the walls of a pregame was electric and promising in ways the bar scene never was. We teetered on the edge of lucidity, as we began to get more intoxicated by anticipation than anything else. Where would we go? Who would we see? What does the night have in store for us in this southwest Virginia mountain town with three whole bars?

Although many nights would feel so dull compared to our outfits, our hype, our hair, or even just dull compared to our patent-leather peep-toe pumps against the streetlights' blinding glare, every time, I genuinely believed maybe this night would be different. It didn't matter if it was before a sorority formal or a Tuesday night in January, we were equal opportunists when it came to hoping for the best night ever. Even though the world would often prove to be harsher than the one we could control indoors, it didn't stop us from creating an immaculate experiential primer every single time. Living in our aimless prologues, simply hoping the night would be one for the books.

The true mascot of a 2000s pregame? One of my favorite millennial

artifacts of all: the "going-out top." I mentioned how we invented cou-
ture previously with our innovative pairing of jeans and a cute top, but
a going-out top was so much more than that. These shirts made it clear
they weren't for staying in; they weren't for the morning or afternoon.
Your outfit can look very rise 'n' grind, but once you incorporate lace,
silk, bedazzling, creative ties, ruching, and/or needless layering, you're
ready to bump 'n' grind. Our battle cry was "YOLO." Our shoes were
Payless BOGO. Our expectations were as high as the tops' price points
were low. And night after night, we'd watch our dignity and hems rip
at the seams from fashions faster than the speed of light.

Why did we buy such cheap going-out tops? Two reasons: 1. This
was the era of the designer jean, and I was determined to not just be
a regular college student; I wanted to be a Citizen of Humanity or a
person who represented All Mankind with 7s. I'm sure Hester Prynne
was rolling over in her fictitious grave watching young women like me
spend $150 for an "A" emblazoned on our ensembles. The way it felt
like a sin to not splurge on "A" pockets is a real reverse Scarlet Letter
we don't talk about enough. The problem was, I'm not sure 7s were
"for all mankind" at this time; they seemed to be made for people who
fell within a very small size range and had large amounts of disposable
income. But on theme with this book, if I felt included, I wasn't asking
questions, and while I didn't have the money, I finally felt the right size.
As a tall kid who always was stuck with inadvertent clamdiggers, the
added length of designer pant legs was a major fashion breakthrough
for me. Until that point, I had to rip out the hems of my jeans, pretending the artful tearing and ombre blue wash was a product of intentional
distressing. The more distressing part was how the added length likely
served as a walking dustpan to bring a parking lot's latest and greatest
into my home. While I did genuinely need longer jeans, it was also very
in style to walk on the extra fabric until the heel wore out, rain or shine.

A core memory for me is looking down at my feet to find a drenched bell-bottom that would make you think I was playing hopscotch in a swamp. In retrospect, it's poetic; I was in college and just getting my feet wet with adulthood. But in reality, it was troubling because it was a gateway to jean cuffing, an era of DIY capris where I exposed my shins and listened to The Shins all the while being expected to forget the many years of inadvertent non-DIY short pants I had suffered through. Though I suppose the silver lining of this high-water phase was the comfort of the twin XL jersey-cotton sheets we claimed were pants and wore around town, dubbed "gauchos." In my opinion, the only garment that can hold a candle to a going-out top in terms of its mid-2000s iconography is the gaucho pant. Gauchos were a time. Gauchos were like buying curtains you didn't measure correctly and then wearing them on your thighs. Even though they have some aesthetic overlap with a culotte, something about a mid-2000s gaucho look is so delightfully, overtly unflattering, it's almost empowering. Not unflattering because of our bodies, but because these cartoon pants seemed to not be made for human women. However, we were so comfortable we made it work. It was the innovative center of a Venn diagram where we saw an opportunity between pajamas and pants that were acceptable to wear outdoors. Gauchos were basically the jersey-cotton fashion Lemon we wore before Lulu, but honestly better, because these cropped wind socks were never made for the male gaze—they were ours. So few things are, and they deserve our celebration. I hope to see a pair in the Smithsonian someday.

Although I had convinced myself that I needed a pair of 7s to be considered a ten, the jeans only covered half the necessary going-out outfit. The problem was, by the time I devoted all my part-time earnings toward a singular pair of tastefully flared boot-cut denim, I had roughly $10 left for a shirt. Enter the cheap going-out top and its omnipresence on clearance racks at Forever 21, Charlotte Russe, Wet Seal, Express, H&M, and the list goes on. Before having ethical consumption on our radars, you could find going-out tops affordably, wear them once or twice, and then they were treated as community property in a friend group. I'm so picky with what I wear now, but back then, I swapped sequins and silhouettes and would wear any sale-rack item I could afford. I'd take a halter, tube, tank, billowing, asymmetric, tunic, bubble, sky, peplum, anything I could get my Lohan-inspired OPI Lincoln Park After Dark–painted paws on to elevate my denim from day to night. This is a real full-circle moment for me as I sit here quite literally writing this in Chicago's Lincoln Park, after dark. I'd feel proud of how far I've come, but I still think I should be forced to repent for the money I spent on a pair of denim a mall salesperson assured me would be "timeless." Pretty sure I never needed to cut open a pair of True Religions and count the rings to know that a bedazzled fleur-de-lis would immediately backdate me to 2006. I blame Fergie.

The second reason we gravitated toward cheap going-out tops? The perils of outfit repeating following an overdocumented evening. This was 2005 to 2009, aka the heyday of the Canon point 'n' shoot paparazzi, and many of us felt a sense of urgency to document commonplace social functions with exhausting detail. As a result, it felt like your top was immortalized by the internet, making it harder to invest in pricier, long-term items without feeling bored of your ensemble. I know, I know. Landfill, party of one. Now, you curate a photo or two for the whole evening, but back then, your friends would mass-upload every goddamn photo like it was a makeshift animated flip-book of the night's least notable details. Social media wasn't the highlight reel it is today; it was more like bad ongoing CCTV footage captioned with inside jokes. No accidental pocket photo, duplicate, or legally questionable photo of a person underage-beer-bonging went undocumented, much to my hungover horror. Though I will say, there are few things more character building than waking up to an email that says, "You've been tagged 63 times in so-and-so's album 'cuZ tHe PaRtY dOnT StArT TiL I WaLk iN,'" then proceed to supersoak your computer with requests to untag yourself.

This lack of curation makes me laugh nowadays, especially because so many people pride themselves on being "unfiltered." As a millennial woman, I'd like to say, I'll see your curated version of unfiltered and raise you the era where *literally no thought whatsoever* went into what we put on the internet. We thought it was temporary, not that it would impede us from being able to run for office someday. I'm so grateful to my sorority for taking down photos of us underage that weren't exactly framers, as badly as I wanted to show my grandkids that one time my team won a flip-cup tournament at Derby Days.

Millennials invented being authentic online; when you really think about it, poor camera quality was the original filter. I appreciated the days when pics didn't have enough pixels available to pick ourselves apart more than we already were. I like that we were forced to be present; we couldn't upload in real time with our flip phones that were separate from our clunky cameras that dangled from our wrists. Even though some had the company of our T-Mobile Sidekicks or felt sharp as hell with a Motorola Razr, I really think this lack of technological advancement took the edge off the added pressure of needing to broadcast how much fun you're having live. Now I often feel like I'm captioning moments I want to share before they're even captured; social media subliminally makes me engineer moments before experiencing them in ways I resent.

However, it still had its downsides. Now, we have a content-centric social-media model instead of a people-centric one; on platforms like TikTok and Instagram, we passively consume strangers' content and ours can be delivered to them, too. If we want to monetize the platform, we're more incentivized to serve the consumer than ourselves. But in its early days, there was no cash to be made or followers to be gained; it mostly existed to tell everyone you know you were living the dream. Our pregames were fun and supportive, but also served as photo shoots for how we'd perform our lives to the rest of the world, wanting to capture our outfits in peak form before we got more disheveled as the night went on.

Sometimes I wonder what college would have been like without Facebook albums, which were added to the interface during my freshman year. It was hard enough to compare yourself to people in person, but with the advent of social media, it became an exaggerated performance, and I bought it; the college version of popular-girl handwriting was copying the style of the unbothered party girl. Her online presence was so persuasive, it was almost like being sucked into a pyramid scheme.~*~ Specifically, when I became interested in Greek life, the way sorority girls posted photos, it was kind of like witnessing an MLM trying to hard sell PNMs by peddling faux best-case scenarios in the form of mobile uploads, convincing you to "join their team" of their totally attainable collegiate party-girl dream.

~*~ SO Random: Online Downline ~*~

Female beauty and body standards have always been like a multilevel marketing scheme, and we are all constantly in the downline of what's popular online whether we like it or not. On social media, a handful of people set the trends, they trickle down, and we slowly but surely join their team, based on being influenced by their edited semiunrealistic routines. We know people only post the best images of themselves online, but exist somewhere in between knowing it's a highlight reel and in vulnerable moments being convinced it's real. Then it becomes an ongoing cycle where we buy similar products and mimic their behavior because that's what gets engagement, even though very few make it to the top. While we've moved on to an era of more transparency in how we communicate and share our stories, unrealistic beauty and body standards are still alive and well in many corners of the internet. If the clothes or cosmetics don't vibe with us, oh well, it worked for them, so they're not the problem, we are. What's the solution? Eat better. Work out. Make more money. Be hotter. Manifest it. That's all that's standing between you and the influencers at the top who are living the dream by performing that they are just like you, so what's your excuse?

By the time the trends make it to the mass market, the upwardly mobile are tired of them; it's time for inventory turnover, and we participate because we're made to feel dated, basic, void of taste, and ashamed for not keeping up. So what are we left with? Piles of consumer products, aka inventory. What do we buy more of? Inventory! For what reason? Our unmet potential! I'm not sure our drawers of old leggings or skinny jeans or stockpile of cosmetics and serums we were influenced to buy (then grew tired of) are all that different from MLM huns being stuck with unsold inventory and sunk costs.

One reason I zeroed in on Facebook albums of party girls was because I was confused about why I wasn't having as much fun as everyone else. The reason I kept going out and then out-out every night was to chase the "best days of my life" I was told I should be having but wasn't experiencing. When I got to a big college with thirty thousand undergraduate students, I was in disbelief at how there were endless seas of young women, each more gorgeous, brilliant, and fun-loving than the next, and who seemed to have unlimited funds for the trends that churned faster than my DIY skills could attend. I didn't realize I got all my confidence in high school from a specific group of people, and without their support and approval, I floundered. I didn't have a skill, a sport, or a grounding source of spoon-fed companionship and belonging, and my grades were average at best.

So it seemed like partying and getting into Greek life was the leading option for finding identity, and while I made new friends, and I had so many fun moments, I experienced a lot more rejection and isolation than I did back home, and it wore on my mental health and body image in a big way. These are two common issues to deal with, but there was something unique about the 2000s that exacerbated circumstances involving self-esteem; it was an era of harsh beauty and body standards, minimal mental-health conversations, and maximum online performance we were very new to being on the receiving end of. Facebook albums were like the five-star notebook that once showcased PGH, and as my confidence depleted, I fixated on how I could mimic the style of everyone else who seemed to be doing so great. But the standards expanded to what was popular in other towns, other states, and other social classes, and even became more integrated with pop-culture starlets when tabloid sites and the Perez Hilton–types arrived on the internet. The crazy thing is, this is normal now—we're able to see what everyone's doing everywhere, faced with endless sources of comparison, but up until that point, we had seen the other side, where you couldn't see anyone's greener grass online.

Through Facebook albums, I saw every date party I wasn't invited to, every sorority I didn't join, every girl the guy I liked chose, and this expanded to seeing bodies and beauty and trends of people in a much larger pool than ever before, having access to people's high-school exes and friends at other schools. I have a lot of empathy for this being the default world for young people now; when it was new to me, I was barely getting by, and feeling like I needed to absorb, conform, and then perform relative to the standards I was seeing online was a shock to the system.

When I joined a sorority halfway through freshman year, I was so relieved to have made new friends and get invited to new places, but it can take me a while to feel comfortable around people, and I was terrified at first. They were so strict about us being classy and upholding their image, and *Bananas in Pyjamas* over here hadn't figured out yet that I can't drink hard liquor. I spent the first couple years on edge about getting the boot, hangxiety-spiraling after a long night about everything I said or did, cringing with every mobile upload as I wore my bidday shirt, which said on the back BECAUSE CLASS ISN'T JUST SOMETHING YOU ATTEND, giving me more anxiety that a sister would notice I wasn't classy nor attending class. Academic probation was no joke; they'd tell the whole chapter at the beginning of the Sunday meeting whose grades were slipping. Did they *really* need to announce how Sister Vanessica was on academic probation to everybody every single week in order to motivate her? Public shaming is a tried-and-true sorority tactic that is so cruel to people having trouble with grades, finances, or health issues. It feels wrong to weaponize "sisterhood" as an excuse to call out people who are struggling, and the reason I didn't pay all those fines for events I skipped was because I wasn't doing fine, but I'm not sure the officers ever thought to ask.~*~

When I'd try sorority-MLM-hun on for size, I'd appear superconfident and social, posting photos of us hitting the town like it was going out-out of style online, doling out motivational self-help captions like my inventory of good feelings wasn't falling apart and defective. But when I could curate the experience on my end, the new evangelizing I was doing, instead of Christ giving me strength, was my Philippians 4:13: "You're only as strong as the cocktails you drink, the tables you dance on, and the friends you keep." "Love my girls!" was as ubiquitous a sign-off as an "amen," because without holding on to each other for support and social relevance, I'm not sure we had a prayer.

I loved being in a big sorority and loved my friends; many are some of my closest friends to this day. But at the time, I incessantly compared myself to them, carefully surveying their eating and workout habits, asking questions about how they landed a boyfriend over condescending meals of cottage cheese. Online, instead of sharing how I built a "six-figure business in no time!" I shared pictures of my six friends whose figures I knew were smaller than mine. I only posted the ones of myself tucked in the center wearing a loose top, and dragged the rest to the trash on my laptop. I cared so much about how I looked relative to them that to post photos with hotter friends felt almost brave, Kappa Delta's Bruce Wayne, disguising my body in a batwing top.

When I think about the parties we posted photos of after going out-out, the smiles and hand-on-hip bent elbows don't come to mind. I feel a sticky floor, smell stale beer and rejection, and hear a frat guy yelling at me for the elbow rule in beer pong as I was elbows deep in jungle juice trying to fill the emptiness of pursuing "hot" and "fun" as my defining character traits. In between games of F the Dealer and Kings, Never Had I Ever shared the truth that I was slipping into a depressive place and hoping I could drink myself into an unbothered state where I wasn't feeling guilty about what I ate, where I didn't feel crazy for thinking so much of this wasn't fun, where I didn't feel as invisible as the frat boys made me feel. At the time, it was common to claim your life was "in shambles," but I never really knew if that was for comedic effect to express how hard you partied the night before, or if I could find somebody to meaningfully relate to about my crumbling self-esteem. Nothing messed with my head more than people telling me that college was the time of my life, and now I wonder if for most people it was, or like a boss babe selling a lofty goal that only represents the experience of a few, the party-girl "time of my life" was my pink Cadillac just out of reach. I convinced myself if I drank more, ate less, and could make myself better looking, I'd drive off into the sunset.

To this day, I struggle to reconcile how you can have fun times in your life but not at all be having the time of your life. But without the friends I made in my sorority during my junior and senior year, I genuinely don't know where I'd be or if I would've even stayed at school. I once trivialized our pregames and late nights and delirious hungover mornings as careless collegiate behavior, but those were the moments of connection that actually mattered. What didn't matter was how narrowly I focused my attention on my appearance, my weight, my outfits, and wishing I could look or be like someone else. It's an incredible privilege to receive a college education, and I'm so mad at myself when I think about the opportunity cost of how that brainpower could have been used. I could die thinking of how easily I'd skip class and prepare to go to the bar, but if a boy chose another girl over me, I'd study everything about her with a level of cerebral dedication you'd think I was studying to take the bar exam.

My self-esteem issues in college were partially self-inflicted and partially a function of the opinions of those around me, but compounded with how the nineties and 2000s were disproportionately hostile toward women, it's no wonder a lot of the misogyny became normalized in my mind, and I'm sure many other millennials' as well. Of course, women across generations have this in common; the unfair societal surveillance of females and the reduction of their value to their appearance, effortlessness, and body shape is nothing new. But we were shaped by a particularly harsh pop-cultural climate that set the temperature everywhere I went from church to school, and in the mid-2000s, it all came to a head even though I convinced myself I was overreacting and it was all in my head.

It's hard to maintain a sense of self-worth when you get mixed messages about what makes you valuable as a young woman from the outside world. At church, my value was allegedly in my virginity and purity, but with boys my age, it was hotness and how far I was willing to go, and then in the tabloid media, women were only talked about if they were losing weight, got a boyfriend, were feuding with a friend, or stumbling bleary-eyed out of Les Deux. Pop stars like Britney Spears were exploited for their sexuality, and while their musical end product was targeted to young girls, their "not-that-innocence" was paraded in front of straight males, popularizing whatever narrow beauty standard met their gaze. Watching the media debate these young women was incredibly confusing; you had to pretend to be wholesome, you didn't want to be called a "slut," you had to suggest you were open to sexual exploration but not too much. You had to dress in a way men found appealing, existing only for their pleasure, while being denied a right to your own if you pursued it too openly. Whether you were withholding something like Jessica Simpson or too Dirrty to clean your act up like Christina, your sexuality was sold and publicly surveyed regardless of sentiment, and the message was clear: we were to be sexualized without our consent no matter what.

Even if a crime was committed against me, the media taught me I should be the one feeling guilty. If a woman was sexually assaulted, it was followed by "What was she wearing? How drunk was she?" From what I had observed, drinking too much alcohol was a means to justify a man's behavior. But for a woman, it seemed like it was a means to justify what had been done to her. I never heard power or authority discussed in the context of how it can be abused to coerce and harass women; it was weaponized as something women chased for personal gain. Monica Lewinsky wasn't the victim of a predatory abuse of power by a figure of authority, she was a punch line, a temptress. If a celebrity had a sex tape or nude photos leaked, they weren't victims of a sex crime, they were asking for it or being attention-seeking.

When I was college-aged, tabloids tortured young women like Lindsay Lohan, Mischa Barton, and Mary-Kate and Ashley Olsen; their reporting fueled and then fed consumer demand for hypersexual material that could be turned around to shame them, like up-skirt photos that were meticulously engineered for their bottom line, and no one even cared if it crossed the line of privacy or human decency. To respond to the immense pressure and paparazzi meant you'd "snapped" or were "crazy." To show emotion in public meant you were on the verge of a "nervous breakdown." There was no empathy or support for navigating mental-health crises, addiction, or eating disorders; someone seeking help and getting caught en route was the catch of the day, and medical bait was fair game, whether at Cedars-Sinai or Passages Malibu. When young "starlets" lost an extreme amount of weight, the tabloids splashed it everywhere as if they looked great, and I hate admitting this but my dreams for validation went from "You look hot!" to quickly normalizing a look that wasn't healthy, it was gaunt.

My friend Nora McInerny brilliantly pointed out in her book *Bad Vibes Only* that "the tabloids declared Lindsay Lohan and Paris Hilton to be 'scary skinny!' but still presented them as winners of every Who Wore It Best?" This perfectly embodies the catch-22 of what we were Limited To in the 2000s; the same behaviors were both celebrated and criticized. This is just one example of the downsides of loving pop culture; for all the ways I've loved to be entertained, it also is responsible for fueling rampant misogyny and perpetuating dangerous beauty and body standards, while encouraging shame and self-blame for our endlessly trying to meet them, regardless of never choosing them in the first place.

The truth is, most of us weren't okay. I never had an eating disorder, but I'd be lying if I said the patterns weren't still problematic and disordered in many ways; just because it never got clinically bad, it doesn't mean it was good. I hesitate to center my experience in talking about diet culture because my problems were mostly due to negative social interactions and body dysmorphia, and there's a major difference between being influenced by versus being discriminated against due to these body standards. I think my self-image became distorted from picking up on the differences in how I was treated when my weight would fluctuate, from the guy I hooked up with who poked my stomach rolls and asked what happened to my abs to overthinking when girls would or would not say, "You look great." It didn't matter if weight gain or loss had a cause that was physical, mental, or medication-related; nobody cared. The default assumption was that your size was a function of your effort alone, and thinness was rewarded; otherwise you'd be reassured with a "You'll get there."

I think part of the problem was my vague proximity to the conventional standards of beauty at the time, and noticing I *could* get the feedback I'd always dreamed of, but only when I lost weight, barely ate, dressed a certain way, had fresh highlights, was tan, talked less, and partied more, aka things at odds with my verbose, turtleneck-loving Irish core. When I wasn't meeting these allegedly attainable standards, I'd spiral into self-loathing, because it meant I was lazy, not trying hard enough, or I had "let myself go." What was actually happening was my body had been adjusting to a different life phase; it makes sense to gain weight when you stop playing sports that involve two-a-days, your meal options are buffets, and you convince yourself you're hydrating via the Gatorade you mixed with Aristocrat Vodka at a pregame.

I feel sad when people talk about loving college, because learning to hate myself is one of the things I remember most about it. The worst part is, it felt normal. While I don't want to project this onto everyone, from what I observed, it was pretty common to openly talk shit about your body in the mid-2000s. It wasn't a red flag as much as it was idle chatter while salting our Lean Cuisines just enough to cut the aftertaste of pure sorrow. I think back on being in dining halls, dabbing grease off pizza with paper towels and doing mental math about Weight Watchers points and then mental gymnastics to justify what went in our mouth, as if opting for a cream-based dressing was reason enough to announce and justify our choices aloud to the group. Just a bunch of MLM huns, ordering things wrapped in lettuce, no bun, soliciting a lifestyle where dressing that wasn't on the side was side-eyed as a choice that would inevitably prevent me from dressing in cute clothes.

In my opinion, we never stood a chance; we were a generation who could recite "a shake for breakfast, a shake for lunch, and a sensible dinner!" from memory like a nursery rhyme, waking up to SlimFast commercials with KLG airing in the morning during breaks of *Live with Regis and Kathie Lee.* In the media I grew up with, I don't remember anyone really talking about health; it was just about watching what you eat and following the misguided food-pyramid scheme. We were taught to be afraid of anything that wasn't nonfat and to replace desserts with packaged Frankenfoods masquerading as sweet treats. Speak of the devil's-food cookies, I'm still mad about when we were hard-sold those pillowy soft SnackWell's. The non-fat cookies were marketed as a "healthier option," so it seemed like we could eat however many we wanted, but they had close to the same number of calories as a regular cookie. The cookies, the frozen meals, the shakes—none of it was about health or wellness, it was about selling flat tummies and the elusive "bikini body" that implied if you weren't a certain size, you shouldn't be wearing one.

I genuinely can't believe how much breath we wasted talking about what we ate, and I resent how much headspace I still devote to it all the time. And I resent how much book real estate I'm taking up talking about it now. While I may have slightly evolved, part of me will always be SnackUnwell from this time where I spent 360 days a year making myself suffer for the five days of summer when I might be in a two-piece in a group setting, hoping this would be the year I'd agree to be in a bathing-suit photo or would enjoy getting back in the game of playing Kadima without assuming people were seeing every one of my bad choices and skipped workouts with every forehand.

Thinking of the obliviousness of my girlhood makes me want to cry; to the shark-teeth and anklet-wearing version of me on a beach, boogie-boarding in the waves, a bathing suit was simply a practical water-friendly garment that allowed me to swim, and nothing more. It's hard to pinpoint exactly when the tide changed, but one day you show up to the beach and won't get up from your seat; you once were too busy looking out into the world but now all you can think about is who is looking at you. I wonder which day I threw the shark tooth away and redefined that looking sharp meant having clavicles like Cutcos. The knife cuts both ways in the pink-Cadillac campaign; even though pursuing these standards butchered our self-esteem, we sold them, too, suffering from and then perpetuating that to live the dream meant to be thin.

What others ate felt like a commentary on what I ate, and we'd talk badly about ourselves and the other would listen, offering validation in the form of centering the importance of our outward appearances. "No, girl, you're so hot! You're so thin! You look amazing!" was offered up for the taking, and while it didn't sustain us, in the moment it's what we thought was right. How could it not feel right when you're validated by plans for weight loss or exercise or dieting at every turn, by girls and boys alike? This is how commodified girl power works, where you only deserve to be empowered if you operate within a narrow set of standards you endlessly pursue, and you're made to feel noble in your efforts to be forever under construction. We were programmed to believe it was what's on the outside that matters, and it's no wonder our worlds revolved around others' words to fuel our self-worth. I guess this is the flip side of always going out in more ways than one; I felt so desperate for out-outside validation, it slowly made me feel more and more vacant within.

What got us down wasn't just ourselves, it was what we were held to, and being reassured against those standards felt helpful at the time. If I'm being honest, it still can be helpful now, and this is where my feminism breaks down. I know this isn't the right thing to say, but sometimes I hate when people say you should *only* compliment women on being smart or being talented, and dodge their appearance altogether. It's condescending to say I don't know that I'm smart or talented; I eventually learned I was in other ways the school system didn't always validate, and I had confidence in other areas that I could lead with, but the 2000s media-and-magazine machine fed the trickle-down misogyny that made us feel like our looks were what we should lead with to add value. But unlike grades you can get or boxes you can check, beauty is different in how standards are arbitrary and shape-shift. And I can only speak for myself, but as a victim of this time, I feel like it's oppressive to expect I should know how to reprogram my mind and not care about my appearance. I struggle with my own piecemeal brand of feminism; the kind where when we talk about the male gaze, I could rage all day, and when I got married I didn't change my last name, because if the insecure girl on these pages ever did something with her life, I wanted her name on it. But I'm also a human who is healing and wants to be told I'm, like, really pretty, because when it comes to why I don't always believe that I am, I don't think I'm the only one to blame.

But I am to blame for not noticing how chasing these narrow standards would make another person feel if their skin color, body type, abilities, socioeconomic situation, or sexuality excluded them from whatever mold I was perpetuating because it felt within reach to me. I was vulnerable, but I didn't do my part to understand that people were affected by this to different degrees. If you felt othered by popular-adjacent girls or seal girls or sorority girls like me, who promoted things like stick-straight, bleached-blond Sun In hair; an obsession with thinness; and a commitment to prioritizing and perpetuating the moving target of male-focused beauty standards as the norm, I'm genuinely sorry for how I participated and wasn't paying attention. I was so caught up in trying to survive, I didn't even understand that my version of "survival" represented issues that were remarkably cushy, and I could die thinking of spending all my time looking into mirrors instead of helping the people who probably needed to feel seen the most. Like the girl power I was first introduced to in Limited Too, it took me far too long to realize that a lot of the pleasant feminist ideals I bought into were only empowering me to consume, and it took me way too long to understand that the hollow and surface-level ways I was taught to empower women only prioritized women whose experiences were nearly identical to mine.

I've been using an MLM as a loose metaphor for how it felt being in this life phase because I didn't question the beauty standards' attainability or misrepresentation. I blamed myself and doubled down and worked harder to be someone I wasn't, hustling and literally grinding enough in frat basements to have the glamourous life of male attention I aspired to. I tried to get drunk, lower my standards for boys, pretend I was a wilder version of myself, and partied and socialized enough to be distracted and get out-out of my head. But like salvation or promises of success or "hot and fun" people on Facebook vaguely living the dream, you can't prove any of it isn't reality, so you can forever peddle the formula. So in a fake-and-bake-it-till-you-make-it world I chased it, and in the photos I never smiled bigger, looked tanner, and acted more content, hoping if I buried that I was unhappy and unhealthy, it would go away.

Point being, I see myself as both a perpetrator and a victim of the things that motivated me at the time, like diet culture, narrow beauty standards, and peddling the party-girl dream to make everyone want to join my proverbial team. I try to see it both ways, because when we criticize social media, we're quick to blame the "highlight reel" or the women showing their bodies or their fitness routines or what they eat in a day. Just like we're quick to blame the women who peddle wet leggings with holes in them or predatory essential oils who were told it was the secret to changing their lives. But we're pointing to symptoms, not at all the root causes. Vulnerable people fall for systems that keep them oppressed, and they may sell the pink Cadillac, but they were never the ones behind the wheel.

We've thankfully come a long way in the health-related vocabulary we use, the way we talk about food, and the types of beauty and bodies we platform, but to say I'm cured from this time for the sake of feigning personal evolution would be a lie. And it would undermine how pervasive diet culture was for many millennials, because these beliefs weren't necessarily a condition of a temporary environment; they were a product of yearslong conditioning. Just when I think I've moved on, I often find myself regressing the deeper I get into my thirties, especially as my body continues to change with age and fertility treatments affect my body in ways I can't control. The one thing I'd still love to lose is the weight of the shame that makes me believe that allowing myself to change or to show signs of my age means that I must be failing.

Some of these chapters represent life phases I've moved on from, but others represent things I still have to work on every day, and that's okay too. I wish I came with fewer reflections and more solutions, but the point is that I'm trying to hold space for the ways I didn't know better, to criticize the ways I was set up, to take accountability for when I should've done better, and, all the while, to allow myself to acknowledge the ways in which it was fun. It's confusing how I see this time period as a source of personal remorse and also a magical time of generational lore; I'll add it to the list of my many millennial contradictions.

Even though I had deeper things going on that I needed to work through, the energy and effort we spent building each other up, however shallow or sincere it was, served its purpose for the time. It was almost like at the pregames we'd reinflate our depleted self-esteem in ways that felt light and breezy at dusk but failed to carry weight at midnight. That quintessential party-girl enthusiasm we felt early on in the night would word-vomit (and sometimes actually vomit) itself hours later and present as feelings of inadequacy and harsh self-surveillance; I think deep down we knew we were meant for more and settling for the lowest common denominator of collegiate fun. It was a safe space where we could unbutton our pants and listen to "Buttons" while we danced, navigating the reality of pants meant for standing, while we waited for music and drinks to slowly morph us into our party-girl personas, however performative they were.

Eventually, you find out the flip side of being seen, and for all the ways it's good and fun, you realize existing to be looked at isn't fulfilling either, nor is collecting compliments and heavy pets and late-night texts to prove you are enough. I was delightfully distracted in ways I can honor and laugh about now, but the process was thankless and repetitive, having surface-level fun once we came undone, then having to come back to our friends to replenish self-esteem after making questionable choices. Regardless, the connections we made were real, and the safe spaces we created were important. We knew what we were to each other meant more than canvases that reduced our friendships to "living for the nights we'll never remember with the friends we'll never forget," but we hung them anyway. I guess this essay is a testament to that quote perhaps being the one thing that was true. I don't remember the places we went out to, I don't remember the parties, but I never forgot the pregames because that was the time we were focused on each other. Back in the daybed, friendship got you through the night, but in college, it got me through the nightmare of feeling like I was the reason for missing out on the best days of my life, unknowingly experiencing them in the moments while we were waiting to go somewhere else.

I feel so fondly about the art of the all-female pregame because those are the only times I remember feeling brought back to life, thanks to my sorority sisters who didn't give up on me somehow. As I write this, I'm on my way home from Las Vegas, where I went with my college girlfriends Hannah, Jasmine, and Claire to celebrate Hannah's and my thirty-fifth birthdays. It's funny how old friends remind you of who you are, even though you don't identify at all with who you were back then. Once we went out-out into the world and scattered, it was easy to lose track of one another, and everyone has a drastically different experience based on where they go, and I hope we always make it a priority to come back together afterward like the old days; to remain friends is to metaphorically find our way back home after a long night. Even though I can look at this through a critical lens and have mixed feelings, we still made it out the other side. None of the things that made us feel bad about ourselves stood the test of time, but we did.

It was a full-circle moment when we got to Vegas, ready to hit the town. Finally, we had the cash to spend on the top shelf and the confidence we wanted back then that didn't make us feel like we weren't as cool as everybody else. Despite being set up for the best-case scenario to go out-out, we laughed about how we actually flew there mostly for reasons that involve staying in bed. Forget the crowds and outside stimulation, we just wanted to lie awake and giggle about our memories. To celebrate meant to be together; to do something out of the ordinary meant to stay in-in.

Going out-out, we always hoped the night would be one for the books, but we were too quick to write off our girlish pregame paradise, as if it only served as the prequel to social functions involving men. But in my book, let the record show that I think we had it backward. The moments we supported each other when we were barely getting by are the memories I cherish more than the parties that came and went. They may have wanted us to believe we were just the opener, but all this time, maybe we were the main event.

~*~ SO Random: Sorority Cult-ure ~*~

Speaking of groupthink behaviors in MLMs, I don't think it's acknowledged enough that sororities have a cultlike element to them where they love-bomb you with gifts and attention, entrust you with secrecy of ritual, and make promises of eternal sisterly support as long as they receive your undying loyalty and ongoing purchasing of $12 philanthropy T-shirts in return. If you cooperate, your experience is very "it's not four years, it's forever," but God forbid your grades slip, you can't afford dues, or you're too busy with academics to attend some pancake breakfast or slip 'n' slide for the children. In which case, you're dead to them. I loved being in a sorority and had a mostly pleasant experience, but it was disproportionately demanding for an at-will club that I'm paying them to be in, and weird they can demand more free labor as a debt for accepting me. Part of my body-image issues came from seeing spreadsheets of T-shirt orders full of "XS" and "S" letters, almost as if it was a qualification for wearing our letters, but there I was: a brave Gildan medium, an American Apparel large, both actually still too small, and to quote my little Claire, it left us feeling like we're too big, endlessly tugging at the seams of our Hulked-out arms.

Needless to say, this cultish mindset made me skeptical in my postreligious era, so I became my sorority's formal chaplain so I could lead prayer requests (again, I love to get the scoop) and infiltrate the chapter with vaguely secular messages about loving yourself instead of fearing God's wrath. But I shake my head at this now, because there I was bowing my head thinking I was doing something of service, but the weird part is having Christian rituals baked into a social organization where not everyone is Christian. I don't even think anyone mentioned it had religious origins during recruitment, and it was entirely irrelevant to how we operated other than rituals and formalities.

Sororities being obsessed with ritual is kind of like people who are obsessed with the Founding Fathers, conflating elements of yesteryear's restricted worldview for wisdom. Some things can and should modernize as the world changes, and Greek life should have evolved by now in many ways. It's a bizarre microcosm of systematic exclusivity that works really hard to make it seem like everyone is included, despite being fundamentally at odds with principles of inclusivity. I think we're all kidding ourselves if we don't admit that the process of "mutual selection" may work to find birds of a feather, but by design, it discourages individuality and diversity, lauding sameness as organizational distinction.

While I met many of my best friends to this day in my sorority, and most of the women I came across were genuinely warm and well-meaning up front, there was also a weird understanding that as a collective, the sorority didn't have your back. I watched people get cut out of the inner circle in an icy manner without the context provided to the rest of the chapter, and some days I felt genuinely supported, others I waited to be the next on the chopping block. The thing is, the women I know from my sorority are all individually kind, empathetic humans who wouldn't behave this way unless we felt like we had to uphold arbitrary rules for social relevance, and this groupthink is just one reason why Greek life can be so toxic.

I would now be very loud in the circumstances where I felt they were insisting we overhaul our instincts in a manner that favored maintaining an image over kindness. But we all knew we'd be kicked to the curb in an instant if we did something to make the group look bad. We cheered to raising our glasses and raising our standards, but then would most likely dance on a raised surface instead, therefore getting sent to Standards, and wonder why the hell this was a social organization that penalized us for socializing. Our loyalty to them had to be unwavering, but their loyalty to us was more fragile than the emotions of the sister chosen to give a testimony on Pref Night. Even though we were allegedly part of a sisterhood, it felt weirdly every-woman-for-herself, and this still confuses me. I'm convinced that's why we subliminally did so many arm-linking exercises. If you made the grave sorority-girl mistake of locking your knees in a standing ritual, that was the only time I genuinely felt like if I fell, you're going down with me.

7

Serotonin, Plain and Tall

While I shared Teen Talk Barbie's interests, I didn't exactly share her breezy disposition; I've had an obscure undercurrent of melancholia for as long as I can remember, which I've been told served as a surprising contrast to my interests. I used to sit on my back deck when it was raining because I felt more at ease in overcast weather and loved to feel the rain on my skin, which I suppose was a foreshadowing of my devotion to *The Hills* when Natasha Bedingfield demanded I do the same. I remember ditching my friends on the playground while they were screaming and swinging and playing Red Rover and feeling like it was a "bit much" for me and running home so I could read my parents a poem I had written about the moon.

I even have a distinct memory of walking up the hill to school in second grade and seeing a mom dropping off her kid at school holding the hand of a cute toddler, and wanting to cry because I felt bad for my mom that she no longer had a toddler, and I felt sad thinking about her being sad that I was growing up too fast. I don't know why I need to see something in passing and have those intense thoughts when I could just let it pass through me, but that never felt like an option. My dad didn't even work in the stock market, but I remember seeing him express his dissatisfaction upon seeing the Dow in red on TV, and I correlated it with his workday being green or red, good or bad. So I would turn on a news channel with the Dow Jones index after school, calling it "Dad's mood meter" so I'd get a vibe check before he got home from work. This is another reason I'm not a woman in STEM; correlation is not causation, and this was entirely irrelevant to his work. But I wonder if my sensitivity led to me wanting to be prepared in case I needed to balance the energy in the room, which is something I still try and do. What if someone had a bad day, and I needed to come prepared with a poem about the moon?

My emotional side would show up in my entertainment choices, and I'd have to learn my limits for consuming tragedy and sorrow. Forget the two types of people in the world that entertain and observe. As far as I'm concerned, there are two types of people in the world regarding sensitivity: those who watched the second *Titanic* VHS from the box set during a rewatch, and those who never touched it following their first viewing. In life and in *Titanic,* I realized that was just the tip of the iceberg in navigating the waters of adolescent hypersensitivity. As previously mentioned, I'd masochistically read *Meet Kirsten* repeatedly and proceed to weep when her BFF Marta died of cholera on that low-budg riverboat (RIP, girl). And as much as I loved AG dolls for the consumerism in the catalog, I feel like back in the day, I had a thing for the trying times of nineteenth-century heroines in general. I'd take my talents to books of the *Dear America* series, which were basically a round-robin of tragedy and waterborne illnesses; and one of my other favorite 1800s girlies was *Sarah, Plain and Tall.*

Upon revisiting, the book's summary is a cornucopia of silly girlish fun; the core themes are "loneliness, abandonment, and coping with change." Another trinity to add to my gospel besides boats, music, and snoozin'. It was about a widowed farmer who put out a newspaper ad for a mail-order bride, and between that and the piña-colada song, I love a plotline that centers on a romance-related newspaper ad. The mail-order bride, Sarah, describes herself as "plain and tall" in her letters to her future spouse to manage his expectations about her appearance. And while she is plain and tall, she is so much more. Sarah is caring, artistic, kind, and thoughtful. And if my memory serves me, like many of the female protagonists I revered (then realized I maybe shouldn't), she primarily serves to bring the male character back to life, à la the "manic pixie dream girl," but I didn't care. When I first saw the middle-parted woman with similarly colored mousy roots on the front cover, I wondered if it was me in some parallel reality. Despite my dense inner world, I felt quite dull on the outside, punching up my vibe with Sun In and trendy clothes and tanning beds throughout late high school and college. I always thought of Sarah when describing myself in childhood, plain and tall being my defining character traits, and even when I got older and went out of my way to veer from plain, it's still how I felt. She was a reminder that there's more than meets the eye, and it was comforting to feel represented by a leading lady leading with her average vibes.

I don't mean to make myself sound more interesting than I was on the inside, either; it's hard to explain that I was deep but also remarkably shallow—my artist's manifesto would be more like I was painting *A Portrait of the Artist as a Young Fangirl*. While the James Joyce novel explores how an artist experiences their surroundings in a way that their commitment to their truth can yield social alienation, the story I'd write would be about a complex girl who was creative and intense and absorbing her surroundings in great detail but willing to drop it at a moment's notice in the name of social acceptance via hitchhiking bandwagons. Despite my early interest in the category of suffering 1800s chick lit, my ability to read sophisticated literature stopped at YA novels, but for some reason I did read *A Portrait of the Artist as a Young Man*. I was bored senseless by almost every classic novel we were forced to read in school, trying to pretend I'd read the book, probably thinking

I was slick by saying things like, "My favorite part of the novel was how mad those grapes seemed. *So* full of wrath!" But until I read that book, which was written from the POV of a hard-to-follow interior monologue, I hadn't experienced another brain that felt as chaotic as mine and wouldn't again until I met Lorelai Gilmore, which is way too big a compliment to myself. If I'm honest, my disjointed career path and interest in yummy bartenders are screaming that I'm more of a Kirk.

Joyce pioneered stream of consciousness as a narrative technique, and while I was plain and tall on the surface, on paper in my journals, I exhibited somewhat of a mainstream of consciousness of deep thoughts about my incredibly shallow experiences. Reading them now, I can't tell if they are chaotic and intense because of early signs of my mental-health issues or if I was worried they would get published if I died. Like a thoughtful posthumous queen, I wanted to provide something of substance. Per PGH, I never knew how to self-identify because most female pop-cultural figures I looked up to were pretty easy to figure out from a series of tropey traits. Sensitivity was painted as weak, and existing in my multitudes made me feel like myself, but I thought it was a sign of indecisiveness that meant I lacked a sense of self.

Sometimes my being so sentimental and emotional would make adults call me an "old soul," but I felt like it didn't apply to me because I don't like old movies or classical music; I fell asleep during our field trip to the symphony because I needed lyrics to be interested. However, one exception made me feel sophisticated: I played a lot of "Heart & Soul," the official anthem of suburban millennial girls who skipped too many piano lessons. In case you aren't familiar: more elevated than "Chopsticks," though not quite requiring the technical rigor of an "On Top of Spaghetti," "Heart & Soul" is a stunning key-pecking number from the 1930s that can be performed solo or as a duet. I find that most people do not know that, nor do they know the lyrics, yet somehow the kids I knew born in the eighties fancied themselves concert pianists when they saw eighty-eight keys in the wild. Legend has it that every time "Heart & Soul" plays, not unlike a bell ring, a person with the middle name Marie, Elizabeth, Lynn, or Nicole gets their wings.

As I previously detailed, I had a great childhood, supportive family, positive environment at home, and close friends. Since I had all the fixings of a happy life, I always felt like something was wrong with me for how intensely I'd react to things. My sensitivities and depressive tendencies made me vulnerable to other things in my environment, regardless of how fleeting or allegedly insignificant they were, and I felt pathetic for internalizing them the way I did. One reason I've spent so much airtime revisiting toxic elements of the zeitgeist, my social interactions, or the pop-cultural backdrop over the years is because of my desire to understand how much of a product of our environments we can become, even if we're set up to not succumb to their influence. I guess I'm telling you this because I still feel a little weird that I struggled with mental health so much; it didn't and still doesn't feel like my problems were ever big enough to justify it. But I also share this to contextualize something I've learned that I have to remind myself of often: mental health doesn't discriminate, and even though I knew I had very few reasons to feel sad, it didn't make me feel any less sad at certain points in my life.

While I always knew I tended to feel blue, it was more like a tint or hue, rather than a consuming saturation of sorrow, until college. But there was a part of me that didn't feel allowed to feel blue, and as I got older, this disposition is something I started to hate about myself; it represented ungratefulness. I am incredibly grateful for a pleasant childhood that gave me the space to house these big feelings in the good times, but I don't necessarily romanticize the role my sensitive nature and mental health have played in how I retained bad feelings in the dark times. It's hard to explain that you've had a mostly happy life and are surrounded by things that make you happy, while also acknowledging that you don't necessarily self-identify as a person with an overly happy disposition. I'm cringing as I type that; it still sounds like a choice, but it's always felt beyond my control. The best way I can explain it is that it's incredibly easy for me to hold on to good memories, but incredibly challenging for me to hold on to good feelings. They pass right through me, and misery loves the company of my brain. Maybe that's why I hold on to the good memories so tightly, as my reflection upon them gives me the good feelings I couldn't always manufacture in real time.

I don't know if other millennials feel this way, but I didn't know anything about mental health until the 2010s, when I started to hear people talk about it more. I thought the contents of our minds were a cause-effect formula dictated by our surroundings, like the Dow Jones, or our experiences alone, or represented a punishment-reward system from God. So when I would be in a dark space, instead of getting help, I just felt guilty, knowing my life wasn't that hard and assuming if I felt bad, it was my choice, or I deserved it. When I read my journals from college, all I talk about is how I should be having fun, I shouldn't feel sad, and the only conclusion I could draw is that I must be shallow and ungrateful for what I have. This was a theme for years, being mad at myself for feeling down and like I should be able to "snap out of it," think positively, or express gratitude to make it go away.

The way I saw mental health portrayed in pop culture and media was a stream of stigmas and extremes, from *Girl, Interrupted* to NSYNC's "I Drive Myself Crazy" video to the headlines I mentioned earlier about women expressing human emotion on camera and being labeled as having a "mental break" or "nervous breakdown." Colloquially, somewhere in between people being depicted as stored in a "basket case" or "loony bin," those struggling with mental health or displaying strong emotional responses existed on a spectrum of stereotypes, making me assume if I wasn't on the level of *Fatal Attraction* or *American Psycho* or *A Beautiful Mind,* I was probably fine. I mostly saw examples of disturbed, often violent characters with an underlying message that they weren't to be trusted or treated with dignity.

Nowhere did I see examples of people who were just kind of blue, who reacted disproportionately strongly to heartbreak and killed time between steamy reads about waterborne illnesses. Or even an example that taught you there are degrees of butterflies fluttering when we're nervous versus when it's potentially an anxiety disorder. You really should be taught the difference between good nerves and feelings of impending doom, between heart attacks and panic attacks, stomach aches and physical manifestations of anxiety, and to take note when your days being filled with gloom could be clinical and out of your control. Similarly, why it might be helpful to lead with empathy and not take it so personally when coming across people who are in a bad mood.

Except for a few eras, for the most part, I've been so used to a semi-gloomy disposition it never felt that serious. I remember feeling so frustrated that during special occasions or milestones or in good company, I'd theoretically be doing something that made me happy, but I couldn't control if I was in a good or bad mood and it was hard to shake. I remember listening to Sheryl Crow on the radio and hearing the lyrics "If it makes you happy, then why the hell are you so sad?" And I didn't know why she had to call me out like that. The first time I saw *Garden State* in college, not only did I think being able to share that I liked that movie would make me seem deep and indie, it also was one of the first movies that addressed (what I saw as) high-functioning mental-health issues head-on, where a person moved through the world and felt completely numb. Unfortunately, the resolution in that film was exposing the evil psychiatrist parent who was overmedicating Zach Braff's character, and when he chose to not get help, he started thriving. Not a great message for me to internalize at the time. Great soundtrack, though!

I think I looked to media for depictions of mental-health challenges because I knew no one in real life who (admitted to) dealing with them. It was part of the artifice of Facebook albums; the same goes for what we wanted people to believe about us in real life. For as emotionally available as I am, I didn't wear my heart on my sleeve in public. I did, however, think the answer to my problems was to wear my heart on my neck, in the form of a Tiffany's toggle necklace, so everyone knew that even if I was lost, please return me to Tiffany's, where I totally belong.~*~

~*~ SO Random: Breakfast at Trffany's ~*~

One summer, I went to New York City with my sister, and we headed down to Chinatown to marvel at the treasure trove of faux designer goods, saying, "This looks like the real thing!" as if we had ever stepped foot in Louis Vuitton. It's hard to walk in the shoes of a wealthy person when you're wearing Rocket Dogs, and I'm sure our being kicked out of a Louis Vuitton store would have been as Speedy as the purse we were looking at. But I wasn't after the highest-end labels like LV or Hermès, I was after what I saw on Mischa Barton, a rainbow purse with two letters serving as my Dooney & Birkin. But the neckpièce de résistance was when I spotted a faux PLEASE RETURN TO TIFFANY & CO. heart necklace I could afford. The problem was, once I got back and wore it only a handful of times, it turned my neck green. But I held on to that necklace like I held on to my secrets, channeling the girl with "The Green Ribbon" from Alvin Schwartz's *In a Dark, Dark Room and Other Scary Stories,* where I learned if you wanted to hide something that was going on with your head, no one will know if you have a green thing around your neck.

Well, I was hiding two things. One, if you looked at the

necklace up close, something happened with the engraving of the letters, making the serif edges bleed together, and it looked like it read PLEASE RETURN TO TRFFANY & CO. It was a quality-control issue that no one saw coming in that white van on Canal Street. But it didn't faze me; I wore that thing at the expense of the green to feel seen, not noticing that the letters on the real thing are in capital letters, and it was a terrible knockoff. But in a way, I was a walking bad knockoff myself, showing up to sorority semiformals and pancake breakfasts with a smile so I wouldn't get a fine while I didn't feel fine at all. Maybe I worried if I was myself, I'd be found out, and like the girl with "The Green Ribbon," heads will roll. That sounds so dramatic, but I heard someone once say that social anxiety is like believing in conspiracy theories about yourself, and that's basically what it was. Thinking that I would only fit in the more I looked the part, never addressing what was going on with my literal or metallic heart. I feel bad now that those people running a "flap-jacks for the children" type of event thought they were there with me, but little did they know, they were at breakfast with Trffany's.

Even though I had journaled my feelings my whole life, and was open with friends about them to a degree, something changed in college. But it wasn't the kind of feeling I could place or knew how to explain. Suddenly, when it came to addressing things on the inside, I was inexperienced and appropriately green, which was also the color of my envy for people who seemed to be thriving. I knew I didn't feel like myself, and felt sad all the time, but didn't know at what point you label it as a broader problem. I understood anxiety and depression in the colloquial way we used them, and I'd say things like "I was *so* depressed" when my fake ID would get rejected, and I'd have to miss a CEOs-and-

office-hoes party (progressive!), but I never thought of myself as clinically depressed or anxious until I went to see a psychiatrist in the early
2010s and she told me that what I was describing was the textbook
definition. This is why I should've probably read more textbooks and
gone to fewer pregames.

It was so helpful to understand that my melancholic disposition also
predisposed me to hold on to dark feelings; it wasn't all my fault. I came
to understand depression as a heterogeneous disorder with the possibility of various underlying causes, from chemical to environmental, and
there are different solutions you can pursue, from therapy and learning tools to cope, to taking medication like SSRIs that can help by increasing serotonin levels in the brain, among countless other treatment
courses that are entirely dependent on the individual. I think when
you're suffering, there's so much hope to be found in simply having options, and knowing they existed made all the difference, even if it took
a while to find what works for me. It also helped with my self-loathing
for my perceived lack of gratitude; I can't express how important it was
for me to understand that the way I felt wasn't fully my choice.

This isn't a medical explanation, but the way I think about it, a common situation may cause the lights to flicker in another person's brain,
but it could serve as a circuit breaker for mine. It was life-changing to
understand that I wasn't completely in power when the power went
off. It helped me better care for myself, get medication when I needed
it, and look out for signs and symptoms to intervene before it became
severe. The first time I went on antidepressants and felt the fog slowly
but surely lifting, I couldn't believe how acclimated I had become to the
bad weather without realizing it; I had forgotten what it felt like to feel
good, to wake up without dread. And to believe you deserve that dread
or you are causing it (despite your desire not to) makes it so much worse,
and this is why I take issue with a lot of self-help literature that preys on
people who may be at a place of desperation for solutions.

I've been there; in these downswings, I read a lot of self-help.~*~ I think focusing on themes like the power of positive thinking and/or a mentality of choosing to rise above the problem can be helpful, but only to an extent. Their inability to work on me made me feel worse, and their tough love's lack of empathy just reminded me of how pathetic I was before I realized that I wasn't the issue. My problem was clinical; therefore their advice was not the solution, nor were they qualified to treat the symptoms of my condition. And self-help is very steeped in toxic positivity, which I think is the type of advice a lot of us are used to hearing, which is designed to minimize your response to bad feelings instead of validating their existence.

Happiness merch is always thriving in the zeitgeist, from every T.J. Maxx sign telling me to be positive in some way, to CHOOSE JOY, or maybe that HAPPIEST GIRLS ARE THE PRETTIEST, which is honestly just rude. I'm already struggling, I don't need this makeup pouch to remind me that I'm unhappy and that's why I'm not cute. Jokes aside, forcing happiness at all costs was a common response for how many of us treated negative feelings in most of my millennial experience. I'm nothing if not a lobbyist for silver linings as a result, and you've probably noticed my willingness to find meaning in just about anything, but I think it's a learned behavior from being a depressive person blinded by a "look on the bright side" culture that didn't validate my experience.

~*~ SO Random: Girl, Boss Your Face ~*~

There was a time in my mental-health journey when I got into self-help gurus who crossed over into boss-babe territory. In hindsight, it never sat right, because it convinced me to overwork, blame myself for not having more time or money, and then when I wasn't happy tell me to "interrupt anxiety with gratitude," thus cycling me back into further self-loathing, where it must just be my ungratefulness that makes me miserable. This type of guru is allegedly there to help you, but more often can only help people who are in identical circumstances to theirs, or who have minimal personal or systemic barriers they're facing, making oversimplified solutions work in their favor. But sometimes, what sounds like encouragement and that you're "made for more" can serve to reinforce that you're not enough, and I think it's a category that can be really predatory, baiting the same vulnerabilities repeatedly, promising the unknowable, and blaming a person who is already suffering for their choices while ignoring their circumstances.

If I may be an advice-giver (while I criticize advice-givers), from what I've observed, a lot of self-help experts co-opt the language of psychotherapy, but without the many years of education, training, and clinical experience that makes them qualified to practice. So it can be good in theory, helping in high-level or mild situations, but mental health is inherently nuanced and personalized, and there is no one-size-fits-all solution. While I acknowledge access to and affordability of mental-health care is a huge problem, I do believe you deserve to have someone who is properly trained to explore the nuances of your feelings and mental state, who can treat you from a behavioral and/or diagnostic standpoint, and you deserve to understand the options that could work specifically for your circumstances. Not the bed-in-a-bag solutions that are overpromised to work for everyone, shouted in an arena, where people are jumping up and down to "Fight Song" and fed messages about supporting women, when oftentimes the only woman being supported is the one at the helm teaching self-help, while helping herself by profiting off subjective solutions that bypass mental health. I'd say sorry for this hot take, but I was told to stop apologizing.

Once I saw the signs of depression, it opened up my eyes just like Ace of Base promised, and I started noticing so much about my college experience I had ignored. For instance, at one point during senior year I hardly got out of bed and I taped a blanket to my window like a vampire while I repeatedly watched *Twilight* and DVDs of seasons of *Friends* or *Gilmore Girls*. (The Logan seasons; him calling Rory "Ace" was my home base for self-soothing. Even though my collegiate melancholia wouldn't ever have yielded me Yale social status, I really subscribed to the kind of lifestyle that's *so* In Omnia Paratus.) I defaulted to my comfort shows and comfort foods and subsisted off wonton soup, white runny queso to-go, and Wendy's spicy chicken sandwiches. I was twenty to thirty pounds heavier than usual, which there's nothing wrong with, but in the going out-out life phase, I wasn't focused on how I wasn't well, I just beat myself up for eating too much kettle corn and not doing enough with a kettlebell.

I wrote poems about how I wanted to sleep in and not be around people, and how it bothered me that my friends asked me to go outside. I didn't see the look in my creative-writing classmates' eyes when I read it aloud because I was embarrassed, but I got an A that said I shouldn't be, so I went with it. I kept accidentally oversleeping and skipping class and missing assignments; I still have dreams of waking up in that room and not having studied for any of my finals, my entire future hanging in the balance because I couldn't get out of bed.

I still tried to go out a ton, though, genuinely thinking it would help clear the fog, but as I'm sure you can guess, being depressed and consuming a depressive substance in excess isn't helpful at all. But I'd never learn; instead I'd try to get home first, often crying on my walk, so I could get in bed with Easy Mac and listen to Coldplay to reassure me that no one ever said it would be this hard. Maybe I'd dream of going back to the start. Not of my life, but a few months prior, when I spilled an entire thing of wonton soup, like a full quart, all over my mattress. I ate the dumplings, and then I just shrugged and fell back asleep. I didn't know how to clean up a jug of soup absorbed into the depths of my only safe space, and when things felt too big, I'd just try to pretend they didn't exist. To the rest of the world, I was lazy and hungover. And like, really into *Gilmore Girls.* Which was partially true. But I was also depressed, had no idea that I was, and it wasn't a cliff so much as it was a gradual slide into being so used to feeling unhappy, it felt normal. Even though clinical depression wasn't on my radar, it seems like it should be pretty obvious from the volume of times I was listening to "The Blower's Daughter" by Damien Rice on repeat.

A big part of the issue was that I felt crazy watching everyone love an atmosphere so much that made me feel invisible and understimulated. I went to Virginia Tech, which I genuinely loved as an educational institution and am proud to have attended. But it also happens to be a big football school, and if I'm honest, I still feel such a disconnect watching other people enjoy themselves so much at a football game. Like, are you seeing what I'm seeing? Men in capris wearing helmets bumping into each other? And you're telling me it's weird that I'd rather sit inside and watch my *Along Came Polly* DVD? I learned quickly that a huge selling point of the school for most people was not for me, and used my tickets for the first couple of games, but then I started selling them at an ungodly markup to tailgaters so I could go buy snacks and get back in bed. At least I was honoring my truth, even though in hindsight it's a symptom of not being in the healthiest headspace. Now I can find joy in watching other people experience their interests; I genuinely like just being around people who are energized and celebrating something for the sake of pleasure. The version of me now would have just gone and LOLed at the intensity of the male-capri spectacle, happy for them that they've got their thing. But I wasn't able to do that then, and I was incredibly negative toward my surroundings, and I'm not sure that I gave it a fair chance.

I feel bad for even highlighting how badly I felt because I don't want my friends to think I didn't love our time together. I have butterflies (the good kind) as I type when I think about driving down Interstate 81 through the Blue Ridge Mountains to the town I called home for four years. But the other thing that may not have come across in the Facebook photos either was the fallout from feeling robbed of comfort and safety in the place you call home. I hesitate to bring this up, because it affected thousands and thousands of kids, and I'm the farthest from most severely impacted, but in recent years I've understood a little better the way it buried itself in my brain while I did my best to disassociate while feeling confused about my deteriorating mental state.

In 2007, I was a sophomore on campus on an unassuming Wednesday in April, and the deadliest school shooting in history occurred a stone's throw away in Norris Hall. It was often referred to by the media as "the Virginia Tech massacre," which to me seems to be so harsh and unfeeling. Most of us just refer to it as the date, 4/16. That was the day thirty-two of my classmates lost their lives when they went to class that morning, just like I did, in a building where I had classes the semester prior and whose layout I knew well. It's something so tragic, so unimaginable, that to this day when people ask me where I went to college, I sometimes pretend I didn't hear them, because people ask questions about it like I wasn't there, forgetting one person's detached true-crime curiosity is another person's tragedy. I left Virginia fourteen years ago, and out-of-state, unfortunately, that's the event most people lead with like a game of word association when you bring up VT. In Virginia and surrounding areas, so many people went there that people associate the school with so much more than its darkest day. But somehow it still gets brought up to me all the time in small talk (living in Illinois), and

I wonder if it makes me think about it more than I usually would. I understand the curiosity, but it's just not something that's easy to have a passing conversation about without feeling gutted about how, as the years go by, you're more and more aware of what was taken from them as you experience more of your life.

But curiosity can cross a line, and my conversations about this with people over the years (paired with the media's treatment of us on campus) are why I don't usually talk about or glamorize the genre of true crime on my podcast or social media. I'll never forget watching the news media descend on our town, and sensing the ratings chase for capturing B-roll footage of despair, doing things like zooming in on a student's red, tearstained face while they mourn on a curb or in a classmate's arms, in a moment of privacy they deserved. The days after are fuzzy for me, but I remember being shocked by how invasive and inhumane the coverage felt, and I won't give this sort of thing a platform if it's there for clickbait more than it is to educate. That's why I hesitate to even bring it up here; I don't want to center myself, but in the context of the millennial experience, the threat of this nightmare has been our generation's reality ever since Columbine, when school as a safe space was first compromised, and we became the first generation to practice active-shooter drills in school. Even though this is personal for me, data shows it's a major source of generational anxiety for many millennials and now Gen Z, who don't know a world where our public spaces aren't jeopardized by the looming threat of gun violence.

It was the kind of unimaginable that my worst nightmares wouldn't have been insidious enough to craft, and even though I was far from the most personally affected, I think I learned you move forward differently after the worst thing you can ever imagine happening actually happens. I don't think I processed it at the time; in fact, I was in shock and frozen. The university was so focused on moving forward, and you didn't want to be the one standing still. It almost felt like disassociating was the right thing to do. I've since learned there's something interesting about group tragedy that makes it really hard to place your feelings. You experience a collective loss, but all grieve differently, and your proximity to it makes you feel guilty for reacting. And it's something so big you can't comprehend, and nothing will ever compare to its size or scale, so you feel terrible for finding any reason to complain, thus ignoring your very valid pain. As I was slipping into a less and less mentally healthy place for other reasons, any processing was intercepted in my mind with "at least you're alive," and I felt pathetic for having such strong emotional responses to things that were nowhere near the level of magnitude of literal life or death.

I've heard others who were present for tragedies of this kind echo a similar sentiment in terms of their shared implications. It profoundly affects your sense of safety and security, and your relationship with public places and crowds. And you sometimes feel like you should have a polished answer for people, but the truth is, I still don't really know how to talk about it; I pushed it down and tried not to talk about it for the longest time, and its lasting effects mostly surfaced in my discomfort in large group settings, lecture halls, movie theaters, stadiums, etc. When I started touring for my podcast and I was onstage and responsible for a large group, I thought about it all the time.

Revisiting this event now more than I did back then is another thing I've found hard to learn about mental health; the idea that we "get over" things and move on isn't always true. And when we can't, it's not that something's wrong with us—it's that we weren't developed enough to handle it at the time. I'm horrified by a lot of what I did in college that was my choice, the binge drinking and recklessness, the obsession with validation, the taking for granted of my education and oversleeping. But I think a lot of us were dealing with some big stuff we weren't ready for, and compounded with the existing challenges of that life phase, it made for a hard time in life to try and have the time of your life. But more so than anybody, we were acutely aware of the equal opportunity for any one of us who went to class that day to be robbed of this life, and I think I had a misguided idea that to really be "living it up" was to party, live for the moment, have another drink, YOLO, likely living out a Pitbull song about tonight being all we have. And thinking about doing that to cope, like the reason we had to, just is so incredibly sad.

All of that to say, I learned that the state of one's mental health is a combination of multiple factors, and several impacted the collegiate experience for me that had to do with both my environment and my wiring. It was completely lost on me that I should honor or explore my own needs, or not minimize my pain just because it isn't unique. Maybe it was okay that I didn't like what other people did or that I didn't enjoy football games. Maybe there was a reason I felt empty after late nights and drunken hookups, after years of neglecting to figure out what I desired in favor of simply being desired. Maybe I should have talked to someone about how when everyone else moved on, the tragedy felt like a stain on something I once wore with pride that now just reminded me that if I had been a few buildings away, I wouldn't be alive. When I couldn't make myself have as much fun as everyone else, when I felt constantly rejected by love interests, when my grades weren't making me stand out, and my activities felt joyless and obligatory, I genuinely believed that I was destined for the purgatory of my own apathy and there was nothing in store for me because I was so unimpressive relative to people around me.

When you're young, you have trouble understanding that how you feel in the moment isn't static. I wanted to express how much fun I had going out-out, along with the harsh cultural backdrop that makes me scratch my head now, and fill in some of the context with my personal journey with mental health, because all of these things can be happening at once. I feel like I only hear stories of "OMG BEST TIME EVER" or "Hated it, one star" when it comes to the way people represent their experiences, and it is hard to explain how something can be a little bit of a lot of things. And that's okay. For me, college was the best of times and the worst of times. Has anyone ever thought of writing that in a book before?

If I'm going to be here spilling the tea, I should at least be honest about a couple of things, the first being the soup. I feel like I should do what I didn't do then and come clean: I have spilled a full quart of soup on a mattress not once but twice. It's been ten years since I had to walk away from this habit and toward a table, where soup eating belongs, and I'm proud of how far I've come. Nobody said cutting bed soup out of your life would be easy; they just promised it would be worth it.

The other thing I should be honest about is I may be more aware of all of this now, but I'm far from evolved. I'm still learning a lot about myself and my own mental health, especially navigating the challenges of infertility and loss, which I'll talk about later, and trying to prepare myself for how hormones play into mental health, among other things in this life phase. I actually don't think I'm that evolved; in fact, I keep cutting this essay (along with other intense parts in other chapters) out of the book entirely. I can't shake feeling guilty for bringing down the room, for making something "about you," for choosing to share things that are sad or hard when I am so privileged and when I could choose to keep it upbeat. I feel guilty taking up the pages by talking about myself, like my experiences don't matter because compared to what a lot of other people go through, I fully realize they are Plain and Small. The whole time I was writing this, all I kept thinking about was people reading it and thinking, *How is this worthy of taking up space? You didn't like parties? You got rejected by boys? You were on-site at a tragedy you weren't physically harmed by?* I know how the tales of a sad sorority girl who wasn't meaningfully oppressed sound, and I convinced myself that's all I was, too. A person defined by their face value and associations, not deserving of grace for having complexities, whose problems' common nature meant they deserved to be reduced. I now know better in my heart, but it's hard to get it through my head.

I can't even believe I've come this far to openly share this all in this book or on the podcast. My online identity prior to, like, 2017 didn't represent my truth at all; I would have never openly admitted to mental-health issues, deeper struggles, fears, or regrets. But the irony is, the only way I got comfortable talking about mental health is by hearing and seeing other people talk about it online whom I related to, and if they could normalize it, so could I. If they could get through it or move forward with it and not be defined by it, it felt like a good sign. Some of the things that cut the deepest take time to even talk about with your nearest and dearest, and finding solidarity with strangers can be immensely helpful.

Before I step off my soapbox, if you're having a hard time, don't be so hard on yourself, and please find someone who can help you better navigate your mind. Mine plays tricks on me all the time, and a qualified, unbiased outside perspective is often the only thing that makes me feel fine. In hindsight, I can't believe the signs I missed in college; revisiting the things I convinced myself were normal are kind of shocking. And soup-er gross. By ignoring it, I robbed myself of a lot of healing I could have benefited from during a challenging time in my life when I was trying to process things much bigger than me.

~*~ SO Random: But First, Zoloft ~*~

The flip side of consuming mental-health content online is that it follows you in ad trackers. And in recent years, I started to see endless merch, T-shirts, mugs, etc., that loudly and proudly shared mental-health issues, and I have to laugh wondering if this is the next iteration of irreverent phrases on merch I thought we were Rae Dunn and done with. I guess we paved the way for relatable merch to thrive, like the toxic-positivity merch mentioned prior, and now that I think about it, maybe we were wearing our issues with mental health on our sleeves the whole time. In my dark days, I felt very "namaste in bed," too. We were forthcoming about how we couldn't get out of bed and had caffeine addictions with "But first, coffee," and no movement speaks to a generation in pain quite like the "Everything happens for a Riesling" wine-mom brigade. I love wine, too, but wonder why no one raised an eyebrow, much less a red flag, when we were buying things that said COFFEE KEEPS ME GOING UNTIL IT'S TIME TO DRINK WINE.

Even the phrase we are ridiculed for, "live, laugh, love," fits into the criteria of literal retail therapy, where we would wear it and hang it all around us to be reminded of how to feel good. When you think about how widely ridiculed that phrase is, it almost makes you forget how it represents three of the most standard and important verbs of our existence: to be alive, to enjoy oneself, to love or be loved. What people forget about the commercialization of the phrase is that it peaked between 2008 and 2012, the era when many millennials postrecession were left picking up the pieces of the world we grew up expecting to inherit imploding before our eyes.

We weren't educated enough to diagnose our own depression in a financial one, so sue us for doubling down on whimsical driftwood decor. Therapy for us at the time was painted makeshift traffic signs in our homes reminding us to experience three basic human emotions. I'm convinced when you look deeper, "live, laugh, love" isn't just a cliché for millennial moms, it's more of a modern battle cry, reminding us to keep calm and carry on and that "We can do it!" as we march toward a lifetime of financial insecurity.

My online feeds are now less littered with promises of proverbial pink Cadillacs and are now full of people and merch and resources that seem to be marked by honesty, and it's genuinely helped decalcify my faux-metallic heart into a real one that doesn't make me feel like my head is hanging by a thread. The ad trackers are listening, because recently I was perusing Etsy, and I saw that I had something in my cart. I don't remember doing this—it must have been a late-night scroll several months back—and there was a necklace sitting there, not representing a silver heart, but something I allegedly lack. It was a design of circles and lines that I thought was pretty, but it also was the visual structure of the chemical compound for serotonin, from a shop that had hundreds of thousands of sales from people who had ordered the same thing. They make jewelry that encourages you to decorate yourself with the things that make you who you are, whether it's something you do well or may lack, suggesting it deserves to be worn with pride around your neck.

The fact that I liked it and put it in my cart is a real 180 for ol' Trffany over here, but to stick my neck out for something real instead of something faux feels right. I may not always say the right thing, but I'm committed to sharing the subtleties I didn't see represented when I was in the trenches between going out-out and looking in-inward. I'm grateful it feels easier to wear my shortcomings with pride now, though being more honest about my mental health and even writing about it in this book is something that feels new to me. I have a long way to go, but for now, just call me Serotonin, Plain and Tall: reporting for duty.

8

Kate Expectations

It makes me laugh when I think of how loved I felt by Jesus, my dad, and lyrics from boy bands like NSYNC and BSB in my earliest adolescence. I was probably like, "Damn, men are so nice! They love me so much! This will never change!!" They all, in their own way, made me believe that by simply existing, someone will swear by the moon and the stars and the sky that they'll be there. This is not a bad disposition; it just never matched up to my actual romantic experiences, where I felt utterly disrespected or rejected in most of my interactions with men before meeting my husband. While I discuss how Jesus and boy bands deliberately led me astray in this book, my dad remained earnest in his plight. I hope every father makes their daughter feel as special as mine always has; I'm charmed by my delusion that made me genuinely think someone would sing "Truly Madly Deeply" to me upon first meeting because I was such a catch.

I often wonder if some of my dating experiences were negative because of their objective quality or more of a function of the delta between my pop-cultural expectations and my reality. Great expectations are hard enough, but I had to learn the hard way that (what I like to call) Kate Expectations were even worse. Unlike familial love from my parents or platonic love from friends, my impression of romantic love from men wasn't grounded in reality or experience, mainly because it was literally a product of consuming fiction. I'm convinced my entire impression of love and romance was built from obsessing over romantic lyrics, charming teen heartthrobs, romantic comedies, TV couples, and other sources of fiction that would cause me to exaggerate, romanticize, main-character, and take things too literally, resulting only in the theatrics of my ongoing disappointment. Worse, I didn't notice what I was doing, and when I'd get rejected, I'd use the opportunity to indulge in more generalized pop culture and read books like *He's Just Not That Into You* or *Why Men Love Bitches: From Doormat to Dreamgirl* to remedy the situation. It's not lost on me that when my husband later referred to me as his dream girl in his wedding toast, I was a literal doormat company owner at the time, and I'm slightly concerned I took the doormat-to-dream-girl pipeline directive too seriously. Regardless, I read those books because pop culture taught me that if you want to get the guy, you need to pull a Sandra Dee or Laney Boggs and change your entire personality.

Outside of TV and movies, I think music was the main culprit for Kate Expectations; it was easier to sneak age-inappropriate music in private than it was to watch MTV on a shared TV in the living room, so that's where I got the juice (shout out to Next's "Too Close" for teaching me the mechanics of male arousal!). It's also where I took the bait for brilliantly generic boy-band lyrics that I could insert myself into, graduating from the likes of *Goodnight Moon* to a nightly swoon over the latest heartthrobs.

Think about it—Backstreet Boys made it clear that they do not care who you are as a person, or where you come from, or generally what you did in life as long as you love them, and I took note. Similarly, Savage Garden taught me that I didn't even have to meet someone first to find everlasting love in "I Knew I Loved You." In the bridge of that song, the lead singer says he sees "a thousand angels" dancing around a woman he just met. "Seems reasonable!!!," I thought. I used to blast All-4-One's "I Can Love You Like That," where they croon about reading fairy tales and how all this time that you've been waiting for a great guy to rescue you, you don't have to wait anymore. Thank God, because I was told True Love Waits and I was famously impatient in the romance department. In NSYNC's "This I Promise You," a seventeen-year-old Justin Timberlake sings lyrics like "I've loved you forever in lifetimes before" and then promises me I will *never* hurt anymore. As far as what I thought sex would be like? It only seems appropriate to direct the congregation to Boyz II Men 2:9. Album 2, track 9: "I'll Make Love to You." That entire album was hypnotically sensual in ways I have to assume that for anyone who plays it, the water is the only thing that runs dry in the room.

When trying to figure out why I found these songs so believable, I had an epiphany. If you recall, I briefly hypothesized that there's one main reason outside of waterskiing that I kept attending church-related functions throughout the years: the music. Maybe I was blinded by the light reflecting off all those studded belts and checkered Vans in the praise band, but when I think back on my religious experience, I genuinely could not tell you if the Holy Spirit was moving through me or if worship songs, like love songs, manufacture a hopeful and emotional state that feels spiritual, making you believe in something that may or may not exist.

Love songs told me all the things I wasn't actually experiencing but desperately needed to believe to maintain faith that I could find a man who could rescue me from myself, and worship songs held me over in a church I often thought about leaving, but the songs were so entrancing I maintained faith that it could rescue me from hell. In both cases, we have hypnotic, transcendental chord progressions, with lyrics that glorify an all-consuming, fulfilling type of love centering the POV of a man who allegedly thinks you're perfect as you are but also kind of projects onto you that you're broken. When you think about it, many worship songs are kind of boy-band love ballads that we are singing to Jesus. "You Are My All in All" could easily be a track off *WOW Worship* or a 98 Degrees song, and I Do (Cherish Both) of these musical categories.

As much as I hate to Carrie Bradshaw for a second time, I genuinely couldn't help but wonder: If this style of music made me deferential to a God above, did the same thing happen with boy-band ballads that mismanaged my expectations for everlasting love?

Before I get more into this theory about how music moved me to believe men would worship me and why I felt moved while worshiping men like Jesus, I should share a few examples of how disconnected some of my early dating experiences were from my favorite romantic crooners. I just described how college was tough, and dating was an added layer to the lack of smooth sailing. I think I went into college assuming I'd finally get to experience the serious relationship I had always dreamed of; I was further removed from purity culture, spent my last years in high school priming myself for a party-girl lifestyle, and I was moving into the only dorm on campus with central AC because surely hot guys would need a place to keep cool. Basically, I was ready to become the one-woman-Christian-brothers-stumbling-block I was told I would be if I sported a deep V. I anticipated I'd find a suitor in the quad—maybe I'd be playing volleyball or reading one of the classics under a tree à la Rory Gilmore, and per Lonestar canon, they'd watch me and tell me every little thing that I did made them feel "Amazed" by me.

This was not the case. Quickly, I went from thinking someone would love me for things like the way I "whisper in the dark" to feeling so in the dark about dating, I was reading self-help books that were some form of *Chicken Soup* for the unrequited lover's soul at the campus Au Bon Pain to soak up my own pain with a weekly broccoli cheddar bread bowl. Though I was genuinely amazed by the experience of the first boy who took me back to his room in college, but for different reasons. We went to his dorm room, and upon kissing, he literally cried, nay, wept to me on his twin XL lofted bunk bed because his high-school ex-girlfriend lived across the aforementioned quad, and told me kissing me is what made him realize how much he missed her. Worse, I stayed there and comforted him because I did not know any subtle way to sneak out, when sneaking out involved climbing over a grown man who was crying while trying not to hit my head on the ceiling as I scaled down a dorm ladder. Somehow I was mostly worried about offending him despite the fact that he had just told me I helped him realize how much he loved someone else through how little he liked me. I was terrified my expectations got mixed up somewhere in the universe; when I said I wanted an Edwin McCain, I didn't mean that "I'll Be" *his* crying shoulder; it's not the same. I was genuinely shocked by the honesty, and now I kind of respect the emotional availability. I just hadn't heard many top-forty songs that represented the experience of someone crying into your mouth, and not to further Bradshaw-down, but I wasn't prepared for such a salty first experience.

After this reverse-McCain, I assume I walked back to my dorm and listened to the Goo Goo Dolls' song "Name" forty-six times until sunrise when I could go to a dining hall and sneak a fountain Sprite in a water cup and hope to get caught so someone would notice me. Like I mentioned earlier, similar to the name of the game with AIM, something about me was less sexy and more emotionally safe that no one could really ever explain. So the scoreboard started at Expectations 1, Kate 0. Actually, it was "Katie" at the time. I spent years trying to drop the "i" in my name professionally throughout my twenties; it's a long story, but tales like this remind me why I probs wanted a rebrand and listened to "Name" all the time.

The second round of being a second choice happened soon after, when I went to one of my first fraternity date parties. I was so excited because lots of my friends had been going to these events, and I knew they were hookup central. After, my date didn't invite me back to his dorm, so I asked him back to mine, and he responded with "No thanks" and literally just walked away. We never went out again. Edwin Mc-Cain had failed me once more; he assured me the strands in my eyes that colored them wonderful would, indeed, stop someone and steal their breath. But this guy wasn't even willing to waste his breath to explain why my womanly essence wasn't making him stumble? It's one thing to not be interested in me in the sack, but I didn't see it coming that he would reject my HVAC.

I can't express how jarring it was to hear "No thanks" after we had just grinded (ground?) in a basement for several hours to Petey Pablo's finest. After this, similar scenarios started to happen all the time. You know when people joke that they're a "ten" in one city and a "six" in another, depending on their perception of location-based beauty standards? That's how I felt with fraternity boys but with floors of a residential structure. Like, to some guys, I had dance-floor make-out-in-a-dark-basement levels of eligibility, but they wouldn't be caught dead with me above ground level at their formals or date parties. I don't want to sell myself short because some boys would invite me back to their room, just rarely the ones I wanted who would lead me on (but never up). I guess one man's subterranean romance is another man's top bunk.

Although I always hoped to come across groups of guys who behaved like boy bands, the groups of boys I came across the most often were fraternity brothers. Most frat stars weren't always as charming or romantic in their plight; I found they mainly were misleading in their interest to get what they wanted, then would show their true Comfort Colors when they did (or didn't) get it, then act like you didn't exist. Meanwhile, they'd strut around campus, feigning a Southern-gentlemanly disposition, as if opening a door and loving their mom are character traits that offset treating women like pawns. If I may exaggerate, to this day, I'm deeply triggered by the sight of a man with flippy bangs and a wet mouth, wearing Sperry Top-Siders with a beer-stained pastel polo, and who likely shows a concerning hue of rage upon a close beer-pong match. I learned everything I need to know about a guy from watching them play beer pong. Specifically, if it escalated to one classic aggressive cliché demand, saying, "Is there beer in that cup????" every single damn time their ball didn't land. Similar to not blaming their aim but their opponent, wondering if they put beer in their cup, when you were their target and they missed, you were to blame for being a tease or a prude if you wouldn't hook up.

For context, this was 2005 to 2009, and the influential pop culture for frat bros wasn't singers of sappy love songs, they were people like Tucker Max (of *I Hope They Serve Beer in Hell* fame). We were sadly in a pickup-artist America, and I've not unpacked yet how normalized blackout-hookup culture was, especially to the degree where men had the audacity to parade their intimate details of conquests, each more incoherent than the last as if it were some sort of sick game to get someone as comatose as possible so you could be like Tucker Max. I know this is incredibly dark and messed up, but that's how I often felt at frat parties, and it alarmed me to hear stories exchanged about other women. This wasn't everyone; I met many great friends and had healthy platonic coed relationships aplenty, but when it came to exchanges with frat bros, I typically had the following experiences: 1. I was dead to them, 2. I felt like a faceless, nameless potential source of friction for their pleasure, or 3. I was their friend, and we'd hook up, then they'd stop talking to me, or things would get weird. So, yeah, in summary, I felt kind of dead to them across the board. If any of you are reading this and feel misrepresented, my condolences, but like our "Fearless" leader once said, "If I'm dead to you, why are you at the wake?," you know?

After quickly learning frat boys weren't living up to my Kate Expectations, I tried to take my talents to a more mysterious creature: the "GDI." A slightly rude way to classify a person who is not a member of a Greek organization, dubbed a "goddamn independent," a GDI intrigued me because I found it sexy not to need validation by third-party social status. Like, you came to college to . . . learn? And not pay for friends? That's hot. Allow me to put on more Damien Rice and do a "Cannonball" into our sea of possibilities and dream about how we may become unlikely star-crossed lovers at the Math Emporium. Most of my collegiate experience was consumed by feeling strung along and heartbroken by GDIs, which is ironic because I was so goddamn dependent on their every whim and every IM. But I quickly learned someone's Greek-organization affiliation had little to do with my luck in the dating department, because most situations started to look similar and their common thread wasn't if they went Greek, it was me.

Whenever I thought things were going well with someone and we'd almost cross a physical barrier, they'd say we were just friends or ghost me altogether. Or, someone would show me a ton of affection and interest while they were drinking and act like I didn't exist when they were sober. Now I genuinely take this less personally and understand how purity culture made me awkward and nervous around boys, or feel like I had to also be pretty drunk to cross a physical boundary, and it makes me shudder thinking about how an effort that was allegedly for my safety gave me no information for going about this safely. But at the time, it wore on my self-esteem; it's tough to understand why you're only good enough for 2:00 A.M., dark basements, or low inhibitions. And it's even harder to stomach why I pined after these people when, come daylight, they'd ignore me altogether on campus, like I was an object worthy of dance-floor pelvic thrusting but not a human worthy of eye contact. How cruel it felt for someone to go so far out of their way to make it clear they don't want a boyfriend title, to barely acknowledge me in public, yet they still felt entitled to touch me in private.

Honestly, perhaps more confusing to me than the world of dating and situationships was the vastly different world of collegiate hookup culture. Even though purity culture made me a late bloomer, there's a lot of in-between hooking up that everyone around me approached so casually, and I tried my absolute hardest to participate in an unattached manner but I always felt so uncomfortable and guilty. My early encounters were disappointing disconnects from my expectations, mostly with the men still acting like Boyz. They'd pour the wine and gaslight the fire; my wish was never their command, but my being "chill" was their demand. There was no love, there was no tenderness, there was no regard or respect for me at all. Hookups were drunken last-minute invites at best, and I'd be flattered and overjoyed if I got so much as a text, while any emotional response I had afterward would make me labeled as crazy or obsessed. Or they were full QAnon vibes for what I now believe is the conspiracy theory of young adulthood: blue balls. I literally marvel at the amount of times I didn't want to go any further and a male would make me believe he was on the cusp of a legitimate medical emergency. The audacity, truly.

Even though I no longer identified as superreligious, I couldn't let go of the belief that my self-worth was a function of what I withheld from men, but in my late teens/early twenties, it confused me how the reality of dating was that being withholding seemed to prevent you from gaining a relationship. It felt like a lose-lose of choosing between loneliness if I didn't hook up with them or shame if I did. Purity culture tells you that your abstaining from sexual interactions is what makes you a valuable person, whereas hookup culture solely values your participation, so it's no wonder at times I felt worthless if my value was as a pawn in someone else's game. In both cases, it requires a level of disconnection from yourself and your body and a tendency to listen to those around you for cues about how you should act, where you should have boundaries, and what your sexual behavior means about you as a woman. In my waterskiing days, I was taught to appear undesirable, and in my going-out-out days all I wanted was to be desired, but not once had I asked myself what I desired until I was well into my twenties. I've now been happily married for six years, but I share these sentiments from a long time ago because it's a less common narrative in the culture I tend to come across; we have a lot of examples of empowered women who own their sexuality, but not many who still are working through residual guilt and shame they never asked for, and it's really hard to understand unless you experienced it.

I feel embarrassed that in the years that were supposed to be fun, wild, and free, these things would happen, causing me to mope around until I hit a Wonderwall that made me seek even more male validation, believing the solution was that maybe, the next one was gonna be the one who saves me. I've since loosely pathologized what I think is a partial source of putting up with these god-awful experiences with guys: my God-given tendency to think it was normal to be broken and to look to a male figure for redemption and validation. Weirdly, there are many parallels between the methods used by the church to make you think you're broken and the spirits moving through you, just as there are ways love songs make you think God must've spent a little more time on you is what someone's thinking when they want to do you.

When I was young and developing my beliefs about love and romance, I was vacillating between worship music and top-forty music that made me think boys would worship me, and I wonder if I was internalizing a deeper message from both sides: I was a woman who needed to be saved. I didn't connect until recently that there's a common thread here beyond frisson-inducing music and collective effervescence that both the church and "the culture" were responsible for promoting in this context. It's a bit hard to put my finger on without aggressively generalizing, but it's almost like a weird form of benevolent sexism that wants you to know how special you are, but also makes sure you know you're broken by default. So much of my favorite music was about being rescued or swept off my feet; several of the boy-band songs I loved operated from the standpoint of you hurting, having your heart broken, not realizing your worth, not realizing how pretty you are, how some other guy didn't treat you right, but this new guy will, etc. I felt crazy consuming romantic music and movies and TV that made it seem like boys would treat you one way, but in real life, many were cruel, unfeeling, or ignored me altogether. It reminds me of how religion can look so grounded in love, light, charity, and acceptance, and how the music creates this insanely spiritual and beautiful feeling, despite people's personal experiences being the opposite when they experience behavior that's hateful and exclusive. Benevolent forms of sexism build you up and tell you how great you are, theoretically, so when you're held back or limited by a male's exertion of power, it makes it hard to argue against because it all sounds so nice and well-meaning. It's a form of female worship that is contingent upon upholding the status quo and adhering to gender stereotypes, positioning male control as beneficial to the woman's implied fragility. This extends beyond love songs and the biblical patriarchy; a lot of chivalrous acts draw a fine line between thoughtful and demeaning. I now listen a bit more closely when women are positioned as pure, fragile beings who are the object of men's adoration. Sometimes it's nice, and sometimes it serves to reinforce and prioritize the male as the more competent party.

At the risk of sounding cynical, I feel like most of the nineties/aughts Lou Pearlman–led boy-band machine I was caught up in was another cog in the capitalism wheel, feeding me what I wanted to hear, making me revere and bolster the role of male attention, making me chase an unrealistic goal of finding a comparably good-looking, nice, wholesome guy who is obsessed with me and respects my boundaries, only for that to not really exist, and I allowed my self-esteem to erode relative to my expectations instead of raising my standards to address the reality I was met with. Somewhere along the way, puberty and pop stars and purity culture oversexualized young people like me in a way that slowly but surely bled into my self-worth, and it all feels interconnected. The media we consumed filled the pages of the magazines we bought that told us we're not good enough, influencing people like me who believed they were a "before" that their tips are how you get promoted to after-hours. And those same magazines would feature artists front and center on newsstands who insisted we were perfect the way we are, saying, "God must have spent a little more time on you" to me in elementary school all the way to being instructed to "look for the girl with the broken smile" in college. These lyrics would make me further romanticize being heartbroken, normalize my dependency on their reassurance to fix me, and conveniently, while I waited to be eligible for saving, I could endlessly self-improve by flipping through the glossy pages that didn't go out of their way to feature things like consent but did give me a crippling fear of TSS.

I'm sure you're thinking, "Is she honestly trying to claim she was indoctrinated into the patriarchy due to JC (son of God) and JC (Chasez) being in cahoots to love-bomb us via Scripture and/or song, causing us to believe these unrealistic highly respectful wholesome men need to 'save' us, thus grooming us to be deferential and 'save' ourselves for them?" Yes, yes, I am. I'm not sure it's working, but these are the things I think about in my spare time. Is this conspiracy more or less believable than blue balls? I digress.

While the church is guilty of this, admittedly, the love songs are a gray area, and I'm musing for entertainment. I was likely drawn to the more heartbreak-centric songs given my melancholic disposition, but talking to me like I'm fragile and in need of rescuing was a consistent enough theme for me to believe it. These unrealistic expectations about gender roles and romance influenced me to excessively chase a form of validation that I wasn't getting, but I was convinced it was real, thus sending me into a cycle of disappointment and self-blame.

I used to cry and sing and hug my pillow and dream of the moment a man would save me from the pain of heartbreak, but in retrospect, it breaks my heart that my youth was wasted wanting to keep my virtue for my knight in shining armor, whom it turned out I never even wanted. Krystal really went for the hard sell on *The Princess Diaries* soundtrack, but I don't think "Supergirl" ever needed someone to save her. It's funny to think I chased that brand of lyrical worship, only to get older and realize that if a person you are interested in actually verbalizes the level of cheese and generic nonsense heard in a love song, it can be a major source of cringe. If I did actually encounter a BSB or NSYNC moment in real life while dating, I probably would sooner assume I was about to get murdered than be flattered if someone I just met claimed to be "drowning in my love." What's attractive about someone I barely know having so few hobbies or interests that they claim everything they'll ever need is in my eyes? Like I'm cute but I'm not that great. Now, I would sniff out this situation quickly; if a guy barely knows you and talks like that, it's not personal, it's not poetry, it's performative. And it's quite embarrassing that despite not knowing these people personally and literally only seeing them perform, that never really clicked. When you don't have a lot of romantic experiences, or don't feel like the community or cultural context you're in allows for safe exploration of relationships or sex, you look to media and friends and magazines to prepare yourself for what to expect. So if you're anything like me, I don't blame us for hoping for the best.

Though I will say pop culture hasn't always done me dirty in the love department; thank God my Kate Expectations were finally positively influenced when I saw *The Holiday* and saw myself in Iris, and realized I, too, was the victim of a Jasper Bloom. It was the worst kind of breakup, where I was dating someone but they didn't know they were dating me, and the only way I knew how to heal was to start writing a memoir (I've since accidentally locked myself out of) called *NyQuil & Chocolate Milk,* aka the items I'd subsist on to survive heartache. Long story short, it was a person I'd hooked up with on and off over the course of four years, while he claimed we were just friends or that he wasn't ready for a relationship the whole time. Naturally, I spent those years watching him be interested in his other friends, get into relationships with other people, as I did endless mental gymnastics to believe it wasn't personal and that he'd see what was right in front of him this whole time in no time. One summer's day when we were back "on," I worked up the courage to have a "DTR" (determine the relationship) conversation and asked him to meet at a fast-food eatery that doesn't get enough credit for its romantic scenery: Arby's. I guess I should've seen it coming that I'd still have beef to this day when he said he still wanted to only be friends and wasn't looking for a relationship after I thought it was different this time. I genuinely believed that he believed dating me would "hurt our friendship" until I logged into Facebook soon after and was notified he was in an official Facebook relationship with a girl who worked at the same place I did. I didn't even know they knew each other. It was then I realized what was happening; he lied. And I spiraled. All of these guys who friend-zoned me were lying. We weren't "too good of friends" to date; I felt like a secret, a side project, not publicly shareable material for a girlfriend or mate. She was good enough for a formal announcement, good enough to click through to see her face, good enough to earn the title because she was the best fit for the cover. Like many friends-with-benefits stalemates, I would have argued he did something wrong by leading me on, I'd imagine he would argue I had romanticized the situation into something it wasn't. It was probably a little bit of both. But what I did know was that I wasn't a best friend. I was a backup plan, a warm body at best.

That summer, I spiraled into self-improvement; I cursed the scale, the mirror, my body, and my face. I started playing guitar and went on a grapefruit diet and then the South Beach Diet. I couldn't even drink legally at a bar but listened to "Set the Fire to the Third Bar" on repeat. I started running to get in shape but also was trying to escape the weight of genuinely believing something was wrong with me or I was unlovable. There's something about a close friend's rejection that cuts deep; in prior situations, I could make myself feel better because they didn't know the "real" me or I was misunderstood, but this person knew me very well and was like, "Meh, I'm good." I was the only person I knew at this point who hadn't had a serious adult relationship with mutually reciprocated affection and all I could do was stay busy, work on my appearance, journal at Barnes & Noble, and watch romcoms at night to try and feel hopeful. I also learned Enrique Iglesias' "Hero" on the guitar and played it every night for my family during our beach vacation so we'd have live music (lucky them!!). The only other song I knew was "When the Saints Go Marching In," and I applaud my range. If I hadn't been on a beer-cart budget, I would've house-swapped like in *The Holiday* with Iris and AmandaWoods (is that all one word?) and tried to leave it all behind. Like many fellow millennials, before I ever went to therapy, I read *Eat Pray Love* and that became my blueprint for a sensible means to process heartbreak. But until I could afford the trip, I streamlined its meaning to provide me with a breakup program with three steps, and I would barely Eat, then Pray to fall out of Love. While the breakup response being rooted in self-improvement is incredibly sad, I can only hope I found my strength with an away message that was something poetic like, "If you can't handle me over a beef 'n' ched, you don't deserve to have me in your bed," because I was heartbroken, but also pretty damn upset to now have a complicated relationship with Arby's.

Around this time, even outside of Christmastime, I was regularly watching *The Holiday* because in the movie, Arthur Abbott says some-thing to the other Kate (Winslet) about her expectations that really res-onated with me, especially as a lover of romantic movies. Arthur says to Iris, "You, I can tell, are a leading lady, but for some reason, you're be-having like the best friend." I feel like this doesn't pack the same punch on paper, but the first time I heard it, I openly wept in a dark Regal Cinemas over my Sour Brite Crawlers. It was the single most-impactful piece of dating gospel I had heard in years and it helped me better navi-gate situations with Matthews, Marks, Lukes, and Johns way more than Matthew, Mark, Luke, or John ever did. Somewhere along the way, I became so used to being treated like the best friend, I would support the people who mistreated me like their best friend, wanting to keep them in my life instead of standing up for myself, hoping they'd come to their senses. Not unlike my experience with AIM, people would open up to me, trust me, spend a lot of time hanging out with or talking to me, and all signs would point to it being a romantic endeavor. But when I'd ask for something more official they'd bail, and I couldn't believe ten years into Katiemae87, I still never Got Male.

I know this all sounds dramatic for a pretty standard end to a friends-with-benefits situation, but that's exactly why I'm sharing it. It is common, but that doesn't make it individually any less gut-wrenching, and people make fun of you for grieving it like a real loss because you were never "official." Actually, I just texted my sister some of these paragraphs, and her response was a great example of how this situa-tion doesn't make you feel a lot of permission to be upset. She replied that she felt bad she didn't realize it was going on; she just thought I was having a very Enrique-forward summer, which was true. Even though I tell her everything, I didn't talk to her about it, or really many people at all, because I felt ridiculous for being shattered over something that was never "real." It's not like my family had met this person as a boyfriend; it was very under the radar, and inconsistent, and I felt very embarrassed he managed to make me torpedo into a summer-long *Eat, Pray, Love.*

Anyone who has been in these unrequited situations knows being strung along by someone who claims to love you as a friend but won't commit to you messes with your head, and society invalidates your feelings at every turn, using your relationship status or the amount of time you dated as a means to gauge if they think your emotional response is proportionate. I now realize why I felt the need to write a memoir at age nineteen about such a commonplace experience on my laptop; it was because I didn't feel permission to be upset anywhere else. I never had grounds to be mad because "we weren't together," and therein lies the psychological warfare of a friends-with-benefits situation. You get strung along, they lead you on enough to get what they want, and when the situation implodes, you're told you're overreacting. Despite this being scattered over the course of four years, at that point, those years represented 20 percent of my life, and literally 100 percent of my early adulthood. I couldn't be mad or sad or emotional, because he didn't technically do anything wrong. While I genuinely haven't had feelings about this situation since I left college, something about its ability to tear through my existence stayed with me in ways I struggle to articulate. Fortunately, Taylor Swift released the "All Too Well" ten-minute version in her *Red* (Taylor's Version) release, and I think I speak on behalf of countless women when I say that scream-singing about someone being so "casually cruel in the name of being honest" healed a generation.

Coincidentally, another holiday classic also taught me a valuable lesson that I put to use once I got into the working world. One guy I had been seeing "unofficially" for several months left his jacket in my apartment, and upon excavating its contents like the breezy gal I am, I found a jewelry receipt from a few weeks prior for a Christmas gift I most certainly did not get. People tried to comfort me and say it could be for his mom or a friend, but anyone who has seen *Love Actually* knows better. She was the necklace, and I was the Joni Mitchell CD. Not to overquote T. S., but I'd literally seen this film before, and I didn't like the ending. I wasn't going to disrespect Emma Thompson and act like her performance didn't have a profound impact on me. Instead of moping around and wondering what was wrong with me, I asked him to meet me during the day sober (!) and drew a boundary (!!) and cut things off. And I stuck to it; I was done. In that instance, my Kate Expectations taught me not to trust this kind of guy, and my rage toward Alan Rickman's character fueled me to stand up for myself for one of the first times ever. I also think this conveys how as a person, I fundamentally changed when I got into the working world, and gained confidence through having my competence validated in ways grades never did. I took better care of myself, and my mental health, and I got to start over. Life was going well. This majorly oversimplifies the situation, but soon after, I met my now-husband, and it conveniently coincided with an era in my life where I was owning my independence, fed up with mistreatment, and still watching *The Holiday* and *Love Actually* a little too much, therefore majorly leaning into my leading-lady era.

Once I got to know myself better, sure, I wanted a husband, but I also realized I never needed to be worshiped, put on a pedestal, or confined to gender stereotypes to be deemed worthy. While it's not usually a bad thing to be made to believe in a great love you have yet to experience and/or to double down on a faith you hope to be true, I do think blindly following high expectations while ignoring your lived experience is unhealthy, and while I draw these parallels for entertainment purposes, I legitimately do think they put me in a position where I would have been in a submissive state of awe and gratitude if a person was willing to love me, and that's why we shouldn't teach young women that they're broken or need to be saved. But if I'm not reading too much into it (LOL), it's worth noting that getting wrapped up in art and culture and observing other people's relationships is a big part of who I am and why I have this job. I'm intense, I'm nosy, I'm idealistic. My exchanges with art tend to extract the hope illustrated more than the reality reflected, but usually, it's not a bad way to live. It's only a bad way to live when paired with reinforcement from sources that connect your romantic and sexual choices to eternal damnation, but otherwise, it's probably chill.

That said, there are no words for how lucky I feel to have found a partner I love, respect, and feel safe with, whom I'm still girlishly obsessed with over ten years later. I'm not one to gush—actually, that's not true, I totally am, but I'm highly suspicious of people who do it in public places, and my husband is so much more important to me than any caption or paragraph could adequately capture, so I rarely feel the need to gush. But I'll say this: my husband's kindness, care, and respect for me made all the difference in the years I was still trying to rebuild the kindness, care, and respect I had lost for myself. It's not that he "saved" me, I just eventually understood that I was never broken to begin with, and he came into my life in such an unexpected, in-passing way that in the blink of an eye, I could've missed him. But I think the saving was done on behalf of the universe, who saved the best for last when I got to end up with him. This book isn't a memoir (unlike *NyQuil & Chocolate Milk*; let's hope that one hits shelves soon), so I won't go into our whole history, but I met him on a cold January night in New York City, literally passing by a mechanical bull at a country-western bar that has since been closed due to rats (cue the *Love Actually* choir!).

It is a sliding-doors moment that profoundly changed my life's trajectory, and it haunts me to think what would have happened if I didn't go out that night, to that bar, and stand in that very spot. I spent so many days of my life posing and performing, trying to simulate a more elegant, sexy, lovable, or different version of myself to offset all the previous ones no one liked before. But around him, I could simply exist, and I didn't feel the need to fake an ounce of my being. Well, after the first few dates, that is; I think I told him I could snowboard at first. Old habits die hard! I wish I could give you advice or a formula for how I found this, but I think the truth is that everybody's different, every dynamic is different, and no two dating scenarios are the same. What I thought was a pattern was just a small sample size of the wrong guys, and it was worth navigating the many situations I struggled to understand to find someone who taught me how much peace lies within feeling understood. Call it the universe, call it random, call it a numbers game. We just vibe well together, to use the technical term. I want to say something profound, but I also just want to blush and say I think he's handsome and smart and cute and funny, and I just thoroughly enjoy his company, his values, his family, and his dedication to me and our Shih Tzu, Tugboat.

We dated for a long time before we got married, although the first couple years were a less serious combination of long-distance, will-we-or-won't-we, and trying to figure out our lives and locations on our own, but there came the point where we realized we could be our own people together, and his companionship was something I couldn't imagine life without. Once we got more serious, we decided to grow in parallel while pursuing our own goals instead of rushing relationship milestones, and I'm really happy we did things our way. The timing of a relationship can't always be simple, and for us, I don't think it was convenient to meet in our twenties when we wanted to do other things, but I guess it didn't ultimately come down to the difficulty of the logistics—it always came back to loving him was easy. I don't always talk about him a lot publicly because our life together is my world, and if this all goes away, I'll know I can still come home, and nothing will have changed. But I'd be remiss not to share that after all of the spiritual trauma, the ups and downs, the heartbreaks and rejections, meeting the right person didn't take nearly the amount of analytics I had to perform trying to figure out all the wrong people.

While the music in this era may have further exacerbated my fragile emotional state and, at times, made me feel helpless, I still believe there's value in how it made me feel hopeful. And I wasn't entirely wrong, because once I found love, I'd argue it exceeded all of my Kate Expectations. Because better than fiction written by someone else, it was real. And it was mine.

Part III

Today

When I think about fitting in
Fitting rooms, not fitting in clothes,
Abercrombie and throwing a fit.
I've fit and flared, I took the stairs,
The way survival of the fitness goes.
How fitting it is
What fits into a size or standard
Is not our choice, stays in motion.
They move the target, raise the bar,
I shop at Target,
Don't go to barre.
I leave my shorts on by the ocean.
I'll think I've evolved from one-size-fits-all
Bed-in-a-bag self-esteem.
If the shoe doesn't fit,
Drop-kick it.
I've cut ties with who I'll never be.
But the train is a trap,
Mind the thigh gap.
I can hear a part of me scream
Into the pillow that covered,
Now smothers my lap—
Pinocchio, those are strings.
When I get condescending emails from men,
A polite-girl fuck-you is how I get my kicks.
You've Got Female, how does it feel?
I reply:
I don't think this is the right fit.

9

B There in Five

After college, when I got into the working world, I was thriving. Is there such a thing as reverse Peter Pan syndrome? I loved parts of my adolescence, but wowza, I was meant to be an adult (as evidenced by my use of "wowza").

When I was little, and we used to "play," I don't remember being very interested in the usual trades like doctor, lawyer, or teacher, and I didn't love playing "house." I remember pretending to have three careers in my playroom: newscaster, vague office worker, or fashion designer. I was scared of popular mean girls, but I idolized a certain type of leading lady: a businesswoman. You know, a *woman* who means *business.* Even from a young age, I loved a fictional boss bitch with a can-do attitude. I rarely knew what she actually did, but I did know she wore structured blazers and pencil skirts, gave pensive stares, clacked in spiked stilettos, and lived in the big city while being married to her job. Buried in paperwork, wearing glasses and pj's on weekends in her apartment to show her human side, often seen blowing a singular piece of hair off her face because she's exhausted, but her charm is that she glamorizes the turmoil.

I remember thinking, *She's just so good at her job!* watching this type of woman, though I'm not sure where I got this imagery. It probably started with Charlotte Pickles on *Rugrats*. She wore her hair in a tight pony, had blue eye shadow and red lipstick, and wore skirt suits more perfectly pressed than her cell phone was to her ear, all while sporting the highest of heels despite being in the throes of a vague nanny-share situation. She was the CEO of Mega Corp, and you could sense she was struggling to balance her career and her strong-willed offspring, Angelica. I was also watching a lot of *The Mary Tyler Moore Show* on Nick at Nite in the nineties because my mom liked and approved of it. I forgot about MTM when writing about Jessie Spano; she was probably my first positive feminist heroine. The people around her didn't make jokes at her expense about her desire to be independent; she just exuded independence.

Moving through high school and college, it seemed like every movie I watched that wasn't about a wedding was about a career woman's journey to romance. I *loved* it. Usually, it was a woman unlucky in love or a career woman with no time for love. My favorite was the latter, your Andie Anderson how-to-girl types from *How to Lose a Guy in 10 Days* (*HTLAGITD*) who works at *Composure* magazine, a fave fictional publication next to *Runway* in *The Devil Wears Prada* or *Poise* in *13 Going on 30*. Andie has a fierce wardrobe, access to cosmetics samples if brokenhearted, goes to cocktail parties in backless dresses, hops on motorbikes with strangers like an adult embodiment of the aforementioned Mary-Kate-and-Ashley movie. She has the confidence to nail down Benjamin Barry, love fern and all, and she gets to bone in a Staten Island shower to my favorite sorority-recruitment video song, "Feels Like Home." But she isn't like other girls! She doesn't want to write about "blondes, do they, like, really have more fun?" She wants *Composure* to talk about issues that matter, like bringing peace to Tajikistan! I thought she was a queen and I had that movie memorized after receiving it for my birthday on VHS in 2003. "We really can have it all," I thought.

In *How to Lose a Guy in 10 Days* and other rom-coms from that time, businesswomen in creative fields usually lived in a city with a tremendously high cost of living, with a just-quirky-enough apartment complete with a sofa and teakettle in a statement color inside their ample square footage, while working in one of the following creative industries that are historically *very* well-known for high-paying entry-level work and fair treatment of women: journalism, magazine editing, publishing, advertising, fashion, or PR. Usually, whether in fictional programs or on reality TV, these jobs came with something inevitable: a witchy ice queen of a workaholic boss, who wasn't charmed by the protagonist's youthful ways, à la Lana in *HTLAGITD,* Miranda Priestly in *The Devil Wears Prada*, or, in reality TV, a Kelly Cutrone People's Revolution type.

It was kind of the heyday of the ice queen; I wonder if it was influenced by the trend Simon Cowell started, proving how rudeness drives ratings when attacking the vulnerable. We really delighted in reality-show contestants' humiliation for a minute there. Between the lady who hosted *The Weakest Link,* Olivia Palermo's superior Erin on *The City,* Tyra Banks and Janice Dickinson on *America's Next Top Model,* and Stacy London scolding women for wearing horizontal stripes on *What Not to Wear,* this was a nerve-wracking time for a sensitive soul to enter the workforce in the big city. There was a time on TV where it was chic to be mean and ratings would skyrocket the harsher and more outrageous you were to weaker people. See also: deplorable makeover programming like *The Swan* or *Bridalplasty,* or even *The Today Show*'s "Ambush Makeover" series.

At the time, I was inspired by these shows. I was like, *Wow, Brenda* has *really let herself go. She needs to graduate to a full pant leg and sail away from capris, find a less orthopedic shoe, and add a lace-trimmed tunic tank under a blazer with three-quarter-length sleeves to become a whole person again.* The haircut would never turn out to be as Fantastic as Sam promised because it was probably a shorter cut in a Gosselin-style that was a nightmare to style, a *Jon & Kate Plus 8*–type of product, if you will. But the way she smiled coming out in front of the camera, it was like Samantha Jones New York in the flesh! I was moved! All I want is for people to feel good about themselves, and per the era of going out-out, I'm such a sucker for a story about a "new you." After all, it reignited the spark with her husband, Gary, who had a beer belly, cargo khakis, a Kirkland Signature shoe, and a wardrobe made entirely of moisture-wicking golf shirts from business trade shows, yet he still somehow believed she needed to put more effort and improvement into her appearance to please him, as he was the obvious arbiter of taste. Maybe she has no time because she's too busy volunteering at the local shelter while juggling her three kids and a full-time job, Gar! Maybe get off the golf course!

To get back on topic, in eighth grade, I took a career-aptitude test they'd administer in a course aptly called Exploratory. When I got the results back, it recommended an "air traffic controller." I was confused. Looking up the skills for this job, at the top of the list was *math*. Then, organization? It was all about precision, fast decision-making, and high-performance standards. Again, is it Opposite Day? I can hear Teen Talk Barbie now, "I *love* first class!" "Are there any lifeguards in coach?" I threw it away.

I didn't really know what I wanted to be outside of the rom-com jobs and playroom pretending, so I was kind of flexible when it came to my future. I was a B student and felt more defined by my ability to be good enough at many things instead of being great at one thing, so I didn't have an all-consuming career ambition like many of my peers. When I got into college, I wanted to be an English major, but my parents told me to apply to the business school, and I feel grateful for the fateful day my mom explained what marketing was. I remember her saying I'd be good at advertising because I like to create slogans and rhymes and storyboard things, and she wasn't wrong; it sounded great to me. Marketing it was! I signed up as a business major, and the first two years were a hellish ordeal of calc, BIT, accounting, etc., but I crushed the actual marketing courses, got super into market research and consumer behavior (big observer energy), studied abroad and did a field practicum, and ultimately found the perfect job for me.

Senior year, I heard of something called an "in-major GPA," which really turned things around on the ol' resume, and during my peak depression, my best friend, Hannah, dragged me to a career fair. I was deep in my bed-soup days and very used to being mediocre and unable to compete with all the impressive, glittery people in a large group. I would shut down at functions like career fairs. Hannah helped me put together my resume, got me out of bed with her go-getter spirit, and my God, I owe her everything. She is a gem. I think about these small moments where people supported me, the ones my whole future hinged upon, and I'm just so grateful to have had women in my life who looked out for my potential when I wasn't feeling like myself. That career fair is how I ended up landing my first job after college, and from there, my life completely changed.

The real world wasn't so scary after all; in fact, I loved it. I needed it. Structure, a salary, and more abstract metrics for success made me feel like I was finally having the time of my life. One of the first times I can recall feeling true, unmanufactured happiness in my early adult life was the first year after college when I moved to New York City for work; on my way home, I'd sometimes stop to journal at 71 Irving, then pass by Gramercy Park and listen to "Empire State of Mind" (it was 2009) on my headphones and have all my best thoughts. I remember a specific moment when I took a deep breath in the crisp fall air, and my lungs filled with the kind of hope and safety and satisfaction I'd once found on an autumnal evening walking home from back-to-school night or a Scholastic book fair. I was filled with confidence, wonder, coziness, and feelings of a fresh start that fed my old soul, and as I walked home up Lexington Avenue with the Chrysler Building in view, I thought to myself, "This is my football game." I felt filled with the kind of contentment and joy I had chased through boys or alcohol or popularity that I didn't know my body was capable of producing on its own. I may have been alone, and I may have been in a brand-new place with nothing familiar, but I had never felt more alive.

This is the cheesiest, most predictable arc for a girl from a small town finding herself in the big city, but it's honestly how I felt. And maybe subliminally I chased a life like a rom-com, but that's where I found hope in trying times. I knew I was Mary-Tyler-made-for-more than the opinions of the boys who dumped me, the tests I didn't ace, the clothes that didn't fit, and the parties that told me I should find it fun to watch a bunch of cups flip.

To this day, it's hard for me to believe I was one of seven in the country chosen for this company's particular path of a leadership-development program; they moved us to New York City, then Chicago, then San Francisco to try out different business sectors. At first, I feared they'd figure me out and realize they'd made a huge mistake placing their bets on a scholastically average person. But I learned once I started that it was a type of work we learned nothing about in school, and I mostly just needed to be teachable. I had convinced myself that because I wasn't a genius, prestigious programs like this wouldn't want me, but it turned out that not all jobs need geniuses; some jobs need employees who are good with people, are creative and resourceful, and who make up for their lack of experience with hard work. Those were all qualities I had; I just didn't know they held value until I met people who championed my career and nurtured my potential.

This job changed everything for me. We lost the woman who hired me, Jo, several years ago, and I always think about if I ever get to my McMansion in the skies and see her, she's one of the first people I'd beeline to for a bear hug in the afterlife. She took a chance on me, at a really low point, and opened up the door that led into the next several years, where I met myself, got my confidence back, and my career took off. I can still smell her Prada perfume, feel her warm hugs, and hear her saying bye on her way to catch the ferry home to Staten Island. She really cared about us and changed the lives of so many kids, and she taught me that my creativity, curiosity, and communication skills may have never mattered before, but in the right context, these qualities were actually desirable.

I was afraid the women I worked with in the corporate world would be like Miranda Priestly or the lady from *The Weakest Link*, but they weren't. I was so scared to move to New York City from Virginia, thinking the city would be so cutthroat, but everyone was so remarkably caring and kind to me, and I felt safe there. I worked for a lot of incredible, brilliant women who championed the hell out of my career when they didn't have to, and they're the ones who made me feel valuable and smart, loved my PowerPoints, puns, and attention to detail. My boss for several years, Sheryl, really believed in me and worked hard to get me more visibility, more recognition, and higher compensation. When she left the company, she went out of her way to make sure I was taken care of with a promotion and a roster of huge clients, making me a director at twenty-five years old.

I feel the same way about my manager and close friend Courtney, who is the engine behind today's version of *Be There in Five*; she worked tirelessly to turn my independent podcast into a profitable venture. She's like family to me and is the only reason I haven't crumbled in this isolating career. My job satisfaction has skyrocketed since getting to share in the experience with someone else who is just as invested, and to me, it's further proof that while I'm the one who has taken a lot of jobs, the people I've met along the way are the ones who've made my career. I also feel this way about the women who worked on this book and believed its contents deserved to take up space on shelves and not just my brain, and all of these experiences lead me back to what Mary Tyler Moore was trying to say in the series finale. She ends with, "Sometimes I get concerned about being a career woman. I get to thinking my job is too important to me, and I tell myself that the people I work with are just the people I work with and not my family. And last night, I thought: What is a family, anyway? They're just people who make you feel less alone, and really loved. And that's what you've done for me." BRB, I'm crying. Maybe it's unpopular that millennials often stray from traditional professionalism; we get a bad rap for being more vulnerable or casual in work settings. But I think it's pretty special to forge connections with coworkers who feel like family. We spend so much of our lives working, and being in good company along the way makes it worth it.

I always thought I needed to be saved by a man, but strangely, I feel like I was ultimately saved by women while working for The Man. While it isn't popular to express gratitude toward capitalism and a nine-to-five in this way, I'd be lying if I said my experience in corporate America didn't have a profound impact on my life's trajectory.

I focus on my corporate career more than my entrepreneurial one because people always ask about my business's story and I've talked about it in several places, given it's the more interesting arc. However, this book is about life lessons learned in the pockets of life moving through the zeitgeist, and corporate America is perhaps the least obvious choice for where a person would find meaning, but it really set me up with the confidence and gumption to actually "follow my dreams" like a true member of my generation. Most entrepreneurs have a story about quitting their job, breaking free from the shackles of meetings and middle management to follow a dream. But my experience was the opposite, where I left a good situation for an unstable one, and it took me a while to be honest about how that probably wasn't the best idea.

While I did love my job, about five years in, I was in a routine, traveling a lot to see clients, and getting a little tired of the corporate grind. I'm a creative at my core, and the more senior you are, the further away you get from the work, and managing people was not for me. Around this time, there was also another word I started constantly hearing in the millennial ethos, and suddenly, everyone started talking about this elusive concept of finding or following their "passion" in life. I liked my job, but did I feel passionate about it? Did I need to? It was such a strong word, one that I associated with strong feelings of adoration, such as my response to Beyonce's 2013 surprise release of her self-titled visual album, or my first viewing of the *Twilight* movie, when I felt passionate about securing a spouse who looked like Forks' hottest, most glittery teenager who was actually 104 years old. I assume I was feeling my limitations with creativity in PowerPoint, and at the time, many postrecession millennials weren't just hitting up Gilt Groupe and Groupons to save cash, we also were trying to make cash by monetizing our hobbies with "creative outlets" that we did on the side.

Like most inspiring entrepreneurial stories, my journey started following a disagreement with my boyfriend. He had just read somewhere that Splenda caused cancer in rats when administered in high doses. He was being sweet (genuinely, not artificially) and brought it up out of curiosity/concern; he didn't want me to get cancer since I was eating copious amounts of Splenda and the article was pretty convincing and inflammatory. He didn't know that for me, this wasn't my first does-Splenda-cause-cancer rabbit-hole rodeo and I had long ago concluded that I don't consume as much as the rats were administered. Honestly, I had been playing fast and loose with the highs and Sweet'n Lows of artificial sweeteners for decades, and some women aren't meant to be Aspartamed. I, for some reason, was very irritated by this. I could do my own research. We'd just moved in together and I wanted to be clear that I'm an independent woman and can poison myself if I want. Like most tiffs, it's never about what it's about. He thought this information would create a whole new world of how I approached my coffee and smoothies, but I already knew about it and carried on in my own world; shining, shimmering, Splenda.

It was a disagreement that maybe lasted a couple hours, but I don't do well with tension and needed to take the edge off. You may think I went and smoked a cigarette, but I don't smoke because those gross lung photos really bothered me in my youth, so I learned to take the edge off the old-fashioned way: arts 'n' crafts. I always loved an arts-'n'-craft station because you don't have to chitchat; it's a perfect introvert's corner where you can celebrate friendship in silence through the bracelet or bead lizard you're making and no one can see through the smile you're faking.

You've probably picked up on the fact that pop culture is incredibly influential for me, and an undeniable touchstone for my sister and me is the show *Friends*. One harrowing plotline I never forgot was when Rachel's hair straightener caught Phoebe's apartment on fire. I don't know about other nineties kids, but the only other trilogy I knew more than Father/Son/Holy Ghost or shake for breakfast/shake for lunch/sensible dinner was stop/drop/roll. I am on *high* alert for fire hazards. So I'm sure I thought, *I'll show him what an independent woman I am, I don't need his input to dictate my Splenda consumption. I shall smash the glass ceiling by getting into . . . flooring?*

I decided to play around with an idea I had, wondering if it could be my passion-turned-side-hustle that would give me an outlet. It felt right to prevent homes from burning down while battling burnout at my job. I started painting "Turn off your curling iron" along with other fire safety or general reminders on doormats, later dubbed "remindoor-mats," so type-B gals like me who are time-optimists (and tend to text their friends "be there in five") would have reminders staring them in the face when they walked out the door. I loved the idea of remindoor-mats; I felt like an "industry disruptor" innovating on a stale category: the welcome mat. They welcomed guests in, but I was the one who lived there! I wanted the doormat to see me on my way out, helping me not agonize over if I burned down my apartment.

I put the mats on Etsy, pinned them to Pinterest with a million keywords, and within a couple of months, they went viral when an Australian radio station made one of the photos into a meme on Facebook and Instagram, and my TURN OFF YOUR STRAIGHTENER mat had two hundred thousand plus likes and thousands of comments in a night. I couldn't believe people liked my idea; the market researcher in me knew it was the free focus group of a lifetime, and I needed to capitalize. From there, I spent the next five years building up (and then scaling down) a doormat business, working backward from the demand I got from this post, which was based on a photo, not an existing, viable business model.

The spray-painted doormats I made for the prototype didn't look very good in person, and I needed to fulfill the demand, so I took my mats to every screen printer I could in Chicago. Quickly, I was met with no flexibility, no interest, and was just told no. To get what I wanted to be manufactured at the price point I could afford, I would've had to get them premade in China, but the minimum order quantities would have put me under, having to put all my capital in inventory, not even knowing what SKUs would sell through and not having a warehouse or logistics system to take on that kind of volume. I wanted them to be pretty and decorative area rugs, not traditional coir doormats, but found out that wasn't realistic. One manufacturer said painting each letter myself was my best bet for producing a decent SKU mixture without holding inventory, and I think he meant this jokingly. After all, who paints on an indoor pile area rug? It's not exactly an ideal canvas.

But you know who would take the time to figure out how to letter phrases on a new canvas? A gal who used to spend hours on end practicing lettering in her spare time, trying to find her place in the world with a fresh set of pens and a dream. I'll be there in a five-star five-pocket! I was pretty good at any type of lettering at this point, and once again, despite my talents being few and far between, this untalented and ungifted gal kept finding herself in comically cosmic circumstances, stringing together motifs that I would have never thought to connect myself.

I didn't know anything about sourcing or screen printing or dye sublimation or floor mats and the importance of their backing material and pile height. But the orders kept coming and coming, and in order not to get in a financially compromising position, I decided to set up the infrastructure to just be a handmade shop over the course of a couple years, first hiring my mom, who single-handedly kept me afloat for a year, then contracting the part-time help of some local students who were lovely and flexible and willing to roll with the punches of my obscure passion project. This business model allowed me to charge a premium and capture the margin I wanted while I took time to vet manufacturing solutions to find a sustainable one, all while not losing the momentum from the viral post. I knew better than to wait for that to happen again, and it never did; but trust me when I say just one post can change your life *that* much.

Nothing surprises me more in hindsight than that I even had the audacity to start a company; it was an exhilarating but brutal process trying to navigate how to start a business from scratch and do it on the side of my nine-to-five, completely bootstrapped.~*~ I met sides of myself that I didn't know existed; in this context, I was a person who was much more strong-willed, confident, and resourceful, and my existing verbal and client-facing skills made me get a lot of media opportunities since people were salivating for a girl-boss story. I got to speak at a global Etsy conference on two panels, I was in every mainstream publication I've ever dreamed of, I sold thousands and thousands of units, and started a wholesale division that was distributed at Wayfair and in Nordstrom stores. And I'm not even attempting to oversimplify here; it happened fast. That's the nature of virality, something that was new to me at the time. When lightning strikes, you shoot your shot. It was an interesting story, and on paper, it sounded pretty damn good.

~*~ SO Random: The Fine Blueprint ~*~

Thinking back to me doing press early on is concerning; I had no idea what I was doing, yet I was being treated like a paragon of entrepreneurial excellence. I'm sure I was like She-Believed-She-Could-So-She-Did Talk Barbie, repeating the same four infantilizing phrases about women in business that you heard over and over in the 2010s. While I won't diminish the tremendous effort I put into getting the mat business off the ground, now, I'd never tell anyone to do what I did without a big fat asterisk saying something like, "She believed she could, so she did, but also, outside of just believing in herself, she also had a lot of time on her hands, a college education, a financial safety net, and faced minimal systemic barriers, along with having a boyfriend who was splitting her rent, so the stakes weren't that high and maybe keep that in mind when comparing yourself to others' anecdotes of personal success?" But I'm not sure there's room for that on a sassy mug.

I was and am still proud of this phase of my life, but I also made a vow to talk about it more realistically going forward. I think I fell for a lot of lofty inspirational stories back then that oversimplified what it takes to succeed, especially the stories that didn't offer much transparency related to their starting point. In my opinion, there are only two things that matter if you want to start a business: having either 1. a lot of time or 2. a lot of money. And my career, wing to wing, is the product of having a financial safety net to get started and then, following that, a disproportionate amount of free time to reinvest and figure out how to navigate new industries and find different revenue streams to sustain me. In the spirit of transparency, I started the doormat business with about $250 in materials to make the first prototypes, and from there, put profits back into the business to grow the handmade operation, but it would still take me a little while to pay myself, so I lived off savings of about $40,000 that I had mostly banked from corporate bonuses after I quit my job.

And regarding the time element, living in Chicago, I didn't have many people from my personal networks in town, I didn't have family that lived here, I truly had no one asking me to be anywhere, and I don't have children. My responsibilities the past decade were quite limited and I sank all my free time into my career. Eventually, I would learn the hard way why this is really unhealthy, but I think my baseline of having a disproportionate amount of free time is important to clarify before I would tell anybody to do what I did. If you have money or can get funding, you can pay experts to make you money faster and you don't need to be self-taught, but most people aren't in that position. When people say it's about things like hard work, grit, ambition, etc., that's true to a degree, but entrepreneurs who share their in-spirational stories often don't realize their lives are not like most people's and they aren't providing the full picture of what actu-ally drives growth. In my opinion, if you're following someone else's blueprint, it's important to understand as much as you can about their baseline, e.g., if they had easy access to capital, a net-work of relevant mentors, if they encountered any systemic ob-stacles, if they're in good health, have available childcare, among other things that affect a person's ability to have more time and/or money. Not matching someone's personal situation doesn't mean you can't do it, it's just important to be aware of the role certain advantages play when you're incurring personal financial risk because the outcome may not always be as straightforward as the one people are selling. A blueprint doesn't always apply if your foundations are different, and I think it's helpful when inspirational stories are forthcoming about how they funded and figured out their ventures through money and time.

About a year and a half into the business, I was so overwhelmed that I had to leave my corporate job, and I hoped if it didn't work out, I could go back. Eventually, I found out that it looked cool on paper, but it was impossible to make the kind of paper I made before, where I worked a *lot* less, had the privilege of caring less, could take PTO, and would've had maternity leave, among other benefits. I'm probably the only entrepreneur who tells people to "keep your day job!" but I really want people to know how hard it is to become profitable, stay that way, and how little you get paid after you pay everyone else and reinvest it back in the growth of the business. I reached a point where to be more profitable, I would've had to scale up tremendously to drive my costs down; otherwise, I'd never make any more money. I was just increasing my workload and expenses with a stagnant margin. I knew I didn't want to do this for the rest of my life, so ramping up terrified me. I felt stuck. Overworked, underpaid, and alone, while on the outside, everyone applauded me for allegedly living the dream.

After two years of self-employment, I feared I had made a mistake. I started applying to corporate jobs again but wasn't getting called back. There was a lot of turnover in my old team, and I had become irrelevant to that role. I realized passion and fulfillment are cool, but I also wanted to have a personal life and be able to save some money, too. Honestly, I wanted to experience true passion again by not having it tied to income. I felt like I was lied to about finding "a job you love and you'll never work another day," because I followed a job I loved and I hadn't stopped working since. Burnout exists whether you work for yourself or for someone else. Being your own boss is not a quick fix; it's a long, high-pressure haul. It has rewards, too, but this was an important lesson for me to learn: when you leave your job, you're not immune to the frustrating parts of work you dealt with before. Sometimes they're worse because there's more at stake, and you can't walk away.

I had a specific turning point that made me feel differently about "hustle culture," and I'd say it hit me like a ton of bricks, but it actually literally almost hit me like an SUV. One night during the craziness of the holiday season, I was moving so fast, working nonstop, and never remembering to eat or drink water until I felt like I was about to pass out. I ran to get a protein shake to hold me over because I preferred drinking my sustenance; it was faster. I walked into an intersection, I looked to my right, and a car was *flying* at me. If you live in Chicago, you know about the insane six-way intersections, and despite having a WALK signal, this person flew through the intersection, and I was so scared trying to get out of the way quickly, I slipped on black ice, falling literally directly in front of the car in the dark, in a fully black outfit. My thought in that split second was that I couldn't believe I had done this to my parents, whose lives would never be the same. And for what? Doormats were hardly a good enough reason to become road-kill. When I saw my mom and sister at the airport the next day when I came home from Thanksgiving, I sobbed. I think I told Kelly that if I died, I would've felt bad for ruining her Christmas, which is a funny Hallmark-esque instinct, because they, too, equate having Christmas cheer as a matter of life or death. I'm honestly still not over it; I can feel the bumper tap my right shoulder every time I cross the street; maybe it was a light tap from God who was finally willing to spend a little more time on me by giving me a little more time. I do not understand the physics of how they were able to brake that fast. If I ever get a car, as much as I want a Geo Tracker or Pontiac Sunfire, now all I care about are the brakes. The worst part is, I was in such shock, I still went to pick up my protein shake. I had prepaid for a peanut-butter upcharge! If I was goin' down, it would've been a waste to pay the markup. A Lisa Frank leopard seal doesn't change their spots.

When people ask what led to me starting a podcast, there are countless factors I could point to, but at the heart of it, it was a desperate attempt for reinvention. I was just one millennial, in front of a mic, at a crossroads in my career when I had nothing to lose. This crossroads was more like a crisis, both financial and identity—ironically, the two things I was told to look for in a job. We're a generation who promoted the pursuit of purpose in our careers, told to find a job we loved and we'll never work another day. But I left my job that gave me space and time to do the things that I loved on the side, to take a job that I loved, but it left me in the dust when I gave it everything and it still asked for more time.

As I mentioned in the intro, millennials are known to have been told they can be whatever they want, and I'm not totally sure why that's a bad thing. I guess the weird part about my career now is that I did ultimately do what I wanted, but not because I have unlimited resources; in fact, it was the opposite. What no one told me about self-employment is that life becomes a game of reinventing yourself over and over, not because you're disjointed or unambitious, but because you need to go where you get paid. My career is in such close alignment with the things I like at my core, because when you're scrounging to be valued somewhere, sometimes you have no choice but to follow what you know.

In the process of trying to scale down the mat business and stay on my feet, I did a bunch of different things, scrambling for a couple of years to find a way to foray my self-taught experience into another career. I sold artwork, I did private consulting, I ventured into party supplies, I got paid to build websites and write slogans and name businesses. After a while, stringing together ad-hoc income streams became such a grind, I decided to return back to the things I've always loved, that gave me peace, and that got me through times of uncertainty before in life. Something about a personal rock bottom makes you go back to basics.

Having nowhere else to go, I asked myself: If it were up to me to rebuild my career from scratch, what would I do? I thought about the playroom: the newscaster, the vague businesswoman. I thought about the worlds I would create behind closed doors with poems that my classmates made fun of me for. I thought about my love for magazines and celebrities and pop culture and popular girls, and the female millennial zeitgeist I spent my days obsessively observing.

I selected a two-pronged approach: books and a podcast. Even though I had scaled down, I was still making the doormats and doing consulting in the background to get by. I started writing and sending out a bunch of proposals for children's and poetry books, googling how to write one and submit to a publisher. I sent around dozens of proposals of various ideas, usually never to be seen or heard from again. I also became interested in podcasting because they were my favorite entertainment medium; they kept me company during the lonely days of self-employment, and I saw a gap in the marketplace for long-form pop-culture content that covered topics outside of modern entertainment news stories. What about our favorite nostalgic pop culture that deserves to be remembered? What about broadened definitions of celebrities, like influencers and social-media stars, whom mainstream entertainment news wasn't giving the time of day? I also didn't want to just talk about what happened in pop culture; I wanted to take the time to explore the nuances of why it matters (like Andie Anderson and Tajikistan!).

I hoped to do the research I was trained to do and pair it with the surface-level interests I was never told to take seriously, exercising the verbal skills I had developed throughout life in a spoken form. I also understood the media industry due to my former role consulting for advertising effectiveness. (Truly, I can't with the buzzwords, sorry. I'm like one paragraph away from talking about synergizing best practices from a ten-thousand-foot view until I can loop back to a paradigm shift without boiling the ocean.) The insights I shared at my corporate job were about consumer behavior and viewing habits, and I worked with data that analyzed how media is bought to reach a target audience. When I started a podcast, I understood how it could be monetized because podcasts are a part of this same advertising ecosystem, but on the "sell" side.

Instagram stories had come out the year prior, and I started using my account to be more about me, not the doormats. I started posting pop-culture theories and Taylor Swift fanfare and internet sleuthing. I posted anything I was naturally interested in, trying to have fun with the perk of a small following. Around this time, it was like fifteen thousand people. Doing this on Instagram made the podcast seem like an extension of my stories, and in late 2017 I bought my first mic. In February 2018 I published my first episode, and around the same time, I got my first response from a publisher about one of my poems. It was a satirical children's book I had written, imagining how a "momager"-type parent would talk to their child about the career of an influencer as if it was a doctor, teacher, or lawyer, called *Twinkle, Twinkle, Social Media Star*. My rampant googling paid off when I got an indie publishing deal, and even though I hoped it would be my big break, it didn't end up paying much at all. I can't tout it for changing my professional life in a big way (even though I hoped it would); however, it did get me out of a dark place, providing me with something to focus on, and I got to see myself accomplish a lifelong dream. I still think the book is insanely cute, and I'm incredibly grateful for the opportunity.

I feel like I'm still too deep in my podcast's story to have the wisdom of hindsight, so maybe I'll save that for another book. But it ended up being a job that I genuinely love, that gave me my life back, and that yielded me the most personal growth. When this book comes out, I'll be close to its six-year anniversary. It's now my full-time job, and it took two to three years for it to meet my corporate salary (which was my goal; I still made mats and did odd jobs in the meantime to get by, and had health insurance through my husband). Now, even though I'd say it's a midsized podcast relative to most, it's exceeded my wildest expectations. It's been downloaded by millions and millions of people, and I've gotten to take it on tour. I did everything myself at first, but the show really took off the last few years after I met my "friend-ager," Courtney, via Instagram (she reached out after hearing me say I was looking for a "Kris Jenner"), and she took over the brokering of ads and managerial back end of the show. The listeners ("The Beths") are some of the most incredible, thoughtful, smart, and interesting people I've ever met; they've taught me so much and they supported my quirky, wordy work even though I wasn't a traditional entertainer. They are so kind: they'll send cards to my PO box in difficult seasons of my life; they'll Venmo complete strangers money for coffee or a pick-me-up if they hear someone's having a tough day in our online communities; they'll bring granola bars to share at live shows. I've had countless venues tell me it's the most well-behaved audience they've ever had, and it makes me laugh thinking about how those away-message quotes can suck it; well-behaved women *do* make history. I don't think this is a testament to my character; they're far better people than I am. It's more like I found a niche of people who are similar to me personality-wise (I'm not sure you could listen to me talk for two hours a week if you weren't). People who tend to be a little more reserved, who want a space to celebrate the things they like, and who love the song "I Knew You Were Trouble" but absolutely hate getting in trouble.

Even though I want to warn people about following unrealistic pipe dreams and calls to action for passionate work, I will say the podcast is what made this whole path worth it, so it's hard for me to feel one way about my career. But life rarely happens in a linear fashion, and I'm now the sum of my parts. I was never good at just one thing, but now the topics I've become known for on my show make me grateful that I'm part wannabe popular girl, part reluctant party girl, part RoXy-QuiCkSiLvRGrL, part megaholy megahottie, part retired girl boss, and even part melancholic waterborne-illness-laden-1800s broad. I like all the parts of me, both shallow and deep, that in my times of need, at any given time could be found writing feminist poetry or rewatching *Katy Perry: Part of Me 3D,* and I think it all got me here. It was the windiest way imaginable to become the playroom newscaster I once pretended to be, and I still can't believe how cool it is that our generation eliminated middlemen and gatekeepers, enabling a democratization of talent on the internet.

Some seem to think it's cringy when you have the audacity to think you deserve to take up space. People make fun of podcasts because starting one means you think what you have to say is important. Most of the odd jobs and industries I've pursued were kind of embarrassing, at first, because they were unusual, and I didn't have permission or proof that they'd work. How would you react if your close friend was leaving a stable gig to start over as a doormat-company owner? Or if that doormat-company owner wanted to quit, and decided their next move was talking into the abyss for two hours about Mormon bloggers' F.U. new construction money? For some reason, I didn't care what anyone thought. Which was abnormal, as I usually care the most about everything. All the Fs, remember? But I had an epiphany when my mom was visiting me about the bigger way this all ties together, and why I've been able to successfully traverse different jobs and industries in the past fifteen years.

My mom has saved a substantial amount of artifacts from my childhood, and recently she's been resurfacing memory boxes to help jog my memory and fact-check the contents of this book. Usually, the boxes she sends me to go through are highlight reels of my artistic pursuits, e.g., drawings, photos, poems, and essays. However, the most recent pile she sent me was different; it was less of a highlight reel and more like the never-before-seen raw footage of my K–12 experience, containing a lot of random schoolwork, report cards, tests, projects, and certificates.

What stood out about this pile of artifacts? To start, not only how many times I attempted to illustrate the complicated couch-bed-outdoor-gate hybrid of a daybed, making me feel validated in my memories of its significance. But I was also surprised by the paperwork and keepsakes from school and sports, though what stood out was not my penchant for overachieving. Quite the opposite, actually. This was an excavation of pure, unadulterated mediocrity. A real who's who of Bs and Cs, abysmal math tests, commentary about run-on sentences (shocking!), evidence of activities I tried for a hot minute, a program from my one piano recital, a cheerleading squad picture of the year I cheered but I couldn't be bothered to attend the team photo. I didn't know whether to laugh or cry when I saw she saved an honorable-mention ribbon from a swim meet on July 6, 1994, where I had gotten twelfth place in a twenty-five-meter freestyle race. *Twelfth!* Aren't there only six lanes in a swim meet? But I turned the ribbon over, and my mom had written "Wow!" on the back, exclamation point and all, even though I came in dead last (of what I assume were two heats), where instead of bringing the fire, I arrived in my signature lukewarm style. In general, this pile honorable-mentioned it all by showcasing how I rarely placed or was the best at something, how comfortably I quit or moved on from something I didn't like, and how little proof I have of any sort of academic or athletic excellence in life. I always knew grades weren't my vibe, but it was almost shocking to me how many things I had tried and how little excellence was on display.

Though my past was buried in insignificance, these artifacts provided me with a level of statistical significance that gave me clarity about my life's common themes. As I reviewed the raw footage, somewhere in between the carbon-copy report cards and mealy construction paper, I felt a deeper sense of understanding about my life and career. I don't think my success in venturing into entrepreneurship and self-employment is the product of excellence. While I attribute it to many things, the one thing I don't talk about enough is that I think I am where I am today because of how effort was praised over excellence in my household. And I think that the biggest influence on me ending up with all that has become *Be There in Five* is the way that my parents allowed me to just Be, ever since I entered school at the age of five. To be me, to support my dreams and gifts outside of the school system, and, most importantly, they were super okay with me just getting Bs.

I remember my grades never being as good as my friends', walking into awards assemblies knowing I wouldn't get recognized, trying out for teams I'd assume I probably wouldn't make. But it never really mattered because my parents only asked for honest effort, and the habit of trying things for the sake of trying really stuck with me in life. It made me see value in the process and in participation more than the end result. When I look back on my career, the only thing that makes me different from anyone else is that I've tried a bunch of different things. I started a business as a creative outlet, and even when I didn't want to keep doing it, I started, stopped, resumed, rinsed, and repeated so many other things to get back on my feet, and I most certainly didn't do all of them well; a few just turned into something worth pursuing. And going through my mediocre memories made me realize that I haven't been successful because I'm the best, I've succeeded because I am okay not being the best. I'm not embarrassed to try things, quit them, and start over. I'm cool with twelfth place. I had a good time, got a cute Speedo tan on my back, onto the next.

What ultimately mattered wasn't validation from the outside world, it was the feeling of walking through the garage and into the back door of my childhood home, hanging up my backpack, and immediately (rudely) asking my mom what was for dinner, while knowing I was back in a safe space, where I was suddenly a genius, even if I forgot to believe it as soon as I stepped back out into the world whose metrics told me otherwise. It stayed with me, and I've always been insecure in many areas, but disproportionately confident about my creativity.

So many pieces I've read pathologize millennial narcissism as being a product of helicopter parenting, saying that parents told us we were too special. First of all, may we all be so lucky to be reminded to celebrate the ways we are unique. I'm not sure why that's a problem. But it wasn't a static disposition I held throughout my life, causing me to have blazing entitlement; it was the opposite. It was a supportive form of parenting that helped me stay afloat. If my parents believing I was special could have prevented me from being influenced by the world around me, that would've been pretty cool, but millennials had endless outside forces that we were held to quite harshly, and if you made it through thinking you were special, it seemed more like the exception than the rule. Sports were insanely competitive, spots in colleges were limited, jobs afterward were scarce, and quantifiable excellence was demanded of those who wanted the chance to be successful. When I was school-age, it was hard for me to believe in the things I was praised for at home if they weren't reinforced in the outside world. I existed somewhere between desperately wanting to be Mary Tyler Moore and wondering if my potential was so low it would make Moore sense to try and marry a guy named Tyler to dodge the workforce altogether.

The truth is, there is not a human on this planet who is void of talent, who has no gifts. And that strategy of labeling kids as "talented and gifted" or not in elementary school was fucked up. We just aren't always existing in the context that allows us to feel that way, and it takes time to figure out where you can shine. But that requires starting and stopping, and I think we put way too much stock in "never give up" clichés. Looking through my memory box, I was defined just as much by the things I quit as the things I did. I think the irony is that in order to never give up on yourself, it actually requires you to give up a lot of things that aren't working for you, but it's daunting to be objectively labeled as a "quitter." So I wanted to share my story, not as a talented and gifted genius, but rather a person who embodies three traits you may not traditionally correlate with success: a habitual quitter, a B student, and a nineties version of an iPad kid. A sensitive soul like me would have crumbled if my parents demanded excellence in areas that didn't come as naturally to me, and I'm grateful they didn't ignore my gifts just because they were outside of what the school system praised.

I also hypothesize that a lack of outside validation scholastically is what gave me the audacity to put myself on the air as a nonfamous person. If someone else had hired me as the talent, I would have been praised for getting a dream job, for earning it. But to say that you think you're talented in the absence of some kind of proof makes people uncomfortable. But ever since I wasn't labeled as "talented" in fourth grade, I've had to believe I possessed it even if I had no formal proof, and believing I could start a company, write a book, and host a podcast was no different. In more concrete fields, education, training, and credibility absolutely matter, but in creative jobs, qualifications aren't as clear-cut, and quality is highly subjective, which means you might have a shot. The "best" doesn't really exist in my job, and a lot of people have trouble navigating subjectivity in the absence of more formal validation, but it doesn't really bother me. On most days.

When I became an entrepreneur and went to networking events, it occurred to me that I was around many high achievers, straight-A students, Ivy League–goers, and people who had been provided institutional validation at every turn. They were in these positions of power, with full jurisdiction over their careers, but without someone else telling them they were important, they didn't believe it. A lack of accolades can get me down, too, but doesn't compromise my identity; it was the first time I wondered if my inability to place my self-worth in institutionalized metrics was actually healthy. The thing about being your own boss is that no one else is going to tell you that you're doing a good job, and I've watched a lot of people suffer as a result. I think I've managed to stay afloat in self-employment because I find the effort gratifying, I'm confident in my ability to figure things out, and I know if it doesn't work out, I'll find something else. I always do.

I'm really proud of my job and my career, even though I don't really have much to point to that defines its success to the outside world. I never got on thirty-under-thirty lists, I still don't have any formal industry recognition or accolades for my podcast or books. I don't have a top-ten podcast, I don't get nominated for industry awards, and my following has grown at a snail's pace. I have chosen not to be a part of a third-party ad or podcast network, even though to some people, my being independent makes my show lack credibility. But those things all have to do with everyone else. To me, a job done well enough is a job well done. My podcast has exceeded my wildest dreams, so it's an A in my book, but relative to how success is defined in the industry, it's more like a B. Well, a B There in Five. And that's okay. While I cared about working hard and doing well, I never needed the A, I needed the eighty-seven, and I believe it made all the difference.

10

The Parent Trap

If you've been around for a minute, you know I'm not the most maternal gal in town. One time I passed Home Depot with my neighbor Mrs. G, and upon reading the signs for the store's departments, asked her, "What kind of parents drop off their kids at the Home Depot nursery??" I'd argue it's maternal in nature to worry that there was a baby nursery near all those power tools, but really it just taught me I know nothing about babies. Or houseplants, apparently. Another time, I was helping with my sister's kindergarten class, and she asked me to tell the class they needed to pack up. I asked them to please "consolidate their belongings" and was surprised when no one took my direction. "Katie, they're five," she said. Apparently, these were not words they were familiar with, which is fair, but I don't know. It's like, get a thesaurus, Skyler?

There were other early signs, like my tendency to secretly favor the lavish lifestyles of nineties stepmom villains like Meredith Blake from *The Parent Trap* or Clarice Kensington from *It Takes Two*. I remember firmly nodding when hearing Meredith Blake say, "Being young and beautiful isn't a crime, you know" as if I was at church, hoping that the blood of Christ would be a Parker Knoll vintage. Even though I had the utmost respect for Elizabeth James and her ability to make me genuinely consider wearing a top hat with my wedding veil, I was oddly drawn to Meredith as a high-powered publicist with a fierce-as-hell hat collection and a license to wed a wealthy wine connoisseur. It was unpopular at sleepovers to say you felt bad she had to sleep in the middle of a lake on an air mattress all alone, but I'm sorry, hating your future stepmom is one thing; sending her out onto the lake on an air mattress after she took a sleeping pill is a true-crime podcast waiting to happen. I'm just saying, if Keith Morrison narrated that camping trip, we'd all see that the nefarious activities performed by the twins are a little less Disney and a little more *Dateline.*

I will say, as a superfan, it bothers me I did not realize until this past summer that my number-one favorite parents from the nineties were *such bad parents.* I firmly believe we were too intoxicated with their good looks and unmatched taste in interiors to see the situation for what it was: an ill-advised custody agreement to separate (and conceal the identity of!) their identical twins from each other, for no reason other than to maintain their lavish lifestyles an ocean apart. Chessy's penchant for khakis and denim button-downs suddenly makes so much sense. How's one expected to make time for shopping in the midst of your employer's gag order requiring you to lie to a child about their transatlantic parent who *chose* not to be in their life and who is also harboring their secret identical-twin sibling? Don't even get me started that neither of them noticed the *one* child they could be *bothered* to parent didn't even return home from camp!! It's still one of my favorite movies ever, but if we can't acknowledge they are the worst parents of all time, take me to the lakes where all the poets (and Meredith Blake almost) went to die, I don't belong.

As I've been writing this book, I'm very much in a life phase where the terms of trying to become a parent have me feeling, appropriately, quite trapped. Between two ways I feel about having kids, between managing my expectations and fleeting hopefulness. Between trying to live my life and "Enjoy it while you can!" as all new moms tell me to do while struggling to enjoy measuring time in between negative pregnancy tests, reminding me that I'm not sure becoming a mom is even up to me. And if it is, I fear my instincts won't kick in. As time goes on, I have to come to terms with the fact I'll never have the natural edge of a Hallie, the refinement of an Annie, or the grace to pull off a neutral skirt suit after getting drunk on a plane like an Elizabeth James. If I'm being honest, I've always known deep down I'm more of a Meredith Blake.

I don't mean I fit the mold for a nineties gold-digger trope; I think her archetype represents what we're supposed to believe when we see a woman who likes to work, hates to hike, wants to make money, and lacks experience with kids. She must be a curmudgeon, a person too distanced from their childlike spirit to be the mothering type. I've waited years to wake up one morning and *Wish Upon a Star*–style switch bodies with a version of me that's ready and nurturing in all the ways I prayed I'd eventually grow into. Approaching my midthirties as I write this, I can tell you, I still haven't felt a moment as simple as flipping a switch, but what I learned along the way was more helpful and reliable than what the clichés promised.

I've spent the past couple of years thinking about how our whole lives, young women are spoken to about marriage and babies like it's an inevitable, guaranteed thing. In many ways, society treats our lives leading up to the point where you get married kind of like a pregame. As if the girlish ways you pass your time and get ready are just efforts to make you eligible to be a bride once you go out-out into the world, leading up to a main event—the way we think of our future identities in the context of being a mom and having kids. When I was the age of those kids whose belongings remained unconsolidated, I was just starting to hear the love-marriage-baby-carriage playground song (you know the one), its primary goal being to embarrass you about having a crush. Its secondary goal is to remind you of your inevitable romantic trajectory. While I don't think this playground folklore was necessarily designed to push an agenda, I think its ubiquity and oversimplification proves how the expectations, order, and terms of marriage and motherhood are embedded into our psyche from a very young age. The nursery rhymes and fairy tales and general fanfare surrounding your wedding and babies start so early, it's less of an option you learn about than it is the framing for what you build your life around.

But when you get into your twenties and thirties, there's often a moment everyone realizes the love-marriage-baby-carriage pipeline (LMBCP) is not as simple and straightforward as you thought, and when the LMBCP bursts at any phase, it can feel like ground zero. While it's a common human experience to navigate departures from our expectations, society often holds women to a different standard, assigning such a high value to our purpose and fulfillment as wives and mothers that it leaves little room for nuance as to why these things may not be 1. desired or 2. guaranteed. Beyond that, I've noticed that when women write into my show about a pipeline burst in the category of love, marriage, or babes in a baby carriage, they almost always feel the need to clarify they are overreacting. They likely say this because they constantly hear people judging women's responses to challenges in their personal lives as if they're a marker of emotional fragility. Bad dates, breakups, divorces, fertility issues . . . these things happen. But for women in their twenties and thirties, this underlying tension involves something more than simply reconciling reality with our expectations. At a point, your personal life feels like less a function of your choices be-cause you're forced to navigate the role time plays for women in having options. Compounded with millennial women being the first genera-tion to share and compare milestones in real time via social media, it's easy to feel constantly disappointed or, worse, ashamed for not living up to timing that's in alignment with this insanely deeply ingrained order of operations, a PEMDAS for women, if you will.

Not to drag My Dear Aunt Sally into this (maybe I am a woman in STEM?), but digital PEMDAS is the best way I can describe the cadence of many millennial women's social-media bios that I've marveled at over the years. I *love* a mom blogger ° O °—they're my modern form of celebrity, and I watch their behavior like I used to watch popular upperclasswomen to serve as a proxy for what life is like in a phase I'm not in yet and am desperate to better understand. And if you read the "about me" section on a lot of popular millennial bloggers' platforms, I think it says a lot about how we project our identities out onto the world. More often than not, it reads something like "Wife [bride emoji]. Mom [kids emoji]." And then, if I'm lucky, a vague religious signifier like "Kingdom Chaser" makes me hit FOLLOW faster than I used to hit on members of the praise band. Eventually, you'll get to why they're there: if it's a public figure, they list their job, e.g., entrepreneur, blogger, influencer, etc. Personal accounts often detail a hobby, interest, community, or cause they frequently engage with on their account. Digital PEMDAS represents an implied order of operations that leads with marital or maternal status before getting to anything central to one's own identity.

Since millennials are a generation marked by being behind and being online, digital PEMDAS perfectly illustrates how we straddle the two worlds I keep talking about, the traditional values we held growing up versus the opportunities that greeted us once we did. Here we are, on a landing page that represents strides in technology, and thus, strides for opportunities for women, but still first self-identifying on those pages as wife and mom before we get to ourselves. This is up to the individual; it's not that there's anything wrong with it. These preconceived roles have been around ever since God first canceled a woman for eating.

But we've come a long way since Eve, and I find it interesting that we're modern enough for it to be normal to create a digital destination that's meant to glorify ourselves, yet we still use it to broadcast the PEMDAS of our lifelong conditioning: that who we are is first defined by our relationship to somebody else.

I don't mean that your career is the most important thing. Or that being a parent can't be the most important thing! Or if your job is a stay-at-home parent, that's not how you should identify. I'm the product of a mom who stayed home and did so much for me, and I want to scream anytime I hear this role undermined; unpaid domestic labor is systematically undervalued and often treated with a frustrating level of invisibility. I am a wife and hope to have kids, and I might stay at home; who knows. I'm a weird contradiction of someone who pursues and values traditions but tries to reject the parts that are oppressive, unfair, or unnecessary, because we can adapt things to who we are, not to who we feel like we have to be. But I can only speak from my vantage point; my digital PEMDAS could be playing musical chairs as we speak. When you're a woman who wants these things, and ultimately learns that wife and mom are more a function of your chances than choices, it can be really challenging to see other people's lives so aligned with the LMBCP you always believed in but can't find. If they choose to lead with those things, are they genuinely the most fulfilling? Or is that what we're supposed to believe should come first?

I realized that when I used to imagine my future, I just thought post-K–12; I'd go to college, hopefully, get a good job, have great friends, buy a house, find a partner, and have kids. But then what? I never imagined having any other life; my expectations for myself went up to my midthirties, but then, my ability to envision what I wanted for myself just stopped; I guess assuming I'd be preoccupied with having a family after I woke up with an all-consuming desire. Two years into trying, no kids, one pregnancy loss, and some frozen embryos later, I'm wondering where I fit in all of this if my goal was to be someone's wife and someone's mom, but I can't fulfill one of those roles.

I think my interest in those who primarily ground their identity in being a wife or mother has always fascinated me because it implies a level of certainty I envy, specifically about knowing you're meant to be a mother. I struggled with knowing if I wanted kids or not for the longest time, and I think that my desire was made more apparent by difficulty and grief, though I don't recommend that route to self-discovery. Sometimes we expect to be all in or all out, but you can't approach every decision with 100 percent certainty. How can you possibly know something is right for you that you haven't experienced before? Ultimately, the boss babe in me just tries to get to 51 percent majority stake in feeling a little more one way than the other for me to be able to move forward. This is different for everyone: sometimes uncertainty is a telling sign of something you don't want; for me, it's usually a function of me stalling or aimlessly weighing opportunity costs. I always hear people say, "If it's not a hell yes, it's a hell no," but I'm not blessed with this level of decisiveness. Or enthusiasm, for that matter. Even wedding dress shopping for me was like, "Say 'I guess' to the dress."

I tortured myself for years thinking that the type of person I was, with qualities like my inner Meredith Blake or the fact I'm always running late, made me not right for motherhood, ignoring that the type of person who is right for motherhood is one who will love, support, and prioritize their children, and I knew I would do that. But for some reason, I convinced myself that because I wasn't super drawn to other people's children (it's the sticky fingers for me), wanted to prioritize my career, and wished I had more time to figure it all out meant there was something wrong with me. While I'm not that into other people's kids, I couldn't love my nephews and niece more, and they are the ones who made it impossible to ignore that I have it in me somewhere, along with my dog, Tugboat. I also love my husband too much not to delight in the idea of him as a father, and as much as I wasn't sure if I wanted babies in general, something shifted when I wanted his. Not gonna lie; I am kind of curious about what a miniversion of me could do with his bone structure and ability to do mental math.

Since expressing these fears aloud on the podcast, countless listeners have reassured me it's okay to not wake up with an overwhelming urge, taught me there's no one-size-fits-all ideal, and pointed out how I just see well-performing-mom content online and assume that's the norm. They've reminded me parenting is an ever-changing role, and this thought was a game changer for me. Maybe I'm not as into pregnancy and young babies, but that doesn't represent a person's entire life—that's just one phase. Regardless of age, I'm deeply drawn to the idea of being someone's mom for the long haul. It's not just about wanting a kid—more importantly, I want to be a parent, to raise a decent human, and to provide for them what my parents gave me. To me, that's what matters more than baby fever. At least I hope. And maybe it wouldn't hurt to have someone young and fun to go to brunch with when I'm old.

Aside from that, part of this trap is feeling like as a millennial woman, I've had more opportunities than generations before me in pursuing personal and professional development, regardless of my future choices related to parenting. I exercised them, in my career, lifestyle choices, the city I chose to live in, and in my journey to self-acceptance. For a while, the limit did not exist. But the further I got into my thirties, something switched. It was like I had all the time in the world until I didn't; suddenly, time was the thing I needed the most and the one thing working against me. I thought I was doing the right thing taking my time; it was what I needed to find peace in picturing myself as a parent. And I got there, only to realize that my human 3D printer never cared about my thoughtful weighing of options or hot takes about if I'm a Chessy or an Elizabeth James or a Meredith Blake. "But I've been to therapy!" I cry out to my dwindling AMH levels, wishing it mattered more to my bloodwork that I did the inner work. Amidst my nitpicking, I almost forgot my clock was ticking, and the reality that no matter what, I'd ultimately be trapped in the facts of (creating) life: time is a finite resource and the one thing we can't control. And I forget this, time and time again, as the role of time shape-shifts with each phase of this process. When I was deciding if I wanted kids, I wanted more of it, when I was trying to have a kid, I wanted to freeze it, and when I experienced loss, I begged for it to pass by more quickly.

Needless to say, for me, motherhood has always been a sore subject. But recently, I've learned pregnancy loss is more like an open wound. Experiencing that changed a lot for me. It's an open wound with the most vulnerable scab, forced to constantly replenish its surface-level protection as it's picked at daily, not by you, but inadvertently by other people's joy. This makes it difficult to be honest about your pain; you feel like a monster making other people's pregnancy announcements, baby showers, gender reveals, and sonograms about you. The thing is, on most days, it's fine, it will scab. But the optics of healing can incorrectly signal those around you the worst is behind you, as it usually would be with the passage of time.

However, now I know time is perhaps the least helpful variable, only serving to remind you of the milestones you would've hit, the trimesters you would've completed, and the date your life would have otherwise changed. After my loss, I noticed so many things I'd physiologically react to that I would have never noticed before, or would have thought was my choice to be affected by. I've never experienced a ping to my stomach so swift and involuntary, brought about by the most innocuous of maternal run-ins. At times I wondered if someone ordered a voodoo doll of me off Etsy and started using cute neighborhood women with strollers at every turn to pierce through my very being. Something about the lottery of who does or doesn't have difficulty rearing children seems uniquely unfair in ways I struggle to articulate. Maybe I'm mad because my impression in sex ed was that it was so easy to get pregnant; I'd get knocked up the second I found myself basking in the chlorine musk of a hot tub near a member of the male species. I assumed this scenario was such an aphrodisiac, it would be a good backup plan as a way to lure a suitor. You know what they say, maybe she's born with it, maybe it's hot-tub chlorine.

I remember having a poignant moment upon going to HomeGoods (the place where I replenish good feelings) after it happened. As I stood there in line, I realized it was the same line I'd stood in only weeks prior when I was buying supplies to tell my husband I was finally pregnant. In my basket was a hideous #1 DAD mug, which was all I could find, along with a proper button-down shirt for Tugboat, so he could accompany me to tell Dad the news on Father's Day. Sidenote: Even though I go there for the good feelings, I did not realize until this moment that my only two core memories from this pregnancy took place at HomeGoods. Clearly, in my version of the simulation, we bookend our milestones a stone's throw from stone-bowl centerpieces.

But there I was, soon after, therapizing my loss with the official HomeGoods "I've had a rough week" starter pack: private-label three-wick candles in off-season autumnal scents, a woven basket that I swear will "really tie the room together," an ambiguous tray that will later serve as a catchall for loose change, earring backs, and my unresolved feelings. Maybe I took a hard left at the aisle entirely lined with twigs to feel the rush of a red sticker and buy two mismatched wineglasses because I keep telling myself I'm going to get into colored glassware. I undoubtedly pass the shocking, I mean shocking, number of tufted ottomans they sell that literally never get discounted, spiraling about the volume of crap that is manufactured in this life, wondering if the overproduction of durable goods, not unlike the 1930s, could contribute to a modern Great Depression. Only to realize that I'm spending a disproportionate amount of time and thought in this HomeGoods because I'm amidst my own not-so-great depression. Without a doubt, once I've scoped some tchotchkes for a new tablescape, I'll have picked up a rogue bag of veggie chips or off-brand sour worms, an important final step. While they are near inedible, I like to have a snack on the way home, forever confusing low blood sugar for what is most likely light-headedness from candle sniffing. When it comes to the 'Goods, I've got it bad.

The moment that felt make or break, far more than designing my latest tablescape, was watching a mother smile at her child in a stroller while I was standing in line. That's it. She literally was just existing, doing the most common of behaviors. And for the first time, I understood a sensation that I would've previously misrepresented as a choice or perhaps a level of compartmentalization I could've achieved. It took everything in me not to sob into a nearby I DON'T WANNA TACO BOUT IT hand towel, not because I was jealous or even triggered about my own experience. In fact, there was no ability to discern even what I was reacting to; I just felt what I can best describe as a gut punch, a subterranean ping to my spirit that I did not want nor even knowingly lean into. It had nothing to do with the woman and everything to do with how the disappointment buries itself so far down, I don't always remember it's there.

I guess what I'm saying is that in this HomeGoods, I realized two things: First, I don't think I understood that the feelings of unfairness about who has children, despite being deeply unproductive and unpreventable, aren't a choice as much as a reflex. It's not that I'm not happy for people; it's just a feeling you get in your stomach I can only describe as an emotional response with a direct line to my soul that my body reacts to before my mind is patched through. I'm laughing as I read back that sentence, as I'm working overtime to basically describe being triggered, but then I would've had to issue a trigger warning for a millennial saying they're triggered, which I've found is ironically the most triggering behavior for those on the front lines of generational wars raging against hypersensitive youths.

Here's the thing: that feeling of unfairness, that fleeting tendency to compare, despite how hard you avoid it, is human. And it happens in all phases of the LMBCP, from dating to engagements, weddings, and beyond. No one can prepare you for the period of time in your mid- to late twenties when your social life is literally only other people's milestones. I used to get such anxiety about going to social functions because people would harp on the fact we had been dating for five years and weren't engaged. But we were so young! He was in grad school, and as one does, I started a rug empire. We were growing in parallel and not rushing things, yet I was looked at with sad eyes like I must be a woman pining for his commitment. It's a frustrating and familiar situation for many of us, feeling like you're defending your lack of personal life news while celebrating someone else's. The reality is, in your twenties and thirties, both social media and our social lives become minefields for coming across other people's milestones. And I'm careful to criticize them as they launch toward my glass house because you know damn well when they happen to me, I'll post about it, too.

While we can be our own worst enemies in believing the lie of LMBCP (that these things are fully within our control), this oversimplification is reinforced by our social interactions constantly. The joke is that the part that is within your control—the ability to decide that you don't want to get married or have kids—is perhaps the more challenging situation to socially navigate. I watch people speak to my friends who are child-free by choice like they are ill-equipped to predict the needs of their future selves, and I firmly believe that choosing to not have children should be viewed as an equally viable option; it's one that I seriously considered and we should commend people who know themselves well enough to make that call.

When I was considering whether or not to have children, I recall conversations being a game of hopscotch between "What if you change your mind?" and "Who will take care of you when you're older?" The latter was asked of me once at a wedding cocktail hour by a new mom when I expressed my indecision about children during that time in my life. As she walked away to pump and expressed her frustration having to do so, I had a realization. She was nursing her child, I was nursing the bride's signature cocktail I waited eleven minutes for (should we maybe not do elaborate eight-ingredient mixed drinks at functions with long lines and attendees arriving at once? j/w), and between these two different types of nursing, the interrogation about nursing homes had nothing to do with me. We were in fundamentally different life phases, and she was probably struggling, too. I wondered if her desire to justify her choices in a challenging phase of motherhood (which she was told would be magical) speaks to the same disconnect in identity and fulfillment I was experiencing. Even if you follow the road much traveled, when your partner or kids don't fulfill you in the ways you thought they would, it can be equally as challenging.

Whether you want to get married and/or have babies or don't, the mere absence of these two things can make everything you've accomplished suddenly feel sidelined for the conversation starters, the pleasantries exchanged at other people's milestones where everyone asks you who you're dating, then when you're getting engaged, married, or having kids. These questions are usually well-intentioned, but the deeper issue is how intertwined our personal lives are with our identities. When you are spoken to about this pipeline your whole life, and social situations reinforce its false simplicity, you feel crazy for all the ways your life falls short of those expectations. When you plan your future around an identity of who you are to other people, then experience a great deal of complexity in acquiring those people to fulfill this alleged identity, it can be disorienting. Speaking to the love-and-marriage piece, it's so incredibly difficult to go on a good date, much less find yourself an ideal life partner. We should be applauding single people for having the courage to leave relationships that aren't right for them. We should be marveling at their resilience in the event it wasn't their choice. Making the right decision for yourself time and time again is a marker of strength and self-worth that gets unfairly branded as being "*still* single," a title nobody should be reduced to outside of a W-2; not spending your whole life in a shitty relationship is a "W" to me.

Pursuing motherhood ended up being my personal choice, but to be clear, it's not what I think is right or necessary for others, nor something anyone needs to be fulfilled. The biggest thing I want to get across, before going further into my era of where I met more of my desire in experiencing grief and loss, is that part of the problem is there is too much emphasis placed on *when* we become wives and mothers, and not enough dialogue about how very beautiful your life can be, regardless of how whens turn into ifs. In my case, I simply didn't understand before what it felt like being deep in the involuntary ifs, and wanted to share some experiences that made Meredith Blake's lizard-in-mouth moment seem among life's least shocking.

Aside from my instinct for comparison, there was a second, slightly sadder moment I had at HomeGoods that day. The bigger pipeline burst when I realized this could be a long road ahead. When I saw the woman smile at her child, I realized at that moment that my moment, when I'd be able to smile at my own kid at a HomeGoods, felt so very far away, with my ability to successfully carry a child very much in question. Beyond that, now when I see babies out and about, I understand the mental chaos that trying to conceive and pregnancy loss leave you with. I cycle through questions I never used to as I look at other women having uncomplicated interactions with their children, standing there wondering if they know what an actual miracle it is for everything to come together in order to have a healthy baby. Does she sit there and think to herself, "I can't believe I was able to get pregnant, stay pregnant, make it through the scans and testing, carry it to term healthily, and deliver it safely"? I'm sure she does, because that's all I think about. I write this misty-eyed and imagine myself asking every step of the way, never relishing in the excitement, just wanting to know if we're *in the clear yet? Good.*

Long story short, the parent trap I've fallen into is waiting too long to wake up and feel maternal, believing if/when I'd have a child would be my decision, only to have a hard time moving forward while grieving a pregnancy outcome that was never my choice to make. But this year, another variable was added, when I had the horrific realization that if it happens again, uneducated legislators could be the ones to make a decision that affects my survival.

I hesitate to share details (because again, I hate to bring the room down), but what I've learned is that for all the ways I could keep quiet to spare people discomfort, I'm also forgoing an opportunity to say something to spare people from a life-threatening situation. I had an ectopic pregnancy (a fetus implanted outside of my uterus that would have never survived, only killed me), which I was told only affects 1 percent of pregnancies. Wish I could find some Occupy Wall Street merch. Fuck the 1 percent, indeed. It was my first and only pregnancy and culminated in a traumatizing and painful ER visit where a desperately wanted pregnancy turned out to not only be unviable, but I also had to choose how to remove it from my body to save my own life.

Following the 2022 overturning of Roe v. Wade, the intervention of nonmedical professionals in my course of treatment could've killed me, as doctors now need to jump through hoops to protect their licenses and minimize liability prior to taking action in situations that can be quite urgent. A hospital's religious affiliation and now a state's laws affect the available treatment options for ectopics, and while most have exceptions for saving a mother's life, there's a level of subjectivity that can make providers needlessly put women at risk of further pain, infection, blood loss, and/or death to prove they're what I like to say "super almost dead" in order to intervene. I use harsh language because that's how it feels to be on the receiving end; like you're not a person with feelings and a pulse or a body you deserve autonomy over. Just a faceless, nameless body they have to push as close to death as possible to be allowed to act in your best interest. Not because it's necessary, but because politicians use abortion laws as a lightning-rod issue to galvanize voters at the expense of pregnant people's lives, writing legislation without a medical background that medical experts now have to prioritize above their own expertise. The medication I was injected with (methotrexate) to terminate the pregnancy to prevent inevitable rupture and internal bleeding is also used for abortions (among other things, like treatment of rheumatoid arthritis), and even though in many cases it's the safer, less invasive alternative to resolving an ectopic (the other is surgery), many have written to me that in their states, providers aren't offering this option because the strict abortion laws make it too murky to administer the medication and prove it was for lifesaving purposes.

While resolving ectopic pregnancies tends to be widely agreed upon as a necessary lifesaving intervention, for courses of treatment involving miscarriages, the same situation applies, where the procedures for abortions are identical to those involved with the medical intervention of some miscarriages, like a D&C or D&E. Most women I've spoken to who formerly were or currently are opposed to pro-choice arguments seem to agree about the danger this poses to pregnant people experiencing complications or miscarriages and that the policies need to be more nuanced, but are hesitant to align with the label. I'm not even trying to make a political statement when I say this, but unfortunately, it's become one, and it's so important to remember this isn't all that complicated.

I think we need to take a step back from the political element now and again to understand that advocacy for choice isn't just about who gets elected, it's about who lives or dies. Having a choice allows people like me not to have to die because of delays in determining which course of treatment will minimize provider liability; by that time, my tube may have burst, causing me to hemorrhage. It also allows any woman you know who has been pregnant or miscarried, since up to one in four pregnancies result in miscarriage, not to have treatments withheld that could save their life or at least minimize the additional physical and emotional pain that would arise from allowing preventable suffering to escalate when they are already amidst one of the most traumatizing days of their life.[8] Having choices allows for decisions to be made between individuals and their medical providers, where they've always belonged, and most importantly, having choices allows for true equality; our basic freedoms rely on our ability to control our reproductive health, and this extends beyond our personal freedoms and plays a major role in racial and economic justice.

I may not say all of this the right way. I'm having to gloss over so much and I know the vocabulary and terminology evolves for how to approach this issue compassionately and correctly, so if a lot of my words fade into irrelevance or come across with insensitivity at some point in time, I genuinely apologize. But the point I want to get across most of all is this: to me, if any part of you believes in protecting people in circumstances like I've mentioned, and if you see the gray areas and the need for exceptions, that is a pro-choice stance. Being pro-choice isn't an extremist position, it simply allows for nuance. Advocates like me are painted as people who want to harm innocent lives, but it's the opposite. I want to care for the precious lives on this earth and ask people to have empathy for the insurmountable challenges like the ones I've detailed that people go through in bringing life here, and hopefully find the humility to admit that we cannot possibly know what is best for everyone and should not be making choices for them.

---

8. https://www.ncbi.nlm.nih.gov/books/NBK532992/

These nuances are one of the many things I didn't know about the process until I experienced it, and I don't necessarily blame people for not understanding. I'm sharing this as a Meredith Blake who genuinely did not even know how to talk to people about children or motherhood before attempting to become a mom myself. I continue to marvel at the endless complexities that make us all operate from such drastically different vantage points, as the topic's sensitivity makes it especially hard to find common ground.

I also don't blame people for not knowing how to talk to people like me, because while I now understand the minefield of milestones a bit better, I still struggle with the tiptoeing that goes on around me when people share their pregnancy news. I fear the tiptoeing does less to preserve my emotional comfort and more to contribute to the bigger problem we have as women: trying to make as little noise as possible. The thing is, there are endless outcomes when it comes to the topic of motherhood. From speculating if you want kids, to being child-free by choice (or not), and throughout the process of trying, conceiving, carrying, birthing, and raising, and any losses we share along the way, I think we have to embrace the uniqueness of pregnancy-related conversations. When a topic sits at the intersection of joy and heartbreak, it's inherently confusing to navigate. My point is that it's rarely personal; rather, it's so individualized that we have to acknowledge the limitations of our ability to understand the specifics and embrace the variability with as much empathy as possible. I like to think there is space for all celebrations and conversations, and it can be nerve-wracking to put this out there when you yourself don't have kids yet, but it doesn't make the process of trying any less valid and consuming.

Several months have passed since I wrote the first draft of this essay; it was one I felt strongly about including, and it all still holds up. I just wanted to say hi from still being deep in my ifs, just now in a new way. As I wrote the rest of this book, I ended up undergoing two egg-retrieval cycles (half of the IVF process), for reasons that are medical- and mental health–related (e.g., bypassing tubes for ectopic risks, issues with egg quality, anxiety about passage of time). Even though the details of our personal choices don't require justification, I share because I've learned a lot; going in, I thought it would be a mostly emotional process for me, and it was. It sure as hell wasn't my first choice, and having to do it twice felt like the end of the world. But coming out of it, I saw it for what it was medically, and I wanted to share this quick perspective about how we frame fertility treatments. To me, pursuing it was medical intervention for my reproductive system not working as it should (like I would for my digestive system, respiratory system, or any other part of my body that I'd like to optimally operate). There's a lot of shame and stigma women can feel, and while I most certainly acknowledge it not being ideal (and have to acknowledge the privilege of being able to swing it financially, and living in a state where coverage exists), I think the more shocking thing is to assume you don't have the right to pursue medical answers or assistance. As if it's selfish, after twenty-plus years of periods and pain and women's issues and not trying to get pregnant, to spend a couple years trying to get the human 3D printer working as I was promised.

And yet, it's just one of many options a person may choose; I fully believe there are many equally valid paths to parenthood, be it IVF, surrogacy, donation, adoption, marrying a partner with children, or otherwise. This worked for our circumstances, and to me, it's not a matter of what it means about me as a woman or wife, or of abstract pride; it was a medical path pursued that, to be fair, comes with a lot of emotion, which you should honor. But for me, feeling the *slightest* bit of control over the out-of-control process of trying to conceive felt like it net out in a place that was proactive, and (on good days) almost empowering, relative to how I felt about the other side, where you're floundering in fertility unknowns, dealing with something undiagnosed and under-researched.

On most days, it was a shit ton of needles, but that part didn't end up bothering me as much as I thought: they were small, Botox vibes, not so bad with ice. And I laughed when I could, trying to share on-line, share with friends in real life, inviting them over to show them the meds I put in a nineties Caboodle. But the biggest LOL I had was when I realized I planned and God laughed once again, and Amelia Bedelia of the skies took me a little too seriously when I wrote earlier in the essay that I felt like a voodoo doll, as mere months later, I looked in the mirror and was literally turned into a human one, stuck with needles on the daily, right in the spot where these issues first emotionally stung.

I just wish someone would've told me not to be so scared, and that even though outcomes vary, it might be okay. Horror stories exist, but so do positive ones. And even in the disappointments (like the first round, learning I wasn't the Pez-like egg machine I secretly hoped I was), I learned so much about my body. I say this as a person who has spent the last two years having to involuntarily speed through my perceptions of not options A and B, but A–Z in terms of what I thought I'd consider and how far I've departed from what I imagined this would look like for me. I feel like I'm in the part of the spreadsheet where the column letters repeat after Z and I'm just kind of tired of the clunky horizontal scrolling. Point being, I'm surprised I'm here, but I also want to make sure to tell you I'm okay with it. This process simply isn't straightfor-ward for a lot of people, and that's okay, too. Getting testing done, ex-ploring options, and learning how to be my own advocate has been the only empowering part of this process, and it was the part I avoided the most. I wish I did it sooner, honestly. I was so scared of looking at options, but to me, they ultimately represented a rare sigh of relief in feeling like there might be a positive outcome when I felt furthest in the Trap.

I wish I had more wisdom to provide, or could provide you with an arc that reassures you I've got it all figured out. Even though I've got options, and am grateful to have some embryos on ice after a couple tries, I'm still deep in my ifs, without a definitive outcome, planning to finish IVF and hope for the best sometime after finishing this book.

Over the course of the past year, the focus shifted elsewhere as options opened, and the stomach pings got better, but didn't go away. Although it's hard for me to tease out my grief from an inconvenient constant trigger I saw: the number twenty-two. I don't know if anyone else feels haunted by due-date numbers, but I sure was, and let me tell you, what a triggering year 2022 was with a due date of 2.22.22. I've had to come 2 terms with the fact that it may forever make me feel a little trapped, feeling Too tied by this elusive number two. When I was shopping around last New Year's, I wanted to cry out, "Are you there, God? It's me, at Target. Weeping in aisle nine over seeing so many New Year's decorations for 2022. Is this going to go on all year?"

Boy, did it ever. I still think about the pings when Taylor Swift's song "22" was ruined, Kylie Jenner's baby was born on 2.2.22, and all the talk of her being so lucky with "angel numbers" (*sob*), cursing every check I had to sign and date. It felt like too much at times, especially when feeling overwhelmed starting IVF, thinking of the kid I already would have had by now, then having to do it twice. I feel pathetic for admitting this; it's not like I'm a numerology enthusiast—it's just another example of a thing I would have never known about loss. Maybe I'll grow out of it, but not today.

I also feel childish for other reasons, not only because I felt the need to share my journey to parenthood through a long, semi-irrelevant *Parent Trap* parallel, but also because I'm actually accompanied by a special guest as I write this, my motherhood muse: a stuffed bunny named Cuppy that I'm likely too old to treasure as much as I do. Cuppy, Hallie's undercelebrated stuffed bunny mascot from *The Parent Trap,* was sent to me by my brother's wife, Emily, whom I consider a sister more than an in-law. She sent it as a congratulations, and as a nod to one of our favorite films; we've always bonded over our Nancy Meyers superfandom.

The thing that's more notable about Cuppy is that she sent it when I told her I was pregnant, and it happened to arrive when I wasn't anymore. When I informed her of the loss, she urged me not to check my mail, likely in fear the gift would upset me. But I ran to the mail room and sobbed with gratitude as I opened up my very own Cuppy she found on eBay from the Disney Store in the late nineties, a store that was my overpriced-stuffed-animal dream (and most parents' markup nightmare). Cuppy is pristine, tag encased in plastic, like it's a Princess Di Beanie Baby, but to me, it's far more valuable. It remains one of my most prized possessions, not only because I assume this means she thinks I'm *such* a Hallie, but also because it's the only thing I have to prove that the experience was real.

Accepting this gift validated that this baby is still part of my existence, of my story, despite never having its own time on earth, and deserves to be honored all the same. It meant a lot to me, and I say that to remind people that sometimes the best way to support someone isn't to ignore their pain. I've learned it means the world to me to be allowed to have my pain exist alongside others' joy, concern, or heartbreak. Like that breezy bumper sticker I once wanted to replace my Jesus fish to prove I was an evolved progressive babe, all of these things can coexist. Over the past year, Cuppy's companionship has symbolized the residency I've established in between my own childlike vulnerabilities and my desire to have a child of my own, two things I'm also trying to allow to coexist as well. Sometimes it's there to comfort me, sometimes I take comfort in that I'll get to pass it down one day, and sometimes it reminds me to talk about these confusing feelings as much as I can, if only to make other women feel like they have a Hallie or Annie with them in this phase of life that can feel like an isolation cabin in its own right. I'll bring the peanut butter and Oreos, you bring the squad of adolescent gamblers and an ear-piercing apple.

In conclusion, there is one thing I know to be true: no matter what, at some point, we've all had (or will have) our pipelines burst in a way that feels incredibly destabilizing as our life drifts further from our expectations. Many of us find ourselves in our own parent trap, stuck inside the maze of the inevitable turns life takes, and if you're like me and feeling trapped inside indecision or the long road of infertility, I see you, and I'm still in the thick of it, too. By the time this book comes out, I have no idea where I'll be. The nursery rhymes neglect to acknowledge the many different paths, orders, and outcomes that exist within the topics of love, marriage, and baby carriages. Most notably, they miss the reality of many people's lives being beautifully fulfilled, not because of those things, but by your life and identity, so it's not defined by the absence of one or more of those things we cannot control. I'm still working on it. The one change I've made is to ask people about their hobbies, families, travels, jobs, hopes, dreams, or anything other than who they are to someone else. I know those questions come from a good place, but it's important to remember that someone's position in the LMBCP involves both their choices and chances, and both situations are worthy of our respect and empathy. Whether your fulfillment of the desired milestone falls short, or a milestone falls short of fulfilling your desires, we've all been bamboozled by this playground song and likely trapped by our own expectations at some point or another.

However, there is good news that helps me on days when I'm battling my rivalry with seeing twos or struggling with my baby-making blues. I take comfort in one irrevocable truth: no matter how intricate the trap, I will never be as bad a parent as Elizabeth James and/or Nicholas Parker. Even though I fully expect to be an iPad mom who has something last-minute conveniently come up every single Saturday morning during a youth soccer game (and will strong-arm my kids to pursue the arts and theater) at least I would not feel comfortable marveling at the aging of a bottle of wine I saved from the *QEII* that I put more thought and care into over the past eleven years than the aging of my own child overseas who has no idea I exist. Compared to them, when it comes to maternal instincts, my Cuppy runneth over.

° ○ ° Pop-up Biblio: To Infinity Scarves and Beyond ° ○ °

After the recession, older millennial women had no choice but to heal our wounds and wrap ourselves in bandage dresses, finding breakthroughs where we could in between breaking in caged heels, as we set out to reclaim our joy through our early adulthood hobbies and Pinterests. And one major bright spot when I think back to the late aughts and early 2010s was the rise of a new type of internet personality. As tabloid culture started to dwindle down, things were getting a bit stale in the hot-goss department. I was growing tired of always hearing how the details of people's personal lives "were none of my business" when I had time on my hands to devote to consuming them. Little did I know, I was about to enter an era of living, laughing, loving, and lurking, as I was welcomed with open arms by people literally in the business of sharing all of their personal business: bloggers. Before the term "influencer" was coined, "blogger" was a more magical moniker for the type of internet personality many millennial women like me were influenced by. They were kind of like living American Girl dolls; many seemed to hold the values of yesteryear and I scrolled through their websites like catalogs, confused by their young age relative to their refined taste in interiors.

There are countless variations of bloggers, from lifestyle to mom to food to DIY, but early on, the term almost became the ubiquitous catchall job title for anyone sharing and storytelling about their life online in a mostly visual format. But unlike editorialized magazines, they weren't fashion models, they were real people. Unlike starlets or socialites, many of their lifestyles were affordable, and their problems relatable. Unlike me, they presented themselves in a way that felt uncomplicated. And unlike the traditionally gatekept pipeline of mainstream fame, they democratized the ability of regular people to gain meaningful reach and recognition, paving the way for entire industries that would hinge upon the cultivation of a digital audience, not unlike my current career. While there are countless ways I could criticize the role of bloggers in their contribution to the "highlight reel" toxicity that plagues social media (and there are many examples of how this type of influence took a turn once it became a lucrative venture), I'd rather take a moment to honor the heyday of blogging for what it was: entertaining.

Whether needing a hobby outside of your nine-to-five or seeking an identity in the throes of new motherhood, blogging was kind of the perfect career for a digital-savvy adult with big yearbook-staff energy who never lost their commitment to the art of a layout and a quippy caption. I respect the hell out of pioneers in the fashion and lifestyle categories; it was a remarkable collective movement of women honoring traditionally feminine interests across categories like fashion, food, home décor, DIY, and beauty, and in hindsight, I'm inspired by these often-invisible domestic narratives being celebrated and written into existence in a modern way.

Pinterest and blog culture in the 2010s is something I'll teach my children about someday, because now in a short-form video (and short-attention-span-content-loving) world, I fear the kids just aren't getting their journalistic fix like we did. Bloggers rounded out my days with flat lays on Pinterest or Polyvore, inspiring me to innovate with clothes I already had. These ladies basically invented fashion journalism that spoke to young Maxxinistas on a budget, whether showing me how to wear denim "day to night," how to use leopard as a neutral, or perhaps how to incorporate more pops of color. They taught me that denim shirts were actually called "chambray," and even though the world made me think this style should be reserved for Tasmanian Devil button-downs at the WB store or reserved for Napa-nanny daywear à la Chessy, it was revelatory to learn I could wear blue-jean material on the top or bottom (and day to night!!).

I used to love long stories about someone's "hubs," whom they married suspiciously young and referred to only with the first letter of his name, as I grew increasingly charmed by his lumberjack-graphic-designer good looks, and incredibly nosy about their financial situation that made broader generational woes seem irrelevant to their lifestyle. Ever since the first time I heard a blogger refer to a space over a thousand square feet as a "nook," I was hooked; the disconnect from reality fascinated me—it was almost like there was a handful of young women who gamed the LMBCP perfectly, moving into a dream house that I might still be priced out of as an Airbnb at age thirty-five. But during trying times and heartbreaks, they made me feel like I, too, was maybe just one elaborate fishtail side braid away from baiting a hot husband like theirs, who wore thick-framed glasses, flannel, had a DSLR, and a dad with a construction company who could build this Polly a bigger pocket.

I used to get lost in the literature beneath vignettes of faux-rabbit-fur throws tossed over a ghost chair in a newly "glammed up" office, relearning my alphabet from Arhaus to Z Gallerie, realizing that it suddenly felt impossible to build my dreams in the absence of a crystal chandelier hanging over a huge-ass iMac on a Hollywood Regency–inspired mirrored desk. Similar to me knowing it would be a smudge fest in real life, this furniture left a mark on me, and I'd spend years being *this* close to dropping my life savings on furniture that was mirrored, acrylic (aka invisible), or lined with nailheads, thinking the ladies really hit the nail on the head when they told me these styles were "timeless." I still fall for "timeless" culture to this day; bloggers can convince me anything is a wardrobe staple or a great investment, as if it's wise to have a diversified portfolio of stocks, bonds, mutual funds, and pebble-ice machines. I also loved coffee-table culture, where for the longest time, feeds were filled with tight vignettes of a coffee table underneath chunky fashion books, an antique tray, a fresh vase of peonies, and a Diptyque candle resting next to—get this—an empty Diptyqe candle jar. Why? To store knickknacks! Matches! Toothpicks! You name it. I love the girl's-girl energy of a person who both burns money like it's nothing with high-end candles, but then saves the jar for crafting purposes. Like a daybed/trundle or a BOGO, we love a two-for-one.

In a precarious job market, we needed these bloggers' aspirations to feel hopeful, but the DIY tips and closet restyling bits were helpful, while many millennials were short on cash, or in my case, succumbing to urgency marketing by treating a Gilt Groupe sale with timed precision like I was disarming a bomb. I'm being sincere when I say that I adored this celebration of traditionally feminine interests on Pinterest, largely fueled by bloggers doing fun crafts for weddings and birthday parties and DIY home projects. It reminded me of the old days flipping through my American Girl catalogs and my *Girls' Life* magazines, while my mom ripped out pages from *Martha Stewart Living, Family Circle,* and *Southern Living,* and we'd plot out our next project for a Halloween costume made from balloons and a clear trash bag (Jelly Belly!) or Christmas ornaments for friends and neighbors, making angels by hot-gluing different uncooked pasta shapes together (penne for the body, macaroni wheel for the halo, and bow ties make the cutest wings!). You don't wallow about your lack of funds as a child the same way you do as an adult, you just figure things out for fun, and this era reminded me of that, because I was finding joy again in pursuing hobbies while I was starting to get more and more burned out with the corporate hustle. I think Pinterest resuscitated for many of us how fun it can be to spend a ton of time on something deeply unnecessary if it means you saved money.

Needless to say, in the early 2010s, I was thriving. I had a rotation of fifteen to twenty bloggers whose style I copied, and I could be blogspotted around town, likely wearing Hunter rain boots I spent my entire paycheck on, ready to fashion blog or wade in a cranberry bog at a moment's notice. As my net worth shrunk, my costume jewelry became increasingly oversized, with a lot of gold vermeil and plastic bangled, beaded, and bedazzled barnacles that were a delight for the eyes and ears. My particular favorite was a famous J.Crew bauble (also referred to as bubble) necklace that featured seven plastic beads on a string that had nineteen various-sized beads cascading below it. It was almost $100, made of literal hollow plastic, and overtook your outfit with the subtlety of kudzu on a Georgian home. To me, this necklace was more precious than the one the old lady dropped in the ocean at the end. I was also committed to wearing a fistful of gold bangles at all times, the largest Michael Kors watch I could find, and the confidence these golden glorified wrist weights gave me reminded me of Wonder Woman's gold cuffs, which allowed her to dodge bullets. Though I failed to dodge the bullet of what I thought made me a warrior in my own right—the one summer I got really into gladiator sandals. To be fair, they seemed so cozy compared to their strappy predecessor I mentioned earlier, the caged heel.

Regardless, not unlike the going-out-out tops of years prior, experimenting with my sense of style helped me feel confident and served as my armor in a transitional time period. Whether it was the colored denim or the ballet flats and loafers that matched my indoor neckwear, to infinity scarves and beyond, or the riding boots I didn't buy for horseback riding but hay riding, hoping to get the perfect cozy fall pic as long as we didn't foil the timing for peak foliage, thinking about this time makes me feel as warm and fuzzy inside as an off-the-shoulder chunky-knit sweater my favorite bloggers would photograph by a window looking outside, while holding a coffee mug as big as their head. Even though our commitment to chevron was tough, I have a soft spot for how bloggers made me want to elevate my everyday look with layers, accessories, and indoor fashion hats that would shade me from the mundanity of corporate reality. Suddenly, our poorly curated Facebook albums looked so pedestrian and left me wondering if I, too, could pull off a fringe boho top with bell sleeves and high-waisted denim and caption it "blue jean baby."

I think it's genuinely impressive that beneath the aesthetically pleasing veneer of traditionally feminine interests that people were so quick to write off, bloggers were en route to doing things like disrupting the fashion industry and overhauling the celebrity spokesperson advertising model. Not only am I grateful for how these women ended a decade by starting a rose golden age, I also want to applaud them for their entrepreneurial contribution that easily gets lost within more modern depictions of influencers. People don't treat influencers like entrepreneurs, and I understand this in the modern day, because you can skyrocket to fame through short-form video via virality that doesn't necessarily favor those who are the most consistent and hardworking. But influencers had to weather through that same stigma that reality TV stars did at first, where consumer preferences shifted, yet many players in the industry refused to dignify their direction. Just like how reality shows democratized fame for those outside of the entertainment world, social media democratized it for normal people, however large or niche their audiences may be. Now exposure, lower costs, and targetability of their channels makes them valuable in ways that rival traditional media.

Watching their lives for free in your free time with ads here and there is no different from websites being littered with ads or having to watch commercials. If you aren't funding the production of the entertainment you're consuming by paying a subscriber fee, then an advertiser does, due to the value of your eyes on the screen, making it free for you and allows people to be paid for their labor. I know most people know this, but sometimes I want to spell it out, because it's not your opinion that validates it as work, it's your consumption. Even if it's not labor you respect, it doesn't mean it can't exist, and I think people should go easier on labeling millennial or Gen Z content creators as narcissistic or greedy ventures when our being entertained by them is precisely why they're making so much money. I don't say this to defend myself—my income isn't directly tied to social media, but it's a promotional vehicle for where I do make money, and podcasts are monetized like traditional radio or TV. But people snarked so hard for the longest time about influencers making money, and still do for every small thing, delighting in labeling their online presence as a symptom of a person's delusion. But if we keep consuming it yet denying its validity, they aren't the delusional ones, we are.

There are plenty of things I could criticize about bloggers, from the frequent lack of disclosure, to the promotion of rampant consumerism, to participating in giveaways that artificially bolster their followings that they monetize, which feels like a form of fraud. I also have to laugh that I know everything about these women—I'll have virtually attended their C-sections, but come a time of political unrest, suddenly, it's too personal if I want to know how you feel about an insurrection? There's endless comedy and concern to be found, and I do that on my show all the time. For now, I'd rather give the pioneers the credit they deserve. It's interesting to think about these women begging brands to take them seriously, brokering partnerships through blog posts and static feed photos without any blueprint for pricing or creative requirements, doing the most while the brand spent the least on them of all mediums, while battling a great deal of stigma from readers and the industries they served. Sometimes I wonder if the content's hyperfeminine nature contributed to its perceived frivolity as a business model; other times I think the bloggers who made their lifestyles look effortless were probably the ones working the hardest to make it appear that way. And of course, I'm not saying unrealistic levels of aesthetic curation are noble, nor am I saying that this is the hardest work. But I think it's cool that we have a whole new advertising channel with ad dollars being distributed to give real people visibility outside of industry gatekeepers.

I'm convinced a lot of these ladies are responsible for convincing fashion houses that power was shifting from people to platforms, slowly legitimizing their role and securing their seat at fashion shows that now are almost exclusively lined with influencers. Celebrities were once valued for their status, but now influencers have something brands want more: reach. Engagement. When we talk about tech disruptors, especially in the space of social media, people often point to those who developed the platforms, but we overlook the women who pioneered the personal economic viability of social media through audience monetization. Early bloggers weren't just influential to their audiences, they were also instrumental in shaping the future of recommendation-based marketing, advertising, and media. For all the ways people ridicule influencers, I think we have to give a ton of credit to the people who built an entire category in the absence of a road map, all while weathering their own dismissal by the very industries their craft supported and audiences they cultivated. A tip of the wide-brim fashion hat to them.

11

Pumpkin Spice Girl

Recently, I was doing some work at a Starbucks and had an incident with a pumpkin spice latte that led me into a shame spiral that ultimately ended in an epiphany about the Spice Girls.

You can't see me, but I just rolled my eyes. Normally, I would delete that sentence so quickly for how, to use a word I hate, "basic" it sounds. For better or worse, it is my truth. I was researching the Spice Girls for my virtual live shows (where I gave PowerPoint presentations about pop culture) because I wanted to celebrate their contribution to the millennial female ethos. I also wanted to reexamine the concept of girl power from "Limited To" as a more evolved human than I was in elementary school.

The way I remember it, in 1997, I formally transitioned from an American Girl to a Spice Girl, using my pioneer skills gained from my days with Kirsten Larson on the Minnesota frontier to forge myself a more modern, provocative image. The milkmaid pigtail braids I once practiced on a baby doll transformed into my own real-life pigtails as I did the only thing I knew how to prevent myself from being dull: cosplay an adult baby. As the blond friend in the group, much to my delight, I often got assigned to portray Emma Bunton's Baby Spice for choreographed basement dances, and I did not take this honor lightly.

None of us did. For millennials, the Spice Girls are kind of like the Magnificent Seven from the 1996 U.S. women's gymnastics team. We didn't choose them, they chose us. Groups of powerful women that allow tween girls to put on costumes and categorize themselves by archetype would inevitably have their status cemented as pillars of generational iconography. In the Spice Girls' case, they feel less like pillars and more like architects, having designed the blueprint for the celebration of female friendship, independence, and fun in a platform shoe, a zig-a-zig-ah at the top of your list of to-dos.

Long before I slammed it to the left politically, I mostly just spent my time doing so while listening to "Spice Up Your Life." They requested you slam it to the left if you were having a good time, and in this fandom, I was having a damn good time. They celebrated individuality while prioritizing female friendships loudly and proudly, insisting that if a suitor wanted to be their lover, they should obviously have to first get with their friends. Their aesthetic was unapologetically girly, their disposition unserious. I hadn't come across a pop sensation at that age with so much emphasis on personality and platform. Also, the song "2 Become 1" single-handedly explained sex to me in all the ways the public school system failed to, so there's that. But the Girls taught me more than just the basic arithmetic of intercourse; being a part of the Spice Girls fandom was one of my earliest memories of the community young women find in popular culture. Dressing up as them at sleepovers, recording our choreography on VHS tapes, collecting loose change to buy their individual Chupa Chups, and waiting with bated breath for the theatrical release of the cinematic (and comedic!) masterpiece *Spice World.* I was in the ten-to-twelve-year-old range at the height of their popularity in the U.S. (and seemingly in the bullseye of their target demo) and I really thought I would "Never Give Up on the Good Times."

Except I completely bailed on the good times. I realized I had a highly concentrated but short-lived stint in the Spice Girls fandom, which is unusual for me. I'm nothing if not a hopelessly devoted fangirl for longer than what society tells me is age-appropriate. But it must have ended due to the Halloween incident I mentioned in chapter one, reminiscing about what was on my mind inside a Limited Too. I have a vague memory of epic plans with friends to dress as the Spice Girls, which resulted in pivoting to a different costume last minute when the boys in my grade made it clear that it wasn't cool anymore to dress up like them, that too many people were this year. I remember my face feeling hot, looking down at my Vans. Maybe it's memorable because it was one of the first times the Enneagram Four in me felt my uniqueness was being compromised.

The boys already laughed at us and teased us with cafeteria commentary about how their music "sucked." I remember feeling like a stupid fangirl who had bad taste in music and wondered if I should rebrand to something they approved, but I didn't know how to dress like a superfan of Chumbawamba or Marcy Playground. The overarching message was clear: the Spice Girls were not cool anymore. Not because they got less cool or because we changed our minds, simply because the boys in our class said so with their imagined authority. So in a comparably choreographed manner, I assume we all got out of formation and took the cue to downplay our public fanfare, taking our talents to exploring costumes that would pander less to what we liked and more to boys liking us for the rest of time. I think I even entertained a Cartman costume at one point despite never having seen *South Park,* which likely got vetoed because the contents of that show made my Baby Spice costume look like my Sunday best. It's interesting to look back on; even though a passing conversation with some boys didn't change how we felt about the Girls, this was the age where I assume we started to think there was something wrong with our interests if others, especially boys, didn't approve of them.

As I was thinking about this, I ordered another coffee while doing my research. I scanned the room as I was waiting for my name to be called, because this particular location is very crowded and in a neighborhood with a lot of young people, and sometimes when I work from there, I daydream about becoming besties with a nearby table of women wearing cute Sherpa jackets and sensible walking shoes. As a transplant in Chicago, I'm quite envious of the friend crews that run this town; it seems like everyone has groups that go way back, sitcom-style, and they seldom take new applicants. I never had trouble making friends until I was in a new city without my long-term girlfriends around, and I felt so nervous and awkward trying to befriend women, I'd find myself not knowing what to do with my hands or face and walking away analyzing our conversations like I had just been on a date.~*~

~*~ SO Random: (My Search for) Friendship Never Ends ~*~

I get why friend crews aren't always recruiting new members; if I had the luxury of living near my friends from back in the day-bed or my going out-out days, I'd likely remain blissfully inside our jokes and oblivious to outside contenders. When I moved away from my existing network over a decade ago, I was so focused on setting out for the big time, I failed to realize the reality of adulthood: at a point, people start to have very little time to invest in friendships. You realize people are suddenly busy; they have significant others, jobs, families, and existing friend groups that supersede the desire to pursue an acquaintance. Gone are the days when you have all the time in the world to invite people over to marathon TV series. Gone are the days when you have a purpose to spend hours crafting theme-party costumes or pulling all-nighters filled with delirious laughter. You realize those lengthy hangouts expedited the friend-making process in a way grabbing a drink never could. You meet up with a potential new friend, and even if you click, it's often weeks (if not months) before you can coordinate schedules for the next gathering. At that pace, it's difficult to get acquainted, much less attached at the hip, and suddenly you realize making BFFs as an adult is a lot harder than it was in your youth.

I find myself wanting to do away with the small talk, the polite laughter, and the mechanics of presenting myself as a likable person. I just want to be best friends already. You know, the "let's just share a dressing room" phase, the emergency contact phase, maybe even the "my unborn children will call you Aunt" phase. I miss that closeness, where no topic is too trivial to pass judgment or too deep to induce discomfort. Where we could have a lengthy conversation about our deepest fears and then have an equally lengthy discussion about the sartorial choices in SEC sorority rush TikToks (turns out, the Pants Store does not just sell pants!). I want someone to "get" me, but I don't know how long that takes or how to get there now that I don't have as much time on my hands. And I know impatience is not the answer, and as much as I want to come out and say "Let's just talk all the time and do everything ever together!" I know that's not real life. As exciting as it was at first to move away and chase a career in a new city, once the novelty faded, I realized how deeply I missed those easy hometown friendships I once so willingly left behind.

I saw someone from afar that I vaguely knew, a friend-of-a-friend situation, with their crew near the counter, and was wondering if I should say hi in case they were recruiting new gal pals. As I had that thought, the barista called out *very* loudly, "Pumpkin spice latte for Kate." For some reason, I didn't get out of my seat. Despite it being standard protocol for a barista to call out your name and order, something about this made my face feel hot, like back when I was told the Spice Girls were not. I wondered why she'd call me out like that, as if revealing my coffee order was akin to committing a HIPAA violation when the pharmacist reads your prescriptions too loudly. If I got up right this second and grabbed it, everyone would know my incredibly basic drink order. Pumpkin spice lattes have been the laughingstock of the meme world for a decade. My inner monologue was cycling through thoughts of, "I swear I'm not like other girls, why didn't I get something more sophisticated?" or "Can you imagine what would happen if I was refined enough to be a tea drinker? They'd probably invite me to a book club!"

I approached the counter in a very delayed fashion, almost subconsciously devising a plan to not be associated with the Kate who ordered a predictable PSL, hoping other patrons would assume I picked up something edgier, like a black coffee. As I sat down to write allegedly empowering material for my live show, I wasn't sure whether to laugh or cry (a common feeling for me), because I still can't shake the reflex to sometimes feel a little embarrassed by the things that I like. The enjoyment of pumpkin-adjacent things is so closely associated with the excessively memeified "basic bitch" (which to me, is a way of calling you the Trefoil of humans, in Girl Scout speak), I've internalized the mockery as something I just have to accept.

Not knowing how to feel, I just sat there. Me, the forever basic b, reeling about how from my Spice Girls days to pumpkin spice lattes, maybe nothing's changed. Remember when, like, a few pages ago I claimed to have evolved? That's the thing, I can intellectualize my response all I want, but the tough part is, my response is what I can't always control. Somewhere deep down, I'm not sure I've come all that far, still caring what people think, most identifying with the Spice Girls' classic callout "Who Do You Think You Are." As I spiraled while perched on a stool, looking out onto the crowd, I thought about how

I've lived my whole life carefully editing my behavior and modifying my interests to match the in crowd. As a result, I've accepted that it's fair for my surface-level interests to detract from my intellect and individuality, requiring them to meet some arbitrary standard to hold value or legitimacy. I know better, but can't seem to get my gut to download the software update.

As a person who has passion for the zeitgeist, over the years, I've learned the importance of controlling the conversation so people don't think I'm not smart or interesting. Questions like "What kind of music do you like?," "What's your favorite movie?," "What do you do for fun?" are small-talk material, first-date conversations, or corporate icebreaker content. These questions, however innocuous they sound, have caused me moments of fleeting panic over the years. Not because I don't have answers, but because I know those answers carry weight. What if I relate more to Andie Anderson: How-To Girl than Wes Anderson? What if I'm more into Danity Kane than *Citizen Kane*? What if my early philanthropic efforts were limited to watching the "We Are the World" music video and sporting a Livestrong bracelet? When Meghan Markle was taking on sexism with Procter & Gamble in 1994, I was bitching that Santa couldn't wrangle my Teen Talk Barbie a new Jeep Wrangler. I hesitate in these conversations, because in my experience, these icebreakers are rarely accurate impression makers, as people use your response to base your entire personality, taste, and intellect off isolated entertainment preferences.

As I sipped my seasonal drink, it was a bit bleak trying to discern what interests were actually mine, fearing I've curated my existence based on how I want to be perceived, not who I am. While it bums me out that the Spice Girls are one of the last times I remember enjoying something without factoring in peer approval, the truth is it became such a familiar experience, I guess I normalized it to the point where I no longer noticed it.

While I'd argue the intensity of female self-surveillance ultimately ties back to the male gaze, the goal was to fit in, so I'd do this in front of boys and girls alike at different points in life. Especially during the peak of hipster popularity in the early 2010s, anyone who made the mainstream their lazy river was ripe for ridicule. And I simply accepted that I deserved to be criticized for going with the flow. As a result, I'd wait fifteen minutes for a pour-over coffee when all I wanted was a Frappuccino. I'd take canvas totes to farmers markets and bask in my moral superiority by "shopping local" and purchasing a $30 jar of artisanal honey. On my walk home, I'd listen to The Lumineers and think about how I wanted to be listening to "Party in the U.S.A." but I needed to get into some folksier tunes in case my hypothetical new friend group put me in charge of DJing at an event I had not yet been invited to. In my peak girl-boss phase, despite being an advocate for closing the gap in female entrepreneurship, I still found myself hiding my *Us Weekly*s on my coffee table and replacing them with *Fast Company* or *The Economist* before a fellow enterprenHER came over, fearful as a female founder that I'd be taken less seriously if I appeared too shallow. I've heard myself say things like "The book is better" even though I almost always beeline for the movie before cracking open the book, and I've joined book clubs that read titles I had no interest in, showing up having read the SparkNotes like a high-school lit class, except in this context I wanted to get an A in friendship and peer respect.

Like many millennials seeking decorative refinement, I put up quotes on my walls from Coco Chanel or Audrey Hepburn. As you know, I didn't own anything Chanel that wasn't from Coco Canal Street. I didn't even like old movies, it just seemed more dignified to claim my favorite Rome-related film was *Roman Holiday* when actually I'd rank that fifth in the category of romance-related movies about Rome.~*~

> ~*~ SO Random: There's No Place like Rome ~*~
>
> A formal ranking of romantic movies about Rome. I will not be taking questions.
>
> 1. *The Lizzie McGuire Movie*
> 2. *When in Rome* (Mary-Kate and Ashley)
> 3. *When in Rome* (Kristen Bell)
> 4. *Christmas in Rome* (Lacey Chabert, Hallmark queen)
> 5. *Roman Holiday* (Audrey Hepburn)

The silver lining of doing this is sometimes I'd pursue things I wouldn't have known I'd like if I hadn't pursued it for the sake of a shared interest with somebody else. For example, I dated someone who drove a pickup truck for a few months in high school and adopted a brief (but admittedly supercute) cowgirl era when I unironically attended a Toby Keith concert. My taste in music has been so all over the place throughout the years, my iTunes library has an at-risk level of range that disables me from publicly playing fast and loose with random shuffle. I tried to plan my hypothetical DJing while walking home from farmers markets because I generally avoid volunteering my phone and it seems like I'm hiding something. But it's only because my iPhone does this thing where every time I plug it in, it automatically starts alphabetically playing "Aaron's Party (Come Get It)" when it's sorted by song title, or the A*Teens' "Upside Down (Bouncing Off the Ceiling)" when sorted by artist. So I'm not being hypothetical when I tell you these Disney-adjacent parentheticals don't always land well as lead singles representing your essence.

I found this took on a new life when I was trying to navigate the workforce. It was already hard to be taken seriously due to my age, and I couldn't roll the dice making my interests sound unsophisticated. To test the waters at an early team meeting at my first job in New York,

I said my favorite movie was *How to Lose a Guy in 10 Days,* and the room laughed. I did not tell a joke. I spiraled thinking of all the other times I was made to feel like an airhead for not caring as much about *Pulp Fiction* as everyone else. But to say I like Tarantino movies would be *actual* fiction, and I hate lying. I distinctly remember all of us having to share what our first concert was, and although I'm pretty sure mine was Clay Aiken and Ruben Studdard, I decided I, too, was "Sorry 2004," so I picked one of my other early concerts and said The Doobie Brothers. I'm a big "Black Water" stan and it was one of my first concerts, but not my actual first. However, it made the middle-aged men open up a conversation with me that wouldn't have happened if I'd picked one of my other early concerts, like Ashlee Simpson. I don't think an elevated conversation about what it really means to make someone want to "La La" would have professionally advanced me in the way The Doobie Brothers did. I truly could not imagine the look on people's faces if I tried to argue for how I considered Clay Aiken's version of "Bridge Over Troubled Water" to be a cultural reset. I mean, it's not like I'm out here as a proud member of Taylor Hicks's Soul Patrol, but regardless, citing an *American Idol* cover song from a nonwinner is a deep cut not everyone is prepared for. Unless it is Adam Lambert's "Mad World," of course, which is up there next to "Spice" in my ranking of top moments in music that involve the word "world."

It's always been a bit confusing to navigate; as a person I value honesty, but I was conditioned to believe my value was in being likable, which requires you to maintain a posture of malleability to cater to your audience. As a result, I would do these on-the-fly calculations, not always feeling like I had another option other than to wave my white flag with its matching lie to avoid professional implications. Prior to my corporate job, the consequences were more social and self-esteem based, but in the working world, the opportunity cost of not being able to establish this kind of connection felt higher and more tangible. In the workplace, the pursuit of likability can shape-shift into something more subversive—trying to be taken *seriously* by male counterparts. It was something that seemed like it could have very real implications on my professional development.

I've noticed (especially in client-facing industries) that male leadership will be wined and dined, taken out to sports games or concerts, and if you weren't a person they thought would appreciate it, you would lose out on a professional opportunity. So it honestly felt strategic for me to self-edit constantly before I saw that it meant I was further deferring to male authority. I'm by no means suggesting that dismissal of what you like is *always* sexist. In many cases it's a function of unfair biases toward things like class, race, culture, or, in this case, age and phase in life, and subjective taste is part of it. But I can't say I've noticed my male peers perform these mental calculations on the fly in the same way I did.

While the experience of feeling dismissed for traditionally feminine and pop culture–related interests in order to feel accepted exists on a spectrum, it isn't new or unique; people have made fun of (especially young) girls' interests for centuries. During my Starbucks rabbit hole about the history of society's perceptions of female interests, I was reminded that many historians attribute the mocking of teen girls' interests to nineteenth- and twentieth-century attitudes about female "hysteria" (unfriendly reminder: "hysteria" comes from the Greek root "hystera," meaning "uterus"), hypothesizing that over time, the stigma of women being "too emotional" contributed to a societal pattern where males held the authority on what forms of music, entertainment, art, literature, etc., were legitimate and valuable versus what was frivolous or in poor taste. I suppose the logic there was that our emotions would cloud us from being able to have a discerning enough palate for public imagery. Forget the rabbit-hole-y spirit, praise be to the Father and Son! Good thing we have the patriarchy to legitimize our interests; I don't know about you, but my period side effects are typically cramps, bloating, and a sneaky inability to ascertain the objective quality of art.~*~

~*~ SO Random: Shop Culture ~*~

As one does in a Starbucks, I researched more historical context that illustrates how events of the twentieth century defined certain elements of pop and mass culture as being predominantly feminine categories. According to a Khan Academy article titled "Women in the 1950s," during World War II, women joined the workforce in unprecedented numbers to support the war effort, only to be pushed out or replaced by returning soldiers once it was over.[9] During the Cold War in the 1950s, mass media filled homes with messages and advertisements linking women's domesticity to national security, reinforcing the importance of women staying home not only for the stability of their families but also the nation. Apparently, part of this in-home patriotism was the embracing of consumerism as a way of waging the Cold War by taking an active role in capitalism. And there you have it, the origin story of "Women be shoppin'!"

There was a connection between the promotion of savvy consumerism as a civic duty and the proliferation of ads for consumer goods on daytime television, both serving to set the stage for the ways people still connect women with consumer and mass culture. The popularity of soap operas (which were literally named for their purpose of using ad space to sell women detergent) seem to be a main culprit for the popularizing of women's entertainment as "unsophisticated." When looking for critical reviews of early soaps, I came across a far more telling

---

9. https://www.khanacademy.org/humanities/us-history/postwarera/1950s
-america/a/women-in-the-1950s

anecdote from a 2015 research article, "Soap Operas and Artistic Legitimation: The Role of Critical Commentary." Apparently, there were very few formal critics of this dishy daytime content because even the TV industry believed the soap audience wasn't sophisticated enough to warrant a critic's appraisal. That same study stated that "while soap operas gained economic legitimacy over time (due to profit-earning potential) and were popular with audiences, they were never widely classified as an art form." I think it's telling that from the earliest days of television, the shows driving network profitability were not taken seriously as long as they were created by women, made for women, or sold to women. This trend continues today, where women's interests are easily ridiculed or sidelined despite their economic viability, as evidenced by romance novels consistently outselling other fiction genres, yet being referred to as "trashy novels," or reality TV dominating ratings, while their predominantly female audiences are labeled as partaking in a "guilty pleasure."

This subliminal reasoning that society reveres male authority in the pursuit of entertainment is fascinating when you consider stereotypical masculine cultural consumption that's widely considered valid. How is a large group of women screaming at a boy-band concert materially different from a large group of men losing their shit over a playoff game? We're all at a large venue celebrating a shared interest, sporting merch, having emotional responses, and finding joy and community in something that exists for entertainment purposes. We're all steeped in the same parasocial delusion that makes us feel like we're being represented by someone who doesn't even know us, like "we" won the game when we just sat there criticizing the athletic performance of sports we can't even play ourselves or the musical performance with tunes we don't have the chops to carry. My point isn't to say one is better than the other, my point is that it's all the same: a function of personal preference in sources of entertainment. But gender plays a role in how a patriarchal society values those preferences, often using popularity and economic viability as more of a reason to dismiss something rather than acknowledge its objective success.

At the risk of generalizing, think of any situation that represents stereotypically large groups of men gathering to express their fandom. Fanatics of sports, *Star Wars,* waiting in line at an Apple store, box-office numbers for DC or Marvel films, Xbox releases, hypebeasts lining city blocks overnight for a limited sneaker drop, attending ninety-plus jam-band concerts, the list goes on. These are just examples of what I've personally seen men lose their minds over, and many women love these things, too, but I never notice anyone weaponizing it to question their intelligence or question the medium's value. Do you know how many group conversations I've been in where a person reveals that they've been to over a hundred Phish, Grateful Dead, or Dave Matthews concerts? The crowd goes wild! They're fascinated, engaged, listening to tales of Bonnaroo and Red Rocks and camping outdoors in dire conditions for the sake of music. Do you honestly think I would receive that kind of group response if I said I'd been to Lilith Fair a hundred times (a dream!)? If I made a personality type out of following the Jonas Brothers on the road? Just last night I was at a dinner and talked about this very chapter. After explaining I was in the midst of working on a several-thousand-word dissertation on the reduction of women based on their interests as told through a Spice Girls anecdote, I watched myself and my book be reduced before my eyes to something they thought was whiny and far-reaching, as someone responded by asking me if I felt like women these days are "not able to take a joke." I am able to take a joke, I just no longer laugh at the ones that aren't funny.

As a wearer of cute distressed band tees for bands whose music I absolutely do not listen to, I've witnessed countless interactions in social settings where one of us conversationally expresses our affinity for something that has a nearby man's approval, only for it to be followed up by an interrogation, questioning the legitimacy of the female's claim to be interested in something the male perceives as legitimate. When you're not interested, you have questionable taste. When you are interested, you're a fraud. While sometimes I do fraudulently claim to like something, it's not to be misleading; it's because I'm constantly negotiating between being made fun of or respected, and for some reason, people only make cool T-shirts about Pink Floyd or Led Zeppelin. But being asked about Led Zeppelin is my stairway to hell, because even naming that song would be too cliché to satisfy most fans wanting to call out a fraud.

Their questioning implies that female interests threaten the quality of their preferred entertainment. Have you ever said you loved a movie, only to be grilled about your franchise knowledge? Said you liked an artist, only to be asked to name a certain number of their songs? I remember playing "Hey Jude" (a song I genuinely love) in my car in college after watching *Across the Universe,* and upon expressing my love for this song, one of my guy friends asked me if I liked the Beatles, then said, "Name five of their songs." I could name countless Beatles songs; my dad raised me on the three Bs: Beatles, Beach Boys, Bee Gees. But in that moment, the reflex of this collegiate male was to assume I was faking it. I'm grateful to those teen girls in the sixties who busted their chops to make the Beatles happen, paving the way for a future teen girl like me to lie through my teeth as I told boys I liked their "later stuff" to conceal my "hysterical" interests, when I actually mostly dig the songs of the "She Loves You" and "I Want to Hold Your Hand" persuasion. That's my second favorite song about hand-holding, next to Hootie & the Blowfish's monster ballad "Hold My Hand."

Speaking of, the history of Beatlemania provides incredibly important context for framing a discussion about how the media has portrayed teen-girl "hysteria" for decades. In an article in *The Guardian* titled "Beatlemania: 'the screamers' and other tales of fandom," I was reminded that before the Beatles were heralded as one of the greatest musical acts of all time, their initial success was fueled by teen girls, whose fandom was ridiculed and patronized by the media. In the article, writer Dorian Lynskey refers to an "infamous" *New Statesman* essay by Paul Johnson, which claimed, "Those who flock round the Beatles, who scream themselves into hysteria, whose vacant faces flicker over the TV screen, are the least fortunate of their generation, the dull, the idle, the failures." In other words, as novelist Linda Grant says, "Teenage girls are perceived as a mindless horde: one huge, undifferentiated emerging hormone."[10]

When I think back on my obsession with Hanson, the Backstreet Boys, NSYNC, Boyz II Men, the Spice Girls, and Taylor Swift (or really most of the fandoms I mention in this book), I realize that I grew up internalizing this same messaging. I assume millennials who were fans of One Direction, the Jonas Brothers, or, more recently, K-pop groups like BTS (among countless other popular acts) have experienced a version of fangirl dismissal, too. I've historically been drawn to mainstream music and media that's coded as feminine, and disliked participating in popular male rituals. But I didn't always feel like I had a choice but to downplay my fanfare, and instead feigned interest in theirs; otherwise, I'd risk being ostracized and left out of adolescent experiences or professional opportunities. When we teach young women that their interests don't matter, that their participation in something makes it less desirable, that their taste or ways of expressing themselves are fodder for mockery, we're telling them that the things they like should be a function of being liked instead of doing what they love. If we tell them

---

10. https://www.theguardian.com/music/2013/sep/29/beatlemania-screamers-fandom-teenagers-hysteria

that what they like is unimportant, how will they understand the importance of their contributions to the world? There are serious implications to having your sources of joy never be taken seriously, and I'm an example of a person who didn't always take myself seriously as a result.

When I was researching the Spice Girls, I realized how I spent so much of my life not embodying the girl power Mel C and the gang taught me, and I honestly felt kind of ashamed. I was posing as a literal wannabe, attempting to embody female empowerment while still feeling the need to self-monitor my interests. It's a little sad to me to think of how young I was when I started to realize how defining a few core characteristics can be how people assign you to your own "spice," and that was a big reason I was so obsessed with the Spice Girls. I longed for the empowerment and individuality they represented in how they were so fiercely themselves.

But as I went on to research the Girls following my Starbucks spiral, I realized I hadn't fully connected the dots. When you read a detailed history of the Spice Girls, one of the most surprising facts is that they did not assign their individual "spice" names themselves: Baby, Ginger, Posh, Scary, Sporty. According to Mel B, in a 2015 HuffPost Live interview, the names were first published in a U.K. magazine called *Top of the Pops* in 1996 by a "lazy journalist" who couldn't remember their names. It's a magazine cutout that says SPICE RACK and jokingly places each woman's head above a spice jar, stating descriptors like, "Sporty Spice: ball control is her specialty!," "Baby Spice: like a baby doll, all soft and fluffy!," and "Scary Spice: such a scary loud voice and a pierced tongue." Mel B went on to say, "He just gave us nicknames, and we were like, 'Oh, well, that kinda works. I don't mind my name. Do you like your name? Baby? Posh?' We were like, 'Let's just go with it.'" Many (myself included) have raised an eyebrow about Mel B's name, and her prevailing sentiment toward its origin is that it was about her being opinionated, stating, "I'm very kind of in-your-face. I was even more so back then. So I guess I could have come off as scary. But I like my name."

So, wait a second. I mean, *Stop right now, thank you very much?* The Spice Girls, patron saints of individuality and girl power, didn't choose their own nicknames? I went into my research assuming their personas were a form of protesting or satirizing this type of reduction, and I don't know if I'm disturbed or comforted by their identities being a product of it. At no point in the "Spice Rack" bit in *Top of the Pops* does it list any of their first or last names; it forgoes their identities while still providing arbitrary, oversimplified distinctions based on a few isolated characteristics. For some reason, learning their message of individuality and independence was dependent on a sexist reduction of their personas rocked my world. On one hand, to feel forced to embrace and find success within an unsolicited sexist trope feels hardly empowering. On the other hand, they took ownership of it to exercise their power, building an empire fueled on messaging that celebrated the same femininity that underscored their mockery. It was then I began to realize my self-diagnosed girl-power outage over the years wasn't in contrast to what the Spice Girls taught me; it was actually the opposite. My entry-level feminist dilemma was embodied by this paradox that had been in front of me the whole time. I now see that this is an example of third-wave feminism in a nutshell, but it took time to make this connection in such an unsuspecting place. For years to come, I'd be attempting to answer the same question that their nicknames' existence was born from: How do we carve out a sense of identity and uniqueness in a society designed to reduce us?

The Spice Worldview I didn't notice until that day is the relatable (albeit privileged) experience of growing tired of the slow progress toward meaningful, systemic equality for women and at times wondering if you should just set up shop in the boxes society puts you in as a sort of feminist halfway house. Having to constantly protest, self-improve, and fight for the resistance can also feel oppressive; some days you want to just be allowed to exist. Sometimes it feels easier to just work around the circumstances. I think this is the nucleus of most faux-feminist movements; having fun and cheering one another on in the most privileged echelons of an oppressed group to make the fact that we're staying in the exact same place just a little prettier and a bit more tolerable. A rose-colored glass ceiling, as I like to say, or perhaps choosing to see what you're not limited to inside a Limited Too. But I realized this is kind of what we've all been forced to do in combating tropes like "basic" over the years. In becoming so culturally ubiquitous, you almost have no choice but to own it, to say the joke first. Like I did in my opening paragraph. It made me wonder if I felt like I had to co-opt pumpkin as my "spice" and approach the world as an individual through the lens of a predetermined stereotype to feign a sense of freedom in my interests. All this time, is that all girl power was?

Daily I scroll through memes with dated jokes about being "basic" (or the flash-in-the-pandemic word "cheugy") that make fun of women with an affinity for things perceived as common or dated. The definition of "basic" isn't just about Ugg boots and pumpkin spice lattes and pashminas and going to brunch and loving Taylor Swift. One of the definitions, upon a quick Google search, is, "one who has no personality; dull, irrelevant," positioning these characteristics as a safe assumption if you like the things I just mentioned. Every time I see the level of engagement on a post that pathologizes a woman's vapidity due to her enjoyment of something as joyful as a PSL, as I said in the introduction, I can't believe we are made to believe this when it's coming straight from people who spend their free time drafting make-believe football teams. Sometimes I click on commenters' profiles, tallying the men who diminish women's existences to "basic" who also appear to wholly subsist off a woman who works her ass off to take care of their basic needs.

For all the days I spent dressing up as and pretending to be a Spice

Girl as a kid, I spent more days trying to make it clear I wasn't a Pumpkin Spice Girl as an adult, horrified the moniker of "basic" would be hurled my way, stripping me of identity and dimension simply due to my interest in cozy beverages. I find it fascinating that for all the ways I've evolved, I still find myself nervous at times to represent my interests in things that are cliché, popular, or quintessentially millennial, watching them be overassociated with an assumed lack of taste before my eyes. While I do find humor in being outed by a PSL, sometimes I wonder if I feel like I have to laugh at the misogyny masquerading as comedy that negatively labels women who like popular things. Like the laugh tracks in popular-boy screenwriting from the nineties, sometimes I feel like I've been conditioned to "sweeten" the circumstances by engineering laughter at my own expense, knowing it's what the masses will expect. And their approval is what I needed.

With my profession being the lengthy celebration of easily dismissed surface-level culture, I have been on the receiving end of plenty of this mockery. I spend my days attempting to not be stuck inside a harsh feedback loop, receiving constant misogyny thinly veiled as constructive criticism about what I talk about, how I talk, my voice, saying the word "like," how I use big words to pretend I'm smart, why "she thinks she's so funny," the list goes on. While I've been privy to this experience throughout my life, I've certainly been overexposed to it in my podcasting career, and the fact that my job causes me to have a greater-than-average sample size of sexist comments makes me feel compelled to call attention to the fact that this mentality is still alive and well. And while I fully believe in not blindly supporting women in the absence of accountability, curbing our desire to shame one another for our interests and outward appearance is important. As long as people aren't using their voices to hurt or exploit other people, most things to shrink or silence other women are kind of shitty, roundabout ways these forces manipulate you to collude with your own disappearance. Even though there's no one right way to be, they shame you for the things they believe you shouldn't be, hoping to turn you into a "mute model."

To call another person a "pick me" girl poses the same issue as labels like "basic" or "cheugy." The problem lies within us wanting others to fall into a "spice"-like category where we can reduce someone's behavior to understand them better, to find them more palatable, to position ourselves relative to them. I think we can make jokes about ourselves, we can own or reject labels how we please, but weaponizing them against other women isn't doing anything other than continuing to follow the male gaze like Waze, ever guiding our compass toward their approval. I don't know much, but I work hard every day not to allow someone else to analyze the value of my interests or labor for sport. Mostly because, again, I fucking hate sports.

Looking back, it's interesting to think about how you gradually adjust to moving through a world where you're a little too aware of being looked at. Back when I was too young to get into bars, I watched the bar for women get higher and the jean rises get lower as I tried to combat being single by double-rolling my Soffes, hoping to triple my chances at being popular by emulating how I saw women portrayed in tabloids, that you were only interesting if you were dating someone, feuding with a friend, had fluctuating weight, or were bleary-eyed walking out of a club.

The name of the game was to be the same as other women. I spent most of my youth avoiding the discomfort of being unique at all costs only for it to cost me the cultivation of my own self-worth and the making of a hospitable environment for other people to find theirs. Now I lie awake at night ruminating on the shame of how my pursuit to be the same as everyone else represented a desirable circumstance for me that was oppressive to other people. My discomfort was in my head, in my height, in my personality, my clothes. Anything that made me feel different, I changed. Now I see what a privilege it was to not have this disconnect grounded in my identity or skin color or sexual orientation or abilities. It took me way too long to stop looking into mirrors and to learn to look out windows again, to prioritize making other people feel seen. As much as I love to laugh about magazines and tabloids and reality TV and pop stars, part of me thinks that as a young woman, I forewent developing a worldview because the male-centric media's surveillance of women taught me to prioritize how the world viewed me.

Although depending on how you look at it, the Spice Girls' ownership of their own reductions wasn't necessarily oppressive; maybe it was the embodiment of doing the best you can despite your circumstances. Choosing what you accept, what you laugh at, what you capitalize on, and what you leave behind, in the process of rejecting a frustrating system that's going to take a while to take down. Maybe they were onto something with choosing to own the labels, but revising the definitions to fulfill their mission.

~*~ SO Random: Millennial Spice ~*~

As I've been writing this book, I've tried to reframe unfair millennial stereotypes in a similar fashion; we take and leave what we want, define them how we please. Maybe we can choose what they mean to us, where we insert the laugh track, and choose not to internalize it. I've often wondered if words like "lazy" and "entitled" look less insulting when they're contextualized from a different point of view. In many ways, we're just misunderstood.

My refusal to do things professionally that may have made me look like Lazy Spice over the years was often a function of knowing they could be done more efficiently, and not agreeing to instructions that were a waste of my time. I also think we are a generation who understands the implications of not taking mental health seriously, and following years of an uncertain job market and corporate burnout, laziness may just be an unfair way to brand people seeking work-life balance, or for those of us just now learning to prioritize our well-being over exceeding our job requirements, realizing it's a thankless grind to give everything to entities who aren't giving us retirement plans, job security, or the long-term incentives of years past. People who haven't experienced job insecurity or periods of unemployment may not have as good a grasp on what it feels like to have a company demand your loyalty who will never be loyal to you. So maybe Job-Hopping Spice isn't selfish; they're cautious, they're ambitious, and they move in between jobs that work for them, because when you're working for companies that make the people who work for them feel disposable, we all have to look out for ourselves.

When it comes to Industry Killer Spice, for products like low-fat yogurt, I'm like, *Hell yeah, keep killin' it, millennials.* Good riddance. The same goes with SnackWell's and any other peak-nineties diet-culture product that completely misinformed the masses by conflating health with weight loss, stigmatizing the word "fat" along the way. I'm somewhat of a Follow Your Dreams Spice, but I wear that proudly; I never understood why it was seen as an undesirable trait to want to find purpose and impact in your career. I don't know why we were ever blamed for wanting to take advantage of the options available to us, as if we shouldn't be allowed to try things, just because those before us couldn't.

I'm also fine with being Delayed Milestone Spice, doing things in the LMBCP later relative to prior generations. To some, it may look like I'm stalling, but in actuality, I also took my time to get to know my partner really well, making sure we were compatible, and we were intentional about being more financially stable prior to trying to have kids. Maybe we're smart for not spending beyond our means to own things just because it aligns with the American Dream; being a renter is awesome when something happens to the pipes and it's not your issue. My husband and I often talk about how it may be beneficial that we waited to have kids. We can break cycles and create new traditions based on having the time and resources to do things our way. And when the time comes, I think we'll be pretty good, albeit kinda old, parents as a result.

And when you think about it, Entitled Spice isn't the worst to identify with, because it's a symptom of how we've broken down barriers and interrupted formerly gatekept industries. Our generation created opportunities, and we should feel entitled to harness them if we can. I'm an example of this; I'm not a writer or scholar by trade, I'm a person who was able to get my voice out there by having direct access to audiences through the internet, who got a chance to follow her dreams because our generation created platforms that made industry gatekeepers irrelevant. So yeah, we feel entitled to shoot our shot, to go after what we want; why wouldn't we? I think we should be proud that instead of pandering to those historically in power, we felt entitled to improve the systems that no longer served us.

Like the Jacob Black to our Renesmee, older generations imprint on us from a young age and define part of our worldview until the common behaviors of a generation develop their own distinction. And while millennials do tend to glorify tragic compound made-up names like Renesmee, unlike her imprinting, I think part of this distinction is how over time, we've lost the need to defer to the way things were done by older generations just because they got here first. Maybe our way isn't wrong; it's revised.

I know that most jokes about millennial stereotypes, along with Bravo and blanket scarves and brunch, are meant to be lighthearted. I don't think any of us are personally victimized by the headlines, and the joke will get old eventually, right? But one of the things that makes the dismissal of female joy so insidious is that it doesn't really seem like a big deal. So what, someone thinks you're basic or your taste in music isn't cool or makes fun of your appearance? I fear that writing off our emotional responses to these small interactions as "not being able to take a joke" or "too sensitive" only puts further blame on our defensiveness, never holding the offender accountable, all while upholding what they always wanted us to believe ever since Beatlemania: we're being too emotional. We're overreacting. It's clouding you from being able to determine what is and isn't quality, what is and isn't funny, interesting, or offensive.

However, we do have that authority as long as we exercise it often and control the laugh track. We do as long as we're willing to take up space. We do as long as we do everything in our power to go out of our way to honor our own pleasure and label it however we want. The solution is not to demand women exist in a particular way; the solution is just to be allowed to exist in your own pleasure in the absence of analysis. I don't think we should have to dissect everything; the very writing I'm doing feels at times insulting amidst a world that seems to demand so much self-regulation from women.

While the "like what you like!" argument is not the crux of feminism, feeling ashamed of and dismissed for your interests or taste is certainly a contributor to dangerous cycles of self-regulation that can impact the confidence of young people, and I wish I'd honored my inner fangirl more often than I prioritized fitting in.

I also wish I understood that for "girl power" to be effective, it needs to operate in the best interest of the collective, not just the individual, and I'm by no means arguing that the solution for centuries of systemic inequality is making privileged women like me feel more comfortable admitting they like 2000s top-forty music. Battle cries for individual-ized girl power tend to gloss over that we live in a society that claims women are empowered, but in reality, they are often dying, barely sur-viving, or hardly supported by way of public policy. I wish I could wax poetic with a Spice Girls metaphor and have a meaningful impact on improving circumstances involving unequal pay in the U.S., being one of the only industrialized countries without paid family leave, or our country's harrowing maternal mortality rates for BIPOC women. I know encouraging you to be a proud fangirl isn't going to combat a capitalist system that exploits care work or assist in recognizing wom-en's reproductive rights as rights, among other far more pressing issues. It's for these reasons I've felt duped by believing in "girl power" in the first place, but this exercise made me realize there's still some relevance in its application, as long as we recognize its limitations.

While remembering the Spice Girls' original message of individ-uality in a world designed to reduce us is not going to solve all of our problems, it at the very least reminds us to prioritize our sources of joy while dealing with the ongoing presence of underlying economic and social inequities. Ultimately, I want to remind people of something so simple yet so overlooked in our existence (and resistance): amidst your efforts to move the needle in this slow, painstaking process of transfer-ring power, please go out of your way to honor your own pleasure. Like what you like, fangirl over it, shout it from the rooftops, take up space, then change your mind, stop liking it, rinse, repeat.

Even though I don't have all the answers, I did find peace that af-ternoon at Starbucks, wanting to move forward more confidently, not as worried about labels, wishing I could haunted-hayride off into the sunset, unapologetically celebrating a cozy fall day and the even cozier feeling of momentary self-acceptance. Over time, I've learned it's not about denouncing others' opinions entirely or ignoring well-meaning feedback; it's about creating a system of values based on what matters to you, and being selective about whose opinions hold the most authority in your book.

In my book, the Spice Girls were important to my female millennial experience, serving as a gateway for me to champion women's interests, regardless if I lost my way honoring a latte here and there. More important than my analysis is the fact that they continue to still serve their purpose, (Viva) Forever reminding me that we should be fiercely individual while also supporting the collective, as true girl power lies somewhere in between our self-respect and advocacy. And maybe girl power isn't too far off from their message in 1997, when they instructed us to perform a call to action that's arguably the battle cry of Entitled Spice. It doesn't matter if you own the labels or ignore them, just don't set what you're Limited To as default, and don't allow As to supersede Mel B and C's creed: live your life doing exactly what you want—

What you really, really want.

12

Light at the End of the Trundle

There were so many themes I wanted to touch on for this book, but there was one big question I kept in mind from the very start: As a person who always felt defined by being average, common, basic, and/or plain, could I look back on my experiences and choose to find the art?

Placing myself back in the daybeds or peep-toe pumps and remembering the pop culture and scenery, I realized that it's the shallow A-pockets of life where I've found the most depth and meaning. And in analyzing why I believed these things weren't allowed to be important to me, through the lens of feeling like a self-involved snowflake, shallow or sinful, boy-crazy, or not talented and gifted, I don't feel like a victim, but rather the product of a time. In tandem with holding myself accountable, contextualizing why or how these things happened helps me feel less frustrated that I can't turn back time. Instead, I can be kind and rewind the footage to rewatch it from a different point of view.

When I do, it does look more artful than people led me to believe. But most importantly, it makes me want to compare it to my definition of art: *The Real Housewives~*~* franchise on Bravo. Sometimes in trying to figure out how to distill stories from my life to fit in each chapter, I felt like a reality-TV producer. Trying to verbally paint the scene the best I could, commenting in retrospect like a talking-head interview, often arguing for plot and drama in the least riveting of places, like AIM or gauchos or 99 Bananas. But that's precisely why I love reality TV: the best parts never drive the plot; the art happens outside of the main arc.

~*~ SO Random: Hits and Mrs. ~*~

The best thing about *The Real Housewives* franchise is it has nothing at all to do with being a housewife or a Mrs. While those roles are important to many of the women, to me, the series continues to be a hit because they find forces of nature that exceed the need to be defined by marital status or a house. Though the houses are a favorite side character of mine; I love a never-finished chateau, a room drowning in taxidermied fish where you can make it nice, only to be topped by a crumbling brownstone with plumbing issues and brown ice. In featuring and furthering the careers of women within an age range often under- or misrepresented on-screen, I've gotten to see real examples of how your life can just be beginning after a "happily ever after," whether a relationship ends, a business begins, you have kids, or your friendships come and go. You keep going, keep reinventing yourself, because when life gives you lemons, you put nine in a bowl.

Similarly, the artful, less self-produced early seasons are a form of still life to me when I think about what the wives brought to the table beyond the lemons, like a prosthetic leg or the nineteen engagements that ultimately made that table flip. I found myself inspired by the imagination required to host a fashion show with fashions that don't even exist. I've felt vicarious rage for being picked up by a family van. I've sneered at the thought of places I've never been, like Quogue or Bass Lake. When I've been stuck with this book, I've thought to myself,

"Use your vocabulary, writer girl," and that usually puts me in my place. It's where I learned terms like "morally corrupt" and "pernicious," internalized how bringing sprinkle cookies makes you look suspicious, and when it comes to raw chickens, to consider first giving them a dish-soap glaze. I've felt ask-believe-receive-seen by Auto-Tuned pop stars living their best "Chic C'est La Vie," even though I forget what that means. I never forget to be mindful of being "Tardy for the Party" or how "Money Can't Buy You Class." But it can fund entrepreneurial dreams, and if you're pouring your net worth into a vague international fashion lifestyle brand, I'm in! Whether commando-in-chief of toaster-oven dreams or putting it all on the line for a line of gold bangles, consider me cuffed to the screen. For me, watching old seasons of *New York, OC, Atlanta, New Jersey,* and *Beverly Hills* is like being baptized in a hotel pool. The women's constant reinvention reminds me that no matter how Scary the Island gets, it's never too late to be brand-new, and we'll have many seasons in life and on TV, even if what the psychic said turns out to be true. The Housewives have proven time and time again that a man may never emotionally fulfill you, but these women sure as hell will. And while my vows to this show don't always renew for every season and city and cast switch, it's not personal, it's just I know vow renewals are a canonical death wish. So shout-out to wives for sharing their lives and teaching us to take it all in good stride.

In Jesus Jugs' name we pray. Amen.

Reading back these chapters was kind of like meeting different characters in the reality show of my life, and thinking about the lessons learned in each season reminded me of a favorite type of *Housewives* episode: the season finale. They often conclude by providing an update after filming, usually in the form of some B-roll with text overlaid, saying something snarky or fun about what the character is up to now in the third person, nodding to things they did during the season. Even though I have no idea what's ahead for me, I thought about trying this exercise for some chapters, to see if I could illustrate my point that sometimes life happens in the most unsuspecting of places, when we're wasting time, rotting our brains, being girlish and allegedly unserious, dressing as a spice, or maybe relentlessly pursuing popularity, boys, or a key to a McMansion in the afterlife.

Here's where the main character in each season ended up in *The Real Housewives of My One in a Millennial Life*:

- *"Passion of the Zeitgeist" represented a twist of fate for Kate she never saw coming; eventually, her career took a heretical turn. She realized her entire job and this book exist at the intersection of the two roles she once believed were mutually exclusive, as she uses her love of entertainment and a lifetime of observing to now entertain people for a living through her observations, disrupting the Britney 6:2 entertainer/observer space-time continuum that goes against everything she once believed.*

- *The You've Got Male Kate now firmly believes this era was the Gateway (2000) to the job she has today, where her entire career and this book are the result of cultivating an online presence. Although she could hardly believe men used to have the audacity to compliment her personality, she has to acknowledge the irony that this is a term now associated with her profession, where she's introduced as a pop-culture and/or media "personality" due to her role as a host and commentator. She wishes she could tell Katiemae87 (or WaFFel77, depending) the very same personality that's making her cry herself to sleep would one day become the reason she's able to live out her dreams, and, more importantly, seek vengeance via the written word for the wrongdoings of Vanessica and Elizabecca. Unfortunately, after being too long removed from AIM, Kate made a grave error in choosing her social-media handles, forgetting the elegant game of alphanumeric dressage that must occur when carefully curating a screen name. Her social-media handles started across the board as @bethereinfive, all lowercase. As a result, daily, she receives messages saying, "Hey, Beth!" instead of her name, Kate, since she's stuck with her modern screen name reading as the handle of a woman named Beth Erin Five. The great thing about this oversight is her podcast community is affectionately called "the Beths," which makes Kate feel like a cult leader, but she doesn't care, because they're truly the Best.*

- *The Kate Whom God Spent a Little Less Time On would go on to consider studying religious people a hobby of sorts, like how other people feel about true crime or sports, but to her, the crime was knowing the perfect imagery put forth by religious influencers was influenced by organizations steeped in oppressive gender roles. Analyzing the behaviors of religious bloggers was one of the first reasons for her podcast taking off; she used her experience in the Bible Belt to examine the behaviors of bloggers in the Gucci Belt, a geographic term she made up to describe wealthy religious influencers in Utah, Nevada, Arizona, and California, where people cite being #blessed for their new construction and fabulous lives. Supporting her hypothesis, there are some people and places where God does, indeed, appear to spend more of His time.*

- *Kate's Expectations were met when her now-husband (without even knowing the story about the jewelry receipt that was her metaphorical Joni Mitchell CD) made a perpetual best friend into the leading lady when, upon opening her door, he proposed to her using* Love Actually–*style cue cards, and in that moment, she finally felt understood and Actually Loved. At their wedding, their first dance was to a middle-school dance floor classic, K-Ci and JoJo's "All My Life," where everyone at the wedding knew the words, resulting in the gospel-choir-chord-progression-frisson-fest of Kate's dreams. All her life, she really did pray for someone like him, who not only wore a watch and loved her unconditionally, but also understood how seriously she took romantic comedies and nineties slow-dance hits.*

- *"Limited To" and "Pumpkin Spice Girl" started as spoken-word poems, then became short essays Kate read aloud during her first podcast tour to gauge people's response. Unable to publish any ideas following her first book, she wanted to see if anyone had an interest in linking superficial elements of nostalgia with existential questions about womanhood, like wondering if it's okay never to be a woman interested in STEM. Ultimately, reading excerpts from those chapters out loud led to the publishing of this book; one night in the audience, there was a very special person in publishing who thought the idea had legs. True to form, Kate thought to herself, "Does that mean my ideas have nice stems?"*

The state of current Kate is probably most accurately captured in Part III of the book, so I'll speak from my POV now (as much as I dig a producer bit). I mostly spend my time working a lot and not learning my own lessons from the "B There in Five" of it all, but not for the sake of hustling, rather usually out of joy and waiting to resolve the ever-present parent trap I'm still in. My day-to-day falls somewhere in between "Saved by the Bell Jar" and "Pumpkin Spice Girl" because these kinds of windy thoughts connecting pop culture and women's interests are my wheelhouse, what I do for fun and for work; sharing my own embarrassing stories and feminist backsliding paired with my genuine desire to represent and defend the interests and rights of my audience is what I think about daily.

With "The Parent Trap," it's tough; it's personal. It's a lot of waiting, ever since wanting to be a mom but not knowing how or when it will happen, and what that looks like for my career, which is reliant on headspace, free time, and energy for the ways I earn income. If we're talking about the writing I'm doing today, now that I've wrapped up this book, my thoughts are best represented by the depths of my iPhone Notes app late at night, which has served as my makeshift journal. And it's safe to say I still feel a bit trapped with this note I just found, even though some time has passed since the chapter was first written, it says:

> *"I feel like it's a *little* convenient that the age you can run for president is thirty-five, the same age women are told their pregnancies qualify as geriatric."*

Something that hasn't changed for this one millennial is that I'm usually still up long after midnight, thinking about a problem I can't solve, struggling to quiet my brain's overactivity as it prepares to dream, like an overtired puppy with the "zoomies." My iPhone Notes are a who's who of these types of aimless questions, ranging from attempting to correlate the maximum range of maternal age to a minimum age of political office to a list of questions I'd ask Taylor Swift if I saw her in person (e.g.: Did you sneak out of your apartment in a trunk? How come there's one "old Taylor" we've never seen sawing off a plane wing in the "Look What You Made Me Do" video? Did you for real own a key chain in 2011 that read FUCK THE PATRIARCHY that was thrown on the ground? Or did somebody say, "Fuck the patriarchy," *then* throw the key chain on the ground?).

But I know this question about thirty-five is kind of a bummer to leave you with; it has the same feel-bad energy as Carole Radziwill saying she has "five good summers left," and although I wish I could tell you otherwise, that's kind of where I'm at. Apparently, I'm the one who's Limited To tendencies of ruminating on my frustration toward these types of dichotomies that I enjoy laying out side by side, a daybed/trundle of the mind.

Seeing this Note on my phone made me realize one interesting part of reading back this book (about how I'm a product of my time) is how I failed to notice as I was writing it, the areas I focused on are very much a product of the time I'm in now. Most of this book is about channeling a younger version of me, starting as a kid. But the whole time I was writing it, I was quite preoccupied with topics relating to having a kid, cycling on and off hormones for two rounds of egg retrievals, and living through the seismic overturning of Roe v. Wade, something I didn't specifically discuss until later in the book, but is everywhere in the topics I cover. My mind was consumed with wanting to reclaim and reframe the time I spent on things related to what I thought contributed to my future as a mother or eligibility to be a bride; like my pursuit of male validation, the misogynistic media, the biblical patriarchy, and the love-marriage-baby-carriage pipeline. I wanted to find value and meaning in the memories gained that centered on what I took away and not what they took from me. There's an irony in choosing to highlight how over time, these things had less power over me as I gained power over myself, while living through such a regressive time that's robbing women of their rights and bodily autonomy, serving as a painful reminder of who is still in power.

On the tough days, at times, it's hard to transcend this weight in attempting wistful writing about girlhood; something feels so insidious about finally reaching an age that represents the stability of character in your eligibility to rule the free world, yet I've truly never felt more Limited To anything as much as I do my biological clock. Admittedly, it's distracting. Especially because when I think about how I went straight from chasing boys to chasing God to chasing popularity to chasing shots to chasing girl-bossery, in search of whatever social currency could make me valuable, the through line of these eras is my tendency to put someone else's opinion first. There has been such freedom found in learning to let that go in recent years. And like my epiphany about PSLs, I don't know whether to laugh or cry when I think about how I got to enjoy a more evolved version of me who learned to put myself first for five whole minutes before the world and/or my biological clock put me back in my place. Second place, to be exact. At least it's not an honorable mention?

I've been thinking a lot lately about how often new parents position their life transitions, saying something like how becoming a mom shifted their perspective, how now "nothing else matters." Sometimes they'll say they don't remember who they were before having kids. Historically, I've taken this as an affectionate comment for how much they care, and I'm sure it is. My world comes to a halt when my dog, Tugboat, has a tummy ache; if I'm half as invested in my child's existence as my dog's digestive system, I'm pretty sure I'll be a very involved mother.

But between current events and personal disappointments, it's been hard this year to not pull out the darker, less desirable trundle half of this argument, where I also hear claims of "I forget who I was before" and "nothing else matters." Some nights it scares me to think everything I've built up until this point, including the life I'm living now, effectively falls into what I may one day refer to as "things that don't matter." What if it matters to me?

A younger version of me (to use her words) would be *SO pissed* if I grew up to be an adult who parroted the thing other adults always said to her: that none of this matters. My life experiences mattered to me then, even when I was told they'd turn out to be insignificant, or that I was being too dramatic or emotional. And they matter to me now, because regardless of something's objective importance, it was important to me and shaped me into the person I became. Many of us spent our whole lives shrinking ourselves, our pain, our bodies, and our existence to make other people comfortable, feeling like our job was to make space for others, and not take up space ourselves. And it turns out, as I've been writing to you, I'm also writing to a future version of me, too, saying, "Don't you dare forget who you were and tell me to shrink when it's taken me all these years to stand proudly plain and tall."

In "Pumpkin Spice Girl," I talked about how I'm tired of sexist reductions and ridicule lobbying for our disappearance. I think these small, day-to-day interactions contribute to an overall theme of invisibility. I'm tired of my body and humanity being ignored on the floor of Congress, I'm tired of having our pain dismissed and our needs under-researched in medical settings, I'm tired of witnessing the invisibility of domestic and cognitive labor involved with motherhood, I'm tired of trying to remain a Polly Pocket–sized version of me, worrying about my body's size and my presence taking up too much space. I'm also probably tired because I stay up all night ruminating over these things underneath the cold blue light of the hotel's Welcome Channel screen featuring Mario Lopez. Even if it's naïve of me to believe my identity won't eventually in some way be eclipsed, I guess my verbal manspreading of female millennial minutiae on these pages is my own form of resistance. To resurrect experiences that previously felt labeled or misrepresented by gender or generation, if only to make a case while I have the headspace that there's so much to our existence worth remembering.

I want people to remember the details of their lives, the things they loved, and honor the ways they passed their time, and to believe they are special, because they are. Not because you're a token millennial, but because they're yours. If you can forgive the self-indulgence of using my own life for the material, ultimately, this book was meant to be a celebration of identity, to remember the things that happened to us in life when we were on our own. And to bring it back to a *Housewives* reference, to proudly "own it" the best I could, even if it's easily dismissed as insignificant or cliché due to generational or gender-related snark. More importantly, I hope you remember not to get caught up in the questions about your choices or chances, and take pressure off yourself in moving through the LMBCP. Being one person doesn't need to be offset with a "just," or preceded by a "plus"; who we are, on our own, as one millennial, is enough.

It's nice to think that even though we're on our own, through sharing our stories, we can navigate the messiness of the human experience as one. It reminds me of the camaraderie I sought with the Up All Night Club™, hoping to find friendship and comfort not in our problems being the same, but in wanting some company to weather the mutual feelings of uncertainty. Though I guess not much has changed; uncertainty was the core driver of what kept me up then, and still is now. In our girlhood, we took cues from older siblings and magazines and movies and went on a fact-finding mission about the world we didn't have access to yet, and now, I obsessively take cues from women around my age on the internet, admiring their career moves and following their decisions and transitions regarding motherhood, trying to piece together what this next life phase looks like for a well-meaning Meredith Blake with a heart of gold vermeil who finally got male but isn't sure she has what it takes.

This brings me to "Back in the Daybed," a chapter I find to be (appropriately) the spookiest coincidence of all in terms of its ability to foretell the thing we all eventually do: spend our whole lives trying to find ourselves, only to realize we were creating ourselves the whole time. Did Audrey Hepburn, Marilyn Monroe, or Anonymous say that, or have I been going to HomeGoods too much again?

The part I thought was coincidental was the sisterhood I sought through bonding over pop culture and existential thoughts in the late hours, the heart-to-hearts too intimidating for the big groups with the show ponies, and my appreciation for the power of connection when the night got lonely. I once spent my sleepless nights talking into a void, despite silence on the other end from friends dozing off, but the important part was I knew they were there. It's not all that different from my career as a podcaster, where I record late at night, talking to no one, technically, just into a mic, while always knowing someone's on the other side. And why I started the podcast, not knowing whom to talk to about these things I felt slightly embarrassed by, but it feels easier when your style of self-expression feels safe, and you find a community that understands you. While I consider myself to be in the business of entertainment, getting the opportunity to be in the business of keeping people company is where I take the most pride, and it's not lost on me that so many people tell me they listen to me talk while falling asleep. It's really cool to be a part of people's routine, during their nights lying awake, or their life's mundane tasks, their long commutes, or late-night feedings: the moments you don't want to be alone but don't necessarily want to have to put effort into talking back. We have too many responsibilities now to have sleepovers, but what a gift to have access to on-demand diversions from the reality of the mind's unfamiliar surroundings, and I always hope to create a friendly, if not wordy, distraction for people, at least enough to forget the metaphorical floorboard creaks and ice-maker squeaks that can serve as the soundtrack to our sleepless nights, catastrophizing uncertainty in ways that rarely serve us.

Even though we no longer have our sleeping bags in tow, it's pretty cool we've found creative ways to find the same solidarity in strangers despite our solitude. Even though no one told me it's tough to get people to stay up late with you for a top-notch heart-to-heart in adult life, I'm grateful to live in an era where women are able to remotely share and scale their experiences through social media, music, books, or any form of art, forming powerful connections that can make the world a hell of a lot less lonely in the late hours. All I ever wanted was for all of us to feel seen, even in the dark.

As I'm wrapping up, I just looked up, saw it's 5:00 A.M., and smiled. I've used this book to wage another war in my lifelong battle to avoid going to bed, spending these hours deep into the night writing my way through an uncertain phase in my own life. I talk a big game about keeping others company, but if I'm being honest, writing this book distracted me through a season of my life that, at times, felt quite dark, like a dead end. I suppose that would make you on the receiving end an official member of the Up All Night Club™.

And even better, that would make this reading our first meeting; welcome aboard! Despite being scarred from Light as a Feather, Stiff as a Board, we still aim to levitate spirits by keeping each other company, and as evidenced by this book's length, we still haven't lost our penchant for paperwork. You may have been expecting answers over an ambush initiation, but the goal of the Club was never to be any one way or even to guarantee it would be okay. It was simply not to go through our dark nights alone. I want this for you, but please know that you being on the other end of my words means a lot to me, too. One thing hasn't changed: there's nothing like the good old days of being distracted until tomorrow comes. Sometimes it's easier to talk to strangers than it is to a friend, and even if I don't know you on the other end, knowing you're there and willing to share in these millennial memories has been a bright spot this year, reminding me of daylight's imminent return.

Thanks for being my light at the end of the trundle.

Until next time, Up All Night Club™ meeting adjourned.

conclusion

I don't know how to, like, end this
It feels like only the start.
I want to remind you to like what you like,
You decide what is art.
When they tell you to act like a lady, think like a man,
They're implying that to be ladylike you must like things ladies
    like.
Likewise, leave all the thinking up to him.
To be a lady liked I was taught to like popular things,
And despite the things I like being sources of my childlike
    wonder,
Teaching me lessons, bringing me joy and the like,
When I got older, I was left disliking myself.
Feeling ashamed of being too much like everyone else.
"Like" aversion, tough from the very first time
How it feels when your likes are lost on someone
Who makes you feel like you've lost your mind,
When it's celebrated to be like father, like son,
But we're called basic when our likes and loves
Are liked by a lot more people than one.

We're told what to like, limited to a shallow selection
Then criticized for skimming the likes of the surface,
God forbid you like your reflection.
A litany of likes is where I leave you, in protest of
Being discredited for saying the word "like" too much
Subsisting on the things that get us likes or thumbs up,
Or questioning our taste if what we like is well-loved.
Of all these likes I've written, if you only take one,
Please, for the love, don't prioritize being liked above
Prioritizing all of the things that you love.

addendum

Pardon the bit, if we may share a plot twist.

Production felt it was necessary to provide one last update about Kate, who wasn't aware of something quite significant when she wrote the conclusion that reviewed the footage as a *Real Housewife* of her *One in a Millennial* life.

After two years of trying to have a kid and the disappointments of 2.22.22 and the difficulty of writing during two rounds of IVF, resulting in a quest for identity that started with what she was Limited To, two weeks before the book was due, Kate found out she was pregnant, out of the blue. Regardless of what happens, she wanted to tell you, because it will always be special to her that she didn't realize while finishing up this one millennial's journey, she had yet to find out she was writing for two.

To this day, it seems Be There in Five still doesn't notice when she's late, in more ways than one, but that would require counting days of the month, and if there's one thing we've learned:

Math class is tough.

acknowledgments

I may be one millennial, but I have so many people to thank for their support in making this book come together.

To my editor at St. Martin's, Sallie Lotz—I'll never be able to thank you enough for taking a chance on this book. I'm so grateful the Venn diagram of our pop-culture references is a circle, and I don't care if *Younger* is inaccurate; to me, you're SUCH a Kelsey Peters. Otherwise, we can settle on our other mutual fave of Hilary's body of work (*The Lizzie McGuire Movie*), because in all seriousness, getting to write this was what my lifelong dreams were made of, and I have you to thank for that. In the movie, Lizzie says that she won't even let her mom hear her in the shower, so she could never sing in front of an audience, and that's kind of how I felt about sharing my longer-form writing with the world. I didn't think I could do it, and your belief in my work and your expertise in guiding this project kept me afloat during an incredibly vulnerable process. You're truly one in a million! P.S. Did everyone write in your yearbook that they liked you a "Lotz"? Because I really do and thank you for everything!

To the SMP team that worked on this book—Jen Enderlin, Laura Clark, Jessica Zimmerman, Erica Martirano, and Hannah Nesbat—I'm endlessly grateful for you championing this concept and for all your hard work behind the scenes. What a gift it has been to collaborate with such talented women in publishing, and I can't speak more highly of my experience. And Hannah, thanks for giving me my "Bluebird Cafe" moment of discovery in NYC when you heard me read "Limited To" in a crowded room. Go figure one of the most profound "sliding doors" moments of this millennial's life took place in a basement. Forever grateful for you having my back and for introducing me to this incredible team!

To my manager and friend, Courtney Heath—ever since you sent me a pic of you as a grown woman wearing a shirt that said "Save a Volvo, Ride Edward Cullen," I knew we would understand each other. Working with you the past several years has truly been one of the greatest joys of my career, and I am convinced Sky Daddy must have spent the absolute most time on you. You are a gem of a human, a Jill of all trades, an incredibly talented businesswoman, and, on top of that, one of the greatest friends I've ever had. None of this would've happened (or gotten done on time) without you, and our daily novel-length iMessages are like having the camaraderie of a coworker, which I've always longed for in this isolating career. Getting to share it with you has made it so much more fun and rewarding. I won't rest until we've completed every single one of our shallow goals on our shared note for what we'll do one day if we "make it," and thanks for being the best of the best and the Beths and for all you do for me and the broader *Be There in Five* community on a daily basis.

To my agent at WME, Haley Heidemann—I talked for years about how I needed to find people to work with who understood me or else I'd never be able to write freely, and your energy toward this project ever since we met in New York has meant the world to me. You're a force in navigating the business side of this, and I'm endlessly appreciative of how you've gone to bat for me in several ways during the past couple of years when I would've never known how to make this dream possible. Having someone like you in my corner is an honor, and your understanding of and belief in this project made all the difference. Thank you for being there every step of the way.

To my husband—sometimes I think about what it would be like to be in your shoes, and to have my spouse year after year announce their nonsensical career pivots, like starting a flooring company and leaving a stable job, writing a children's book about social media, or starting a podcast, and I realize I would have probably stopped me at every turn and thought these were all very bad ideas. But you never even flinched. You were the first to tell me to start a business, support me when I needed a change, and encourage me when I wanted to see if my personality could get me places. You've been unwaveringly supportive and understanding throughout the past decade as I've truly paved the most bizarre career path imaginable, from doormats to Taylor Swift dance parties and everything in between, and I'm endlessly appreciative of your belief in my dreams, in my career, and in me. Thank you for your patience while I had to prioritize writing this book, thank you for waiting to watch our shows until I got home, and thank you for being the absolute best dad to Tugboat. I can't wait for this next chapter of our lives as both partners and parents. I love you so much it hurts.

To my siblings, I know I'm a walking cliché of a youngest child, and thanks for letting me watch and copy your every move since '87. I feel so lucky that my childhood memories are a haze of playroom hangs, manifesting snow through inside-out pj's, housing Fla-Vor-Ice pops on family vacays, an obsession with the holidays, and a dedication to pop culture we all share to this day. It's funny to think about spending our time fighting over who got to use the computer, because I'm now sitting at my computer, realizing what a luxury it was when we were younger and got to hang out all the time. Thanks for being the people I look up to the most and for being the reason I race home every Christmas— what a gift it is to be hallmates again even for just a few days.

To my parents, I don't know if I'll ever be able to find the words to adequately express how grateful I am for the life you provided for me, the confidence you instilled in me, and for the faith you've always had in me to land on my feet. From letting me be myself, to celebrating my getting Bs, to operating as my NC satellite location when I started *Be There in Five* and beyond, you've always held space for what made me unique and supported my creative dreams, even if it meant moving away or telling jokes about my childhood on a podcast or stage. I know it's not a normal experience to have your daughter detail her life in a podcast or a book, and I'm so appreciative of your openness to my unconventional career, and I hope you know that the magical childhood you gave me is the reason nostalgia is such a cornerstone of my work. You've given me everything and still somehow say, "What else can we do?" and when it comes to your dedication to our family, I'll never know how to repay you. I love you so much and will forever be trying to make you proud.

To the Beths, I owe everything to you. No one, I mean no one, asked for a long-form one-woman podcast with a non-famous host who talks mostly pop culture that is *not* current, but you guys have shown up for *Be There in Five* week after week, giving me a spot on the air and helping me find my place in the sky, and I would have never had the confidence to continue to put these thoughts out into the world without your ongoing encouragement. The only reason the words I wrote in this book were able to be put out into the world is because of your support, and I can't thank you enough for everything you've done for me, from sending in your stories for crowd-sourced episodes, to leaving Katelilah voice mails, to the kindness and humanity you show me in DMs, emails, or in person at live shows. It's a true honor to have the privilege of your time week after week, and while this book is about me, it's heavily influenced by what I've learned from you. All I want is for you to be proud of who you are and what you like, and like I said, to never let anyone who drafts make-believe football teams make you believe that your interests aren't important.

To my future child, it's wild to read this back now knowing that I wrote it deep in a place where becoming a mom was an "if," but now it's a "when," just a few short months from now. I'm nervous and excited; it feels like there's so much at stake for this well-intentioned Meredith Blake, but I hope that what ultimately matters is that it's okay if I'm not like other moms—I'm meant to be *your* mom, and I can't wait to meet you and fill your world with all the magic my parents filled mine with. I hope someday this book makes you laugh and makes you cringe, and I hope you'll do the same when you look back on being a kid. If you cringe, it means you're doing it right. Thanks for keeping me company and making sure I got some sleep during the home stretch of this project. While I can't wait for the day I can once again comfortably stretch down to my feet, more important, I can't wait to bring you home.